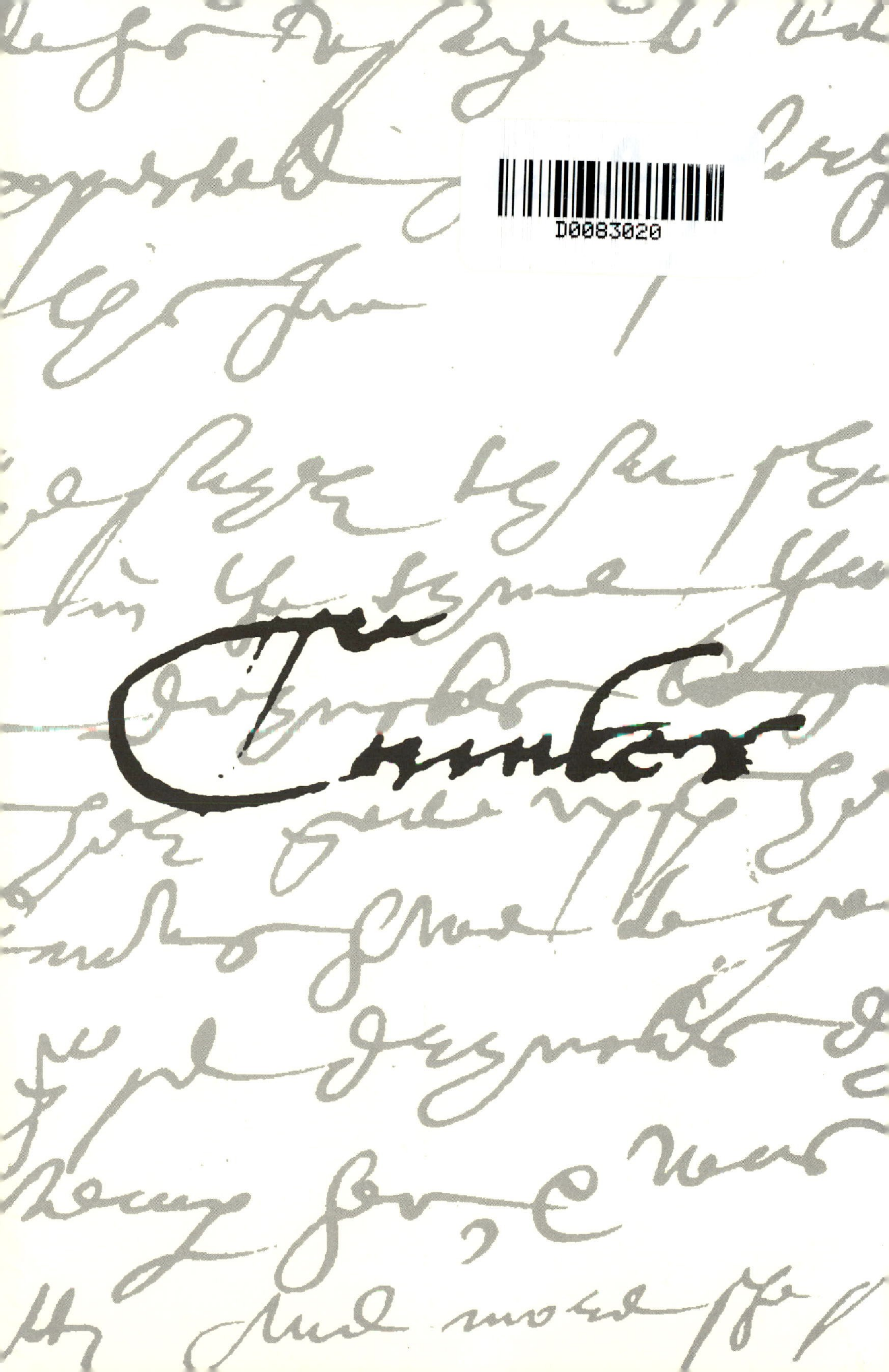

The BEWITCHING of
ANNE GUNTER

The BEWITCHING of
ANNE GUNTER

A horrible *and* true story *of* deception,
witchcraft, murder, *and the*
King of England

JAMES SHARPE

ROUTLEDGE
NEW YORK

Published in 2000 by
Routledge
29 West 35th Street
New York, NY 10001

First published in Great Britain in hardcover in 1999 by Profile Books Ltd.,
and reprinted by arrangement with Profile Books Ltd.
First Routledge hardback edition, 2000
Copyright © 1999, 2000 by James Sharpe.

Printed in the United States of America on acid-free paper.

Library of Congress Cataloging-in-Publication Data
Sharpe, J. A.
The bewitching of Anne Gunter : a horrible and true story of deception, witch-
craft, murder, and the King of England / James Sharpe.
p. cm.
Includes bibliographical references (p.) and index.
ISBN 0-415-92691-2 —ISBN 0-415-92692-0 (pb)
1. Witchcraft—England—History. 2. Trials (Witchcraft)—England—History. 3.
Gunter, Anne, 16th/17th cent. 4. James I, King of England, 1566-1625. 5. Great
Britain—History—James I, 1603-1625. I. Title.
BF1581 .S517 2000
133.4'3'094209032—dc21   99-056590 CIP

10 9 8 7 6 5 4 3 2 1

For Guy

In the hope that he is getting a better deal from his father
than Anne had from hers

He this deponent saith that he ... did not at any time give or cause to be given unto his said daughter Anne either during her fits or before or after any sack or sallet oil ... but this deponent's wife or some of her servants ... did in two or three mornings in the time of the sickness of this deponent's said daughter when she was out of her fits give unto her some sack and sallet oil mixed with spices and sugar candy to comfort her stomach. And this he saith was done by the direction of a cunning woman dwelling at Pangbourne as this deponent was also informed.

Deposition of Brian Gunter to the Star Chamber, 11 February 1606

She saith that in the time of her sickness & troubles she had sack & sallet oil with some other mixtures in the same given unto her by her said father & by Nicholas Kirfoote & his sister, & that when she took this drink she was presently provoked to vomit & to tumble & toss up and down & that the same drink so troubled her senses that she knew not what she said, besides that it made her very sick. And of this she saith her father made her to drink when & so often as he thought good.

Deposition of Anne Gunter to the Star Chamber, 24 February 1606

CONTENTS

Preface   xi
Acknowledgements   xiv

1   Anne's Story   1
2   Some Unexpected Consequences *of a* Football Match   14
3   Many Strange Tortures   43
4   Witchcraft   64
5   *The* Oxford Connection   90
6   *The* Witch-trial *at* Abingdon   115
7   Demonic Possession *and the* Politics *of* Exorcism   139
8   Anne Meets *the* King   169
9   Loose Ends, Tied *and* Untied   197

Notes and References   213
Index   231

PREFACE

E VEN PARED to its essentials, the story is a fascinating one.
In the summer of 1604 a young woman called Anne
Gunter, then aged about twenty, fell ill. She recovered quickly,
but her symptoms, or something very like them, returned in late
October of that year, and this time they persisted. Anne lived
with her parents, a gentleman named Brian Gunter and his wife,
also called Anne, in the small country parish of North Moreton,
some twelve miles south of Oxford. The parents, concerned by
her illness, called in doctors, but they were unable to find a satis-
factory explanation for her affliction, and suggested there might
be supernatural causes. Anne was by this stage showing the
symptoms that the age considered indicative of demonic possession or of witchcraft: she had fits during which she writhed and
contorted; she fell into trances or comas; she vomited and voided
foreign bodies, especially pins. And, as was so often the case, she
called out against her supposed tormenters as she suffered her fits
before an ever expanding audience of fascinated spectators. She
named three women as witches: Agnes Pepwell, who already
had a reputation as a witch, her illegitimate daughter, Mary, and

Elizabeth Gregory, her principal tormentor, who was the wife of a yeoman farmer called Walter Gregory and, on many accounts, the most unpopular woman in North Moreton.

Agnes Pepwell ran away, but Mary Pepwell and Elizabeth Gregory were tried for witchcraft at Abingdon in March 1605. They were acquitted. Matters might well have ended there, but Brian Gunter decided to re-open the case, or at least to gain sympathy at the highest level, by arranging a meeting between his daughter and the King, James I, when the monarch visited Oxford University in August 1605. James had a reputation as a witch-hunter, and Brian Gunter was building his hopes on this when he brought Anne before him. The plan misfired badly. James was in a sceptical mood, while the ecclesiastical politics of the Church of England meant that in 1605 there was a body of extremely influential Churchmen, including the archbishop of Canterbury, Richard Bancroft, who were far from credulous about instances of witchcraft, demonic possession and exorcism. The King passed Anne to the care of Archbishop Bancroft, who in turn put her in the custody of his chaplain, Samuel Harsnett, who had already been a propagandist for the sceptics in earlier cases of supposed demonic possession. By October Anne had confessed to James that she had simulated bewitchment at her father's instigation, to further a feud between him and the family of the chief of the accused witches, Elizabeth Gregory. The feud had begun in 1598, when Brian Gunter had inflicted fatal injuries on two of the Gregorys at a football match.

Probably under Bancroft's guidance, proceedings were initiated at the Court of Star Chamber early in 1606 against Brian Gunter and his daughter Anne for falsely accusing the three women. The dossier resulting from these proceedings, which makes this quite simply the best-documented English witchcraft case, contains the evidence of over sixty witnesses and comprises several hundred pages. Many of the witnesses described how Brian Gunter gave his daughter a mixture of 'sack', or sherry, and 'sallet', or salad oil. The father claimed it was for his daughter's good; Anne claimed it was to make her fits all the more believable. It is Anne's version of what happened, here as elsewhere, that ultimately convinces.

ACKNOWLEDGEMENTS

I FIRST CAME across Anne Gunter while I had a term's sabbatical leave in Oxford in the autumn of 1992, an experience made possible by the generosity of All Souls College in awarding me a visiting fellowship. My initial debt incurred while writing this book is, therefore, to the Master and Fellows of All Souls. My second (and all historians of English witchcraft are indebted to this obscure scholar) is to that pioneer of English witchcraft studies, Cecil L'Estrange Ewen. Early in my term at Oxford I ordered up Ewen's *Witchcraft in the Star Chamber* from the stacks of the Bodleian Library, a pamphlet dating from 1938 that contains a brief account of the Gunter case. That term I was regularly commuting from Oxford to London to attend a Wednesday seminar on early modern mentalities at the Institute of Historical Research, and on my next visit to London I called in at the Public Record Office, ordered up the relevant Star Chamber proceedings, and realized that I had stumbled across a remarkable body of historical documentation.

As my researches proceeded, I incurred further debts. As well as the Bodleian Library, the Public Record Office and the

Institute of Historical Research, I have worked on materials held by the British Library, the College of Arms, the Guildhall Library, Lambeth Palace Library, York Minster Library, the Archivist to His Grace the Duke of Northumberland, the Berkshire County Record Office, the Hertfordshire County Record Office, Oxfordshire Archives, Oxford University Archives, the Archives of New College Oxford, the Berkshire Family History Research Centre and the Family Records Centre, London, while I have also benefited from correspondence with the County Archivists of Dorset, Somerset and Wiltshire. I am grateful to the Huntington Library, San Marino, California, for making available a microfilm copy of a document relating to the Gunter case in their possession, and for permission to quote from it. As ever, my work has depended heavily upon the resources of the J.B. Morrell Library of the University of York.

Numerous individuals have provided help and support, among them Roger Dickinson, John Guy, Ralph and Margaret Houlbrooke, Mark Jenner, Henry Lancaster, Brian Levack, David Scott, Bill Sheils, Sabina Sutherland and Jenny Wormald. I am grateful to Chris Durston, Diana Barker and Rebecca Mullins for permission to cite information from their theses, the various members of the Berkshire Family History Society who corresponded with me, especially Arthur Coles, who sent a comprehensive listing of parish register entries relating to the North Moreton Gregorys, to Mrs J.M.W Morgan, and above all to Professor Gerald Howat for generously bringing his knowledge of the local history of North Moreton to my assis⁄tance. Cliff and Kathleen Davies aided the logistics of research visits to Oxford and provided welcome hospitality. Special thanks are due to my agent, Jane Turnbull, and to Andrew Franklin at Profile. My wife, Krista Cowman, has, as ever, both supported and shown a keen interest in my researches.

I have modernized spelling from early modern documents and
printed works, and have also dispensed with the formal scholarly
apparatus of footnotes; the interested reader will, however, find
full notes and references at the end of the book. I have generally
given modern renderings of Christian names and standard-
ized the spelling of a number of surnames ('Kirfoote', for
example, is spelled about ten different ways in the documentation of the period). I have followed the modern practice of dating the New Year from 1 January. Prices, etc., are given in
pre-decimal currency, with the pound divided into twenty
shillings[*s.*], each worth twelve pence[*d.*]. Translating seventeenth-century costs into modern equivalents is notoriously difficult: in the England of 1604, a skilled workman would be lucky
to earn a shilling a day for his labours, and a quart (two pints or
just under a litre) of ale in one of North Moreton's alehouses
would have cost 1*d.* As a rough indicator, monetary values from
the early Stuart period should be multiplied by a factor of 800 to
a thousand to produce a modern equivalent.

Stillingfleet, North Yorkshire
February 1999

chapter *one*

ANNE'S STORY

ANNE WAS first interrogated on Sunday, 24 February 1606, at the Holborn Court of Gray's Inn. By then the Star Chamber no longer carried out the preliminary examination of defendants at its antechamber in Westminster. As Anne was being questioned she may well have imagined what was to come: sitting before the King's privy councillors or, if they were in a harsh mood, being made to stand before them at the bar in the 'outer' part of the most notorious court in English history, the *Camera Stellata*, the Star Chamber.

This 'chamber' (in fact, two interconnected rooms) had originally been built more than three centuries earlier on an upper floor, facing the Thames, of the royal palace of Westminster. It had been successively improved, with ever more imposing decor, in the reign of Queen Elizabeth, dead less than three years before Anne's trial. By the time of that trial those involved in the court's proceedings found themselves in a large room, among whose rich decorations the arms of the late Queen were prominent, as were the stars painted on the ceiling, from which the court took its name. The privy councillors, acting as a judicial body, heard and deliberated on cases as they sat around a large table, traditionally covered by a green carpet when the court was in session. Those brought before the court could hardly fail to be intimidated, placed as they were in a courtroom designed and furnished to overawe the subject and to emphasize the power of the law and the monarch who embodied it.

By 1606 most of the court's business was transacted at the Star Chamber office in the Holborn Court of Gray's Inn. William Mill, the skilled administrator who became clerk of the council in the Star Chamber in 1587, had realized that the number of cases entering the court had grown so great that the paperwork could no longer be prepared in the busy antechamber at Westminster; he had subsequently moved the court's extensive clerical staff to this new centre of operations. Defendants and witnesses were questioned by one of the Star Chamber's two examiners, and their answers recorded by an underclerk.

The record of Anne's interrogation, written down in the difficult hand of the clerk who noted so much of the evidence in this case, tells us nothing about how the questioning was conducted. We do not know if Anne was subjected to leading questions, to verbal bullying or to psychological pressure. We do, however, have the interrogatories, one of those sets of questions that, adjusted to the peculiar circumstances of each case, formed the basis of all Star Chamber investigations. Her answers to the matters listed in this document were formed into a more or less continuous narrative by the clerk, who doubtless modified her words as he wrote them down. There is no record of Anne having been represented by a lawyer, although she had almost certainly been coached in what to say and how to say it by the various great men who had taken an interest in her case over the past few months. Moreover, although the charges against her were laid formally in the name of the King's attorney-general, this Star Chamber case was instigated by the archbishop of Canterbury, Richard Bancroft, which may well have smoothed the way in which matters proceeded. But what must have helped most was the fact that Anne was an interrogator's dream, a freely confessing suspect. And however intimidated she must have felt in the Star Chamber office, her ordeal there was no worse than much that had happened to her over the previous eighteen months: indeed, the realization that she was coming to the end of a period of lengthy stress must have been a cathartic one.

The initial weeks when she was simulating bewitchment were bad enough. Anne had lain on her bed in her chamber in her parents' house in the presence of an ever changing, ever growing and ever more diverse crowd of onlookers. At first her family and immediate neighbours had come, then doctors, clergymen and more distant relatives, and then a continuously widening body of interested parties, extending indeed to casual passers-by. Before them (for her father had been determined to make her supposed sufferings as public as possible) she had pretended to go into contortions and trances, writhe, foam at the mouth and, by sleight of hand, vomit foreign bodies, notably pins, and pass them in her urine. She had feigned insensibility while trumpets had been sounded near her, as swords had been flourished before her, and yet more pins had been stuck into her breasts and arms to 'prove' her lack of feeling. All of this was stressful enough, but if only it had happened in a familiar place with, if only at first, mainly familiar people present. Even when she was taken to her brother-in-law Thomas Holland's lodgings at Exeter College, Oxford, the doctors, dons and clergymen who came to examine and to help the bewitched girl were disposed to treat Anne kindly; indeed, many of them were already known to her.

But circumstances had subsequently forced her into less

familiar surroundings and made her the object of more daunting people's attention. A few weeks after the trial of two of the women who were supposed to have bewitched her, Anne had been taken into the custody of Henry Cotton, the bishop of Salisbury, who, interested in one of the rare cases of witchcraft in his diocese, kept Anne under close observation and had her examined by local doctors. At about this time she was also lodged with (or, more accurately, kept in the custody of) Sir Giles Wroughton at Tidworth in Wiltshire. But the world really changed for Anne after her father made his unfortunate decision to bring her sufferings to the notice of King James. Meeting the monarch must have been an overwhelming experience for the girl, although from the first there is every indication that he treat-ed her sympathetically. Her statement to the Star Chamber, how-ever, suggests that she was very worried about being taken into the custody of Samuel Harsnett, the archbishop of Canterbury's chaplain and an important member of his middle management, a man with a formidable reputation as a sceptic in matters of witchcraft and as an exposer of the fraudulently bewitched. She stayed with Harsnett for a month, during which time she was medically examined by the physician Edward Jorden. Jorden had been involved in a well-publicized witch-trial in 1602, in which he had given medical evidence in favour of the alleged witch, arguing that her supposed victim, another young girl of good family, was suffering from a natural ailment. When Anne came before the Star Chamber she had already experienced some months of confinement, during which she had been subjected continuously to questioning and medical examinations.

Unfortunately we know nothing of Anne's appearance. The court records give us no information. We do know that while under Bancroft's care in the autumn of 1605 she fell in love, prob-ably for the first time in her life, with one of his servants, and at least one contemporary recorded that the love was reciprocated, and marriage envisaged. Given the capacity of the period's commentators on court affairs to make cutting remarks when they felt it appropriate, we may therefore surmise that Anne was attractive enough. She told the court that she was aged about nineteen at the time of her interrogation, although the parish register entry recording her baptism suggests that she was in fact twenty-one: surprisingly to the modern reader, people in Tudor and Stuart England were sometimes a little imprecise about their age. We know that she could read: she learned how to pretend bewitchment partly by consulting books about such matters, while her statement in the Star Chamber dossier ends with her firm, literate signature. She was conventionally religious. Some of the statements made while she was in her fits (where the sufferer's body turned temporarily into a battlefield between good and evil, and she was expected to voice godly sentiments) demonstrate this. Her sister Susan had some years previously married Thomas Holland, by the time of Anne's trial regius professor of divinity at Oxford University and a well-respected clergyman and academic. A man on that career track would not have risked marrying into an ungodly family. There is, in fact, nothing in either the Star Chamber records or in any of the other sources connected with her story to suggest that Anne was anything other than a normal young woman, an unremarkable daughter in a solid country gentry family, who found herself thrust into rather remarkable circumstances.

Certainly the formal answers she gave to the charges laid against her, dated 23 February 1606, were couched in entirely conventional terms. Anne confessed that under pressure from her father she had agreed to 'feign and counterfeit herself to be bewitched', and more or less threw herself on the mercy of the court, deploying a rhetoric that was patently designed to strike a chord. She was now, she declared, 'very penitent' and had 'often upon her knees asked mercy and forgiveness at God's hands'. She pleaded with the court to 'take consideration of the weakness of her sex, of her young years and that she was and is a child owing obedience to her father that commanded her, and having no means, but by her father's provision, to live, and how she hath suffered much torment and affliction in body and mind by this her offence of counterfeiting'. She had now, the document repeated, 'grown to sorrow and repentance for the same' and 'doth most humbly commit herself to the censure of the honourable court'. This statement was obviously calculated to have considerable impact.

The story Anne told when she appeared in the Star Chamber office the following day, recorded as it was in nineteen pages of closely written foolscap, could not have failed to make an even greater impression. Anne began by going back to her original illness in the summer of 1604. The illness, she said, seemed to her to be 'the disease called the mother', that is, hysteria, which the medical theory of the period held to be a characteristically female complaint, originating from disorders of the womb. At first, she insisted, she did not believe or claim that she was bewitched. It was her father, together with his neighbours Nicholas Kirfoote and his wife Alice, who developed this idea when the illness returned in October; they persuaded her to 'counterfeit herself to be bewitched' and to lay the blame on Elizabeth Gregory, and Agnes and Mary Pepwell. Her father, she explained, had a long-standing grudge against the Gregorys because they held him responsible for the deaths, which had occurred a few years previously, of two members of the family, John and Richard Gregory. There was also a pre-existing enmity between Alice Kirfoote and Elizabeth Gregory. The hapless Pepwell women, especially Agnes, already had reputations as witches and were sucked into the accusation because their supposed complicity would lend credence to the allegations against Elizabeth Gregory. Anne recalled how a Mr Roger Bracegirdle, a physician, reinforced the growing rumours that witchcraft was at the root of her sufferings by telling her parents that further recourse to doctors was pointless, that her troubles were supernatural in origin, and that they should rather seek to help their daughter by consulting 'cunning men', or good witches.

Anne's problem now was how to fabricate a convincing simulation. Knowledge of the symptoms of witchcraft-induced illness and of demonic possession was widely diffused in the culture of the period: people knew what to expect and what to look for when confronted by an individual showing the signs of such afflictions. But Anne needed a more focused approach, and, as she told the court, this was in large measure provided by a lucky chance. Early in her sufferings concerned parties, presumably hoping to give her and her parents some idea of what lay ahead of them, had supplied her father with what Anne described as 'the book of the witches of Warboys', as well as 'some other books which she remembreth not'. Anne's 'book of the witches of Warboys' would in fact have been a fairly lengthy tract entitled *The most strange and admirable discoverie of the three Witches of Warboys arraigned, convicted and executed at the last Assizes at Huntingdon*, which described the sufferings brought on by the bewitchment of a number of children of another gentry household, that of the Throckmorton family of Warboys in Huntingdonshire. This was one of the best known of the early English witch-trials and resulted (as the title of the tract records) in the execution of the three supposed witches in 1593. The case set a pattern for English witch-accusations that was to last into the early eighteenth century, a pattern that was taken across the

Atlantic by English colonists to appear in an extreme form at
Salem, Massachusetts, a hundred years after the original incident.
Anne read this account and from it learned the names given by
the Warboys witches to their 'familiar spirits', those half-animal,
half-demon beings that are so central to English witch beliefs, and
applied those names to the 'supposed wicked spirits' of Elizabeth
Gregory and the Pepwells. She also learned from the book 'the
manner of the fits of Mr Throckmorton's children' and set about
imitating them. It has long been suspected that trial pamphlets
and similar literature helped spread ideas on witchcraft, but such
striking evidence of so direct a connection between a printed
account of one case and what happened in another is very rare.

The techniques acquired from the Warboys book were
supplemented by some basic trickery. Anne recounted how her
parents told her of the superstition that if some thatch from the
house of a suspected witch was burned, the afflictions suffered by
the supposedly bewitched party were lifted. Accordingly, at
pre-arranged times thatch from Elizabeth Gregory's or Agnes
Pepwell's roofs was burned in a chamber of the Gunter residence
adjacent to where Anne lay on her sickbed, and the girl would
experience a convincing, if short-lived, recovery. 'This practice,'
Anne explained, 'was a great means to persuade those that saw it
that Mother Pepwell and Goodwife Gregory bewitched her.'
There was another trick that required Anne, as was usual with
the bewitched or possessed, to show second sight (her father, so
she told the court, was compiling a notebook listing such
occurrences: did he too have publication in mind?). So when
some gentlemen came to the Gunter house to see the afflicted girl,
who was in a separate room, Alice Kirfoote managed, in the
course of general conversation, to find out how much money
they had in their purses. This information was conveyed secretly
by the older woman to Anne, who was then able to tell the gentle-

men how much money they had about them. This, she told the court, 'was made a great wonder'.

But more was needed than a few basic deceptions if the accusations against the three women were to be brought to a successful conclusion. According to Anne's account, from an early stage her father attempted to make her symptoms seem more compelling by keeping her drugged. His first move in this direction was to have brimstone burned under her nose as she lay in her chamber. This treatment lasted for about a fortnight and, as Anne told the court, 'troubled her exceedingly', choking her and making her sick. She begged her mother to make her father desist from this course of action, which she did. Then, 'in the time of her sickness & troubles', her father gave her 'sack & sallet oil with some other mixtures in the same'. When she drank this concoction 'she was provoked to vomit & to tumble & to toss up and down & that the same drink so troubled her senses that she knew not what she said'. Her father made her take this drink 'so often as he thought good'.

Even more dramatic were the effects of a mysterious 'green water' (the official interrogatories suggested this was some kind of herbal brew) that, Anne recalled, was first brought into her home by a neighbour, Robert Tadmarten. He was to bring further supplies once or twice more, although after this Anne's father learned how to make the drink himself, as he 'had it always ready to give her when he listed'. This 'green water' had a more violent effect than the sack and sallet oil. It sent Anne into 'great rages', which were followed by 'heavy dullness', followed in turn by a deep sleep in which the girl was insensible until the effects of the drink wore off. So profound were the slumbers caused by this mixture, which was usually administered when Alice Kirfoote and her sister were present, that on one occasion when Anne had taken the drink the bell of the parish church was tolled for her, as it was feared she was near to death. Anne told how her father normally gave her this 'green water', often against her will, when strangers came to the house to witness her afflictions. He also administered it to her before her interviews with the King in the summer of 1605.

But the abuse Anne suffered as she simulated her fits and trances went beyond being drugged. People allegedly bewitched or demonically possessed were usually subjected to a variety of tests designed to 'prove' that their sufferings were genuine. These often took the form of demonstrations of insensibility. One of the most unpleasant experiments conducted on Anne was having pins (these quite apart from the pins she was supposed to vomit) stuck into her arms to demonstrate lack of feeling. She told how on one occasion Alice Kirfoote and her father stuck numerous pins into her arms and breasts. It was left to Alice (the task was obviously thought too immodest to be allocated to a man) to clean up the girl after this treatment, and Anne remembered that two handkerchiefs were needed to wipe away the blood. When the effects of the drugs administered to her wore off, Anne found that her breasts were so sore 'that she could not well bring her arms together or lift them up without much pain', so that she 'fell a weeping & asked Kirfoote's wife what she had done to her and why she had used her so'. The older woman's reply that 'she had done nothing to her' was as unconvincing as it was callous.

Anne was under terrible pressure during the ten months or so when she was forced to manufacture the symptoms of bewitchment on a daily basis: it is noteworthy that this pressure came overwhelmingly from her father and from Alice Kirfoote. Her mother's involvement was barely mentioned in the girl's evidence, except on that one occasion when she intervened successfully to prevent her daughter having to inhale the fumes of burning brimstone, while Nicholas Kirfoote, once the business had

begun, seems to have faded into the background, making much
less impression than his wife. Brian Gunter kept up the pressure
by constantly forcing Anne to swear oaths to keep the plot against
Elizabeth Gregory and the two Pepwells secret. Thus when she
was about to be examined by a group of clergymen, among them
the vicar of North Moreton and her brother-in-law Thomas
Holland, Gunter took Anne into his study and made her take an
oath 'never to disclose any of those things which she had sworn to
keep secret', an oath whose solemnity was emphasized when her
father reminded her of it as the two of them kneeled together
while receiving Holy Communion in their parish church a few
days later. On another occasion, immediately before she was
taken to stay at her brother-in-law's lodgings at Oxford, her
father again swore her to secrecy, and Alice Kirfoote added that if
Anne revealed anything 'what she had sworn to keep secret', the
devil would come and 'fetch her away both body & soul'.

Physical brutality was added to psychological pressure. Her
father beat her several times when she refused to simulate fits, and
there was one especially violent incident, also recalled by other
witnesses to the case. Anne locked herself away in the house of a
neighbour, Anthony Ruffin, rather than feign convulsions and
comas yet again. Her father was so incensed by her rebellion that
he threw her to the ground and 'spurned' her, that is struck at her
with the heels of his boots. William Field, a neighbour who was
in the street near Ruffin's house when the incident occurred, said
he saw Gunter drag his unwilling daughter out of the house on
her stomach, crying out to her as she lay on the ground, 'What,
you scurvy harlot, will you not come home with me?'

Perhaps Brian Gunter had never liked his last child, who
came into his life when he and his wife were both in their forties,
by which time they probably thought their days of child-rearing
were through. A significant comment was made by Nicholas

Kirfoote in his lengthy statement to the Star Chamber, a statement marked chiefly by his retreat from any past association with accusations of witchcraft launched by Brian Gunter. Kirfoote recounted that before Anne fell ill her father 'made very little reckoning of her and disliked her so much that being sick at Oxford and making his will would have bequeathed her only ten pounds for her portion', information that had been passed on to him by one of Gunter's sons. Aspects of Gunter's behaviour towards his daughter appear abusive to the modern observer, while it is not over imaginative to see in Anne's attempts to comply with her father's wishes a desperate effort by an unloved child to gain her father's affection.

The sorry business took a tremendous toll on Anne. One of the matters of greatest interest to the Star Chamber was Anne's vomiting of pins. Anne claimed that she was trained by Alice Kirfoote to hide them in her mouth before pretending to vomit them, and was insistent that her father played no part in this particular deception. But at one point she swallowed some of the pins, 'hoping by that means to make an end of herself', since 'her state of life was so odious and loathsome unto her'. Her despair was deepened by concern over what her friends would make of her when the dissimulations were revealed, and by messages she received 'touching torment and torture that she was likely to endure with Mr Harsnett'. The consequence of all this was that 'she gave herself over to a most desperate state of mind', and that she was 'so weary of her life that she resolved to make an end of herself whatever became of it'. Her mental condition was corroborated by Alice Buckeridge, servant of that Anthony Ruffin whose door Brian Gunter kicked down when his daughter tried to hide in Ruffin's house. After this episode Buckeridge heard Anne say to Brian Gunter, 'Indeed, father, afore I will have such a life with you I will take a halter and hang myself.' These sentiments would not have been voiced lightly in an age when suicide was a crime under English common law and, perhaps more importantly for a girl with conventional religious leanings, a sin of great magnitude. Living under such massive stress, Anne was slowly driven to acute despair.

While she was questioned by the Star Chamber, Anne was held in Lambeth Palace, the archbishop of Canterbury's London residence, which often served as an ad hoc prison for political or religious offenders (heretics had been incarcerated there before trial in the Middle Ages, for example). At the end of the day's interrogation, the easiest way of conveying her back to the archbishop's palace, which was and is located on the south bank of the Thames opposite Westminster, was by ferry. It is easy to imagine Anne, exhausted but one hopes relaxed after giving her lengthy statement, crossing the river huddled in a cloak against the dank February air, an attendant or two with her as the ferryman rowed his craft. After her experiences that day, her mind might well have been running to the strange train of events that had brought her to her sorry condition, events that had begun in the small village where she had lived since she was a toddler.

chapter *two*

SOME UNEXPECTED
CONSEQUENCES *of a*
FOOTBALL MATCH

MOST OF the men of the village were gathered together that day in May 1598 for the football match. The older, more established of them were to be found among the spectators: Brian Gunter, then in his late fifties, the richest man in the village and its only resident gentleman; Robert Adams, aged about sixty-five, head of one of the richest farming families in the community; Robert Gregory, aged about fifty, member of another of the yeomen farming families of North Moreton; and John Sudbury, aged about forty, a husbandman rather than a yeoman farmer and thus a little further down the social hierarchy, but a man who nevertheless took an active part in village affairs. The players, of course, were composed mainly of the younger men, like Richard Gregory, son of Robert Gregory's brother William, or John Field, a youthful member of yet another of the village's farming dynasties. But younger men were also to be found among the spectators: Brian Gunter's second son William, for example, and John Gregory, Richard Gregory's brother. Also present, although it is unclear whether they were participants or spectators, were Brian Gunter's servants, Simon Watts and John Tailor.

Only in England would a historian of witchcraft have to confront the history of football, a history that, even more than the history of witchcraft, has to be constructed from scattered and imperfect shards of evidence. The nature of this evidence is such that we can form little accurate impression of what football meant in this period, of how and when it was played, and of what if any rules were applied to it. In many instances football simply involved men or boys kicking about a ball or some other spherical object. But frequently what was described as football was more or less institutionalized violence between villages or different parts of villages. Certainly, most of the references we have to football in this period were created either when local authorities feared disruption, or after death or injury had occurred when football was played. Football was, for example, seen as a problem in Manchester in 1608, just a decade after the match at North Moreton. There the town's manorial jury noted that

> there hath been heretofore great disorder in our town of Manchester, and the inhabitants thereof greatly wronged and charged with making and amending of their glass windows broken yearly and spoiled by a company of lewd and disor-dered persons using that unlawful exercise of playing with the football in the streets of the said town, breaking many men's windows and glass at their pleasures, and other great enormities

and ordered that any persons playing football in the town in the future should be fined a shilling (a repeat of this order in 1609, and the appointment in 1618 of officers whose sole task was to stop footballing suggests that the fining proved ineffective). More seriously, in 1576 the authorities of Middlesex took action against a number of men from Ruislip and Uxbridge who 'with unknown malefactors to the number of a hundred assembled themselves unlawfully and played a certain unlawful game, called football, by reason of which unlawful game there rose amonst them a great affray, likely to result in homicides and serious accidents'. The occasional coroner's inquest or homicide indictment demonstrates that the Middlesex justices' fears were not unfounded. One such arose, intriguingly, from a football match played at West Ham (then a small rural parish in Essex) in 1582, when a yeoman named Thomas Turner was accused of violently throwing a labourer called John Ward, an inhabitant of the neighbouring parish of East Ham, to the ground and inflicting fatal injuries. Turner, as was usual in such cases, was acquitted.

This negative image of sixteenth- and seventeenth-century football is reinforced by the strictures of contemporary moralists and social commentators. Football was not a game for the elite. In 1531 Sir Thomas Elyot published *The Book of the Governor*, an important work on the education of young gentlemen. Discussing games, Elyot commented that a number of games were totally unsuitable for 'all noble men', among them 'football, wherein is nothing but beastly fury and extreme violence; whereof procedeth hurt and consequently rancour and malice do remain with them that be wounded'. At the very end of the sixteenth century James VI of Scotland, in a book of advice for his eldest son, Prince Henry, numbered football among the 'rough and violent exercises' that the boy should avoid. The Puritans were hostile to football (although, interestingly, one contemporary noted that Oliver Cromwell was more addicted to playing football than to his studies while an undergraduate at Cambridge). Thus Philip Stubbes, a Puritan pamphleteer whose *Anatomie of Abuses* of 1583 is an impressive attack on the sinfulness of his compatriots, fulminated that football was more

a friendly kind of fight, than a play or recreation, a bloody and murdering practice, than a fellowly sport or pastime ... and hereof groweth envy, malice, rancour, choler, hatred, displeasure, enmity, and what not else? And sometimes fighting, brawling, contention, quarrel-picking, murder, homicide, and great effusion of blood, as experience daily teacheth

We do not know what sort of football was being played in North Moreton on that day in May 1598; we do know that the outcome was one that Stubbes proseletyzed against. When the Star Chamber investigated the Gunters' witchcraft allegations, a number of witnesses testified that bad blood between the Gunters and the Gregory family, into whom the chief of the suspected witches, Elizabeth Gregory, had married, could be traced back to a football match of a few years previously. For once, we have evidence from a variety of sources to reconstruct what happened with a fair degree of accuracy.

The parish register for North Moreton records the burial of John, son of William Gregory, on 20 May 1598, and of Richard Gregory on 26 May. The actual entry, as was usual in this period (plague deaths were an important exception here), did not state the cause of these fatalities. But in this instance somebody, not the vicar, took the trouble to add a note of their own. The hand in which the note was written was an educated one, and clearly dates from around 1600. Although the syntax is uncertain, the meaning is obvious enough. 'Both 2 men,' the interpolator informs us, 'were killed by old Gunter.' Statements, including that of Brian Gunter, in another set of Star Chamber proceedings, dating from 1601, confirm the parish register's sorry tale. Two of the football players, John Field and Richard Gregory, began to fight and 'did ... fall together by the ears'. William Gunter intervened to break up the fight, whereupon he was set upon by Richard Gregory and his brother John. A general mêlée developed, in which Brian Gunter reached over the shoulders of the struggling men and, with the pommel of a dagger he carried in his belt, struck the heads of the two young Gregorys. Gunter claimed he gave them each only 'a blow on the head and no more', and that they 'had little harm' and only shed 'little blood'. But both of them died later, 'within a fortnight' as the note in the parish register informs us.

In theory, all violent or suspicious deaths in England were open to investigation by a coroner; there were normally two appointed for each county. We must, however, assume that many suspicious deaths were simply not reported, and, of course, many coroners' inquests have been lost. But in this instance records survive. Inquests were one of the categories of legal record that should have been returned to the Court of King's Bench at Westminster, and lodged in the King's Bench records is the inquest held at North Moreton on 26 May 1598 on the body of Richard Gregory. The document is faded but unequivocal. The fourteen jurors called by the coroner found that Gregory had died the previous day from 'divine visitation' ('*ex visitatione divina*' in the original Latin of the document), a form of words used by inquest juries to cover suspicious deaths where it was felt impossible or undesirable to bring a verdict of homicide. On this occasion, indeed, the record was anxious to make it clear that Gregory had not died from any wound ('*ex aliqua plaga*') inflicted by Brian Gunter, gentleman.

It is dangerous to read too much into one scrap of documentation, but this inquest does not conform to either the standards of accuracy or the format normally found in coroners' inquests of the period. The inquest on Richard Gregory is in Latin, as most official legal documents of the period were, but it is not written in the usual court hand, the script of the legal document, but rather in secretary hand, the script of the diary and the private letter, and its wording does not conform to the usual formula for inquests. Indeed, it reads and looks like a draft for such a document. And there is that verdict of death by 'divine visitation', which so often masked a dubious cause for a fatality, and that unusual insistence that Brian Gunter was not responsible for the death. There is a sense that the coroner and jury were not too anxious to push matters any further than was necessary in this fatal wounding involving an important man.

Yet homicide was, of course, a crime, and like most serious offences was usually tried at the assize courts. A few weeks after the killing of John and Richard Gregory, three North Moreton men, Robert Gregory, John Sudbury and Robert Adams (the latter two were present at the football match), went to the meeting of the Summer Assizes for Berkshire at Abingdon to give evidence against Gunter in the hope of initiating a formal prosecution against him. In this period accusations of crime were screened by a grand jury, and were then passed on for trial before a petty jury if the grand jury decided that there was a case to answer. Possibly persuaded by the coroner's inquest, the grand jury did not 'find', or accept, the bills of indictment against Gunter for killing the two Gregorys, and so the matter did not go to trial. But there was now bad blood between the Gunters and the Gregorys. William Gregory, the father of the dead youths, gave evidence that after the football game William Gunter came to his house where his two sons lay dying, and threatened them, 'saying that he had not had enough and using many other threatening words'. Walter Gregory, husband of the Elizabeth Gregory who was at the centre of the later witchcraft accusations, likewise told how William Gunter had come to William Gregory's house, and told John Gregory that 'he was sorry he had given him no more hurt, wishing him to come out and revenge himself'.

If one wanted to reconstruct an Elizabethan village community, one would avoid North Moreton. Leaving aside really lucky breaks, like the survival of a parish clergyman's diary or a set of good estate papers from the local lords of the manor, the historian of the early modern English village needs three sets of sources: parish registers, manorial records and Poor Law records. Of these three, only the first, on an initial investigation, seemed to survive for late Elizabethan North Moreton. To make matters worse, quarter sessions records, an essential guide to county administration as well as law and order issues, are missing for Berkshire in the sixteenth and seventeenth centuries.

It is easy to place North Moreton in its general context. It lay close to the border between Berkshire and Oxfordshire (in fact, the Local Government Act of 1974 means that it is now in Oxfordshire) in what was an area of fertile farming land. The eastern half of the Vale of the White Horse, where North Moreton is located, and the adjacent Vale of Oxford, between the Cotswolds and the Chilterns, was an area of mixed husbandry. Cattle were raised by nearly all the richer farmers, while a few sheep were kept, along with the odd pig or horse. Most effort, however, was devoted to arable farming, with much barley being grown, and wheat occupying a secondary position. The inferior grains, oats and rye, were little known, although beans and peas were grown in some quantity. This farming was locked firmly into commercial marketing. There were at least twelve market towns in Berkshire, although most of the produce from the Vale of the White Horse was marketed in Reading or, indeed, Oxford, while produce was also sent down the Thames to be sold to the ever expanding London market. By the standards of the time the region where North Moreton lies was characterized by an advanced, sophisticated and commercial agrarian economy.

North Moreton itself was a small village of 1,102 acres. It is impossible to estimate its population in the years around 1600 with complete accuracy, but it probably consisted of about 200 to 300 people, most of whom, in common with the inhabitants of the other settlements in the area, were involved in farming. As has been said, the farming was commercial and the area an economically advanced one, so we are not looking at an isolated, backward community. The people of the village seem to have enjoyed numerous contacts with larger towns, notably Oxford, which is about twelve miles to the north, Newbury, about twenty miles to the south, and Reading, about the same distance to the south-east. The main manor in the parish, itself named North Moreton, was held for most of the late sixteenth and seventeenth centuries by the Dunch family. They were one of the most important gentry families in Berkshire, their fortunes founded on service at the royal court, with their main holdings at Little Wittenham, a village that lies two or three miles to the north of North Moreton. They seem to have been absentee landlords, playing little direct part in North Moreton's affairs.

The parish church, All Saints', was constructed mainly in the thirteenth and fourteenth centuries, resplendent with stained-glass that had survived the iconoclasm of the Reformation and was to survive the renewed iconoclasm of the Civil Wars. The parish was served by two vicars in the years with which we are concerned. Thomas Heard came to North Moreton in the late 1580s, but was replaced in 1598 by Gilbert Bradshaw, who was then probably aged twenty-five or so. We know little about either of these clergymen. Unusually for southern England in the late sixteenth century, neither of them had a university degree, although Gilbert Bradshaw, described as a 'plebeian' (i.e., of non-gentry origin) and a native of Oxford, had matriculated at New College, Oxford, in February 1592 at the age of eighteen (the slight discrepancy in ages probably results from the contemporary tendency to be approximate in such matters). During his incumbency at North Moreton, he rose to a modest level of material comfort, and his will of 1639 put his wealth at just over £202, of which £140 was in money either kept in his house or held in the form of bonds.

In the apparent absence of manorial records, it was necessary to turn to other sources to find out about the inhabitants of the parish. The records generated by central government taxation and, in particular, parliamentary subsidy rolls make a useful starting point. The subsidy, by Elizabeth I's reign the traditional form of direct taxation in England, was granted by Parliament and raised nationally. It was a progressive tax, falling more heavily on the more wealthy, with the poorer bulk of the population exempted from payment. Of the taxpayers, some were assessed on their lands, and others on their goods, as the local assessors felt appropriate. Subsidy rolls, it must be admitted, offer an imperfect guide to the real wealth of individuals or communities. But they do provide a rough indication of the relative economic standing of the more prosperous inhabitants of the period. Moreover, England's more or less regular involvement in warfare after 1585, when Elizabeth finally decided to offer direct assistance to the Dutch Revolt, meant that Parliament was called frequently, and subsidies were granted regularly to meet the costs of war. There are gaps in the records, but one consequence of this war taxation is that the modern historian benefits from a good series of subsidy rolls for the late sixteenth century.

The rolls provide a series of listings of the principal

inhabitants of North Moreton. In 1600, for example, as in other years, the subsidy roll records a number of names. On the strength of this evidence, the wealthiest man in the village, and the only taxpayer described as a gentleman, was Brian Gunter. He was taxed at £6.16s.0d. on his goods. Edward Field and John Mayne were also taxed on their goods, each paying over £3, while a number of others were taxed lesser amounts on their lands: William Leaver, Thomas Leaver, the widow Joan Leaver, William Gregory, Robert Gregory, Robert Tadmarten, Robert Adams, Edward Spooner and John Sudbury. Rolls for other years around 1600 confirm the pattern suggested here: there was no dominant landlord in this small village, but wealth (and, we may assume, local social power) was concentrated in the hands of a small group of leading farming families, the Adams, the Fields, the Leavers, the Maynes and the Gregorys. These families figure regularly not only in the taxation returns but in the whole range of available records relating to the village.

There is every indication that this was a period of rising prosperity for the yeomen farmers of North Moreton. Whatever the deficiencies of the records, the more substantial inhabitants left a fine series of wills and probate records from which it is possible to gain more detailed insights into both the levels of wealth these farmers enjoyed and what they owned. One of best written wills was that made by William Leaver in 1607. He left his wife, Denise, the household goods, his second-best cow and two pigs. To his daughter Helen went £66.13s.4d., to be received when she was aged eighteen if she married, at twenty if she did not. His son Clement was left £100, to be paid in two instalments when he was twenty-four and twenty-five, while his younger son was to get £50 and land in the neighbouring parish of South Moreton when he was twenty-four. His daughters Isabel and Mary, perhaps already married and thus provided for, received only half a quarter of wheat each. His eldest son, John, married to a Gregory, was left the rest and made executor. As an indication of what this yeoman farmer's substance meant, the £100 he bequeathed to Clement should be contrasted with the £15 that would be roughly the annual income of an agricultural labour-er's family at the time.

The goods left by the North Moreton yeomen were rich and varied. Most of them bequeathed small sums of money to their relatives and, occasionally, to servants, while Thomas Leaver, a yeoman making his will in 1585, left 3s.4d. for the repairing of the bells and bell wheels in the parish church. Quantities of barley, the main crop of the area, were also often left in lieu of money. These farmers, like William Leaver, frequently bequeathed cattle to their wives, and normally a decent attempt was made to pro-vide both for these future widows and for unmarried daughters. Another member of the Leaver family, Raphe, left his married daughter Joan a featherbed, and another daughter a quarter of barley, a brass pot, a standing bedstead and 'one fair chest'. He bequeathed to his brother William (presumably the William Leaver whose will of 1607 we have already referred to) 'my best coat & doublet', one pair of 'venetians' (breeches made of 'venetian', a high-quality cloth), 'my best hat, one pair of shoes & one pair of stockings'. But it is in the probate inventories often filed with these wills that we get the clearest indication of the wealth of these yeomen farmers. Yet another Leaver, John, whose will was made in 1626, was worth £320.18s.6d. at his death. This sum included the value of fifty acres of wheat and barley, ten acres of pulses and vetches, fifteen acres of hay, a plough 'with all furniture thereunto', seventeen cattle, twenty hogs and pigs, along with pigeons, drakes, hens and turkeys, and a plethora of household goods and furnishings.

As the reference to the marriage between William Leaver's

son John and one of the Gregorys suggests, these wills provide evidence not only of individual wealth but also of intermarriages and friendships existing between the leading families. Not too much should be made of either of these matters: friendships die, and interpersonal relations between relatives, not least relatives by marriage, can sour. Yet studying their wills gives us a general idea of the relationships between these families. John Leaver was married to a Gregory, while his father William in his will made 'my loving neighbours' John Mayne and Richard Field overseers of his will. And somebody who will become very familiar as our tale of witchcraft unfolds, Nicholas Kirfoote, was one of the three men made responsible for drawing up the inventory of William's goods. Another Leaver, in this case Nicholas, a husbandman or middling farmer, and thus a rung or two down the social scale from his yeomen relatives, had the same Nicholas Kirfoote as an executor of his will, as a witness to it, and as one of the men entrusted with making the inventory of his goods. It is perhaps not without significance that Brian Gunter figures only rarely as a witness or executor in the years before 1600.

The subsidy rolls and wills thus demonstrate the existence of a wealthy circle within the parish who shared material comfort, intermarried and were linked by friendship and mutual trust. This economic elite, however, in North Moreton as in many other prosperous English villages of the period, also enjoyed a grip on local office-holding. Visitation records for Berkshire for the mid 1590s give details of the parish's churchwardens. These men filled an important post, seen by some contemporaries as carrying greater social status than the parish constableship. The churchwardens' names are, for the most part, familiar: Nicholas Kirfoote, William Leaver, William Field and the less well-documented William French. Despite the general lack of evidence on North Moreton's constables, we know that the parish constable who went to arrest the suspected witch Elizabeth Gregory was Richard Spooner, a representative of another of those substantial farming families listed in the subsidy rolls of the period. And Nicholas Kirfoote was not only churchwarden in 1594 but also served a little later as a hundred bailiff, that is, as an officer working under the county's sheriff who was involved in serving writs, making arrests and carrying out other law enforce-ment duties. Such men, albeit in the limited world of the village, enjoyed wealth as well as responsibility, authority and a degree of power.

We can uncover details of these richer villagers with some success. The poor, in the absence of Poor Law records, remain elusive. Certainly, many of the wills of the yeomen farmers and husbandmen record small bequests to the poor: John Leaver left 6s.8d. in 1626, William Leaver 10s. in 1607, Thomas Leaver, unusually, 4d. 'unto every poor cottager within the parish' in 1587. People are named – in the parish register, in church court cases, in chance records like a coroner's inquest of 1598 – who do not belong to the group of important families, but it is impossible to find out much about them. The poor were there, both the respectable and the not so respectable, God's poor and the devil's, but they figure infrequently in the records. By chance, we know that two of them, evidently members of the undeserv-ing poor, were accused of witchcraft in 1604. The Pepwell women were apparently members of that growing sub-stratum of disorderly, rootless poor that contemporaries were identifying as a major problem. William Leaver, the wealthy yeoman farmer we have already encountered, in his evidence to the Star Chamber told how Agnes Pepwell 'wandered up & down the country & that in such her wandering Mary Pepwell her daughter was begotten of her by one Heywood a lame vagrant as it was said'. The social gap between such people and the respectable yeomen, even in the England of 1600, was already marked.

The volume of the *Victoria County History* for Berkshire covering North Moreton, published in 1923, recorded that manorial court rolls for the village were in the custody of Lord Ashburnham, but these had not been deposited subsequently at the Berkshire Record Office. However, thanks to help from the County Record Office staff, it was discovered that the Ashburnham family had taken the rolls with them when they moved to Hertfordshire, and were lodged in that county's archive office. A visit revealed that the rolls survived in a decent series, starting in 1333 and ending in 1621, and that the documentation was especially thick, with a manorial court roll surviving for about every other year for the last years of the sixteenth century and the first years of the seventeenth. These manorial court rolls provide very important information on life in the village immediately before Anne Gunter's bewitching.

These old manorial court rolls confirm that the village was dominated by a bloc of yeomen farmer families. The sense that the Dunch family, the lords of the manor, were little involved in the affairs of the village is reinforced. No Dunch ever attended a sitting of the court in this period: the direction of business was left to their steward, a gentleman called Thomas Stampe. But in doing business Stampe, the landlord's representative, had to work with the representative organ of the village, the manorial jury. And this jury, normally consisting of ten or twelve men, was recruited overwhelmingly from the top layer of village society, that stratum of rich yeomen farmers from whom the village's churchwardens and constables were also drawn. Thus the jury of 1605 – the year when Elizabeth Gregory and Mary Pepwell were tried for witchcraft at Abingdon, and the year in which Anne Gunter met King James – included several familiar names:

William Leaver, Thomas Leaver, Richard Field senior, Richard Field junior, Robert Tadmarten and John Mayne. This shows again how the village was dominated by a loose grouping of prosperous farmers.

North Moreton, like so many of the villages of the peasant Europe of the period, was in many respects a self-governing community. Every meeting of the manorial court saw the present-ment (that is, prosecution) of a few local inhabitants for minor offences, letting animals stray on the common fields, failing to keep ditches clean or fences repaired, the normal petty transgres-sions that had to be curbed if the village was to run smoothly. To aid this smooth running, the jurors at North Moreton regularly enacted orders, in effect by-laws, for the village. At the 1581 sitting of the court, for example, nineteen such orders were made. These involved the feeding of animals, the regulation of sheep owner-ship, not overgrazing the common, keeping sheep off the cornfields and the inspection of boundaries. Local officers were appointed: Nicholas Knowles as supervisor of animal feeding, William Hoskyns as hayward, and William Leaver as inspector of boundary marks between the lands of the various tenants. On the evidence of this documentation, it was the leading tenants who controlled village government: poor cottagers living on the manor were mentioned rarely, and then only when they were being prohibited from doing things.

The other feature of this documentation is, perhaps surpris-ingly, that Brian Gunter and his family were hardly ever involved in manorial affairs. He was not listed as a tenant of the manor, and appears in the manorial rolls on no more than two occasions. The first came in 1592, with a dispute that shows with complete certainty where the Gunters lived in the village. The second dated from 1600, when Brian Gunter, along with Robert Horsley and Richard Leaver, were fined 5s. apiece for feeding

their horses on the common contrary to a manorial order, Gunter
receiving in addition a smaller fine for not keeping a ditch clean.
We shall return later to these two appearances in the manorial
court rolls.

Even with this accruing body of evidence about North
Moreton, it is difficult to assess the overall quality of life in the
village. There has been some lively debate about the nature of
human relations in the early modern English rural community,
but its outcome remains uncertain. The old myth of the integrat-
ed and co-operative pre-industrial village settlement turns out
to be just that: a myth. There was much greater mobility, and
therefore a greater turnover in the population of any village, than
was suspected before detailed research began, while there is
ample evidence from court records of disputes between villagers.
This has led to converse claims that the quality of human
relations in the typical village was low, and marked by hostility
and competition between individuals. The truth, as so often,
probably lies between the two extremes. Any village had its share
of disputes and could be disrupted by a few troublesome individuals. North Moreton suffered from its quota of such problems.
Archdeaconry court records for Berkshire from the 1590s (and
archdeaconry courts in this period were a forum where many
neighbourly disputes were played out, and where many troublesome individuals were presented by their neighbours) reveal a
fairly typical handful of cases. The vicar Thomas Heard fell into
dispute with William Gregory over tithes. Francis Mayne was
cited for not attending church. John Sudbury was excommuni-
cated for not attending church. There was a defamation case, in
which Mary Leaver alleged that Peter Field was spreading
rumours of sexual immorality on her part, with, as the case
unfolded, Brian Gunter's wife Anne being named as one of those
responsible for repeating the gossip. But these problems and

disputes were typical of the period, and there is no reason to suspect that North Moreton was an especially contentious or dispute-ridden village.

So far little has been said of one of the major sources that survives for the parish, its registers of baptisms, burials and marriages. If we begin in 1604, the year when Anne Gunter fell ill with her strange afflictions, and allegations of witchcraft followed, there are few surprises. There are a handful of entries, as befits a small parish, some of the surnames familiar, others not. But, turning back to the previous year, we immediately encounter something unexpected that still moves the modern reader over a gap of four centuries: there is evidence of a massive disaster that struck this small rural settlement.

The bubonic plague was one of the greatest spectres to haunt the sixteenth and seventeenth centuries. In the mid fourteenth century the Black Death, the first pandemic of the bubonic plague, had carried off more than a third of Europe's population, and the disease, although never so virulent as in its first onslaught, kept returning, helping to inhibit population growth for a century and a half. By 1600, as many of the more analytically minded contemporary observers noted, the plague had become a disease that seemed to hit hardest in urban centres, and especially in the poorer areas of those centres. The Great Plague of London of 1665, so much a part of our historical consciousness through the vividness of Samuel Pepys's first-hand account and the powerful fictional images created by Daniel Defoe, bore this out. But the lasting impression created by these descriptions of England's last great outbreak of plague has obscured the importance of a number of earlier visitations. One of these came in 1603, when the plague carried off 30,000, or roughly a fifth, of London's population, a proportionate loss as great, and perhaps greater, than that suffered in the well-known outbreak of 1665. London, in 1603 as in other years, was not the only place to be afflicted. The plague touched other locations, among them that obscure Berkshire village whose affairs we are investigating.

As Gilbert Bradshaw wrote in the parish register early in 1604, 'it pleased the Lord to visit this little village with great sickness which did continue until the third day of February'. The pestilence arrived on 27 August 1603 at the house of Robert Adams, the head of one of the parish's yeomen families. Bradshaw thought that 'it will never be known how it did first come', although he suggested that it was brought by an infected boy from London who stopped for a drink at the Adams house. If that was so, the family paid dearly for its hospitality. Ten members of the household died: Robert Adams and his wife, two other men named Robert Adams (we may assume that three generations were wiped out) and three other Adams men, along with three people who were probably servants. This disastrous impact on one household suggests an attempt at quarantine in the hope of halting the spread of infection, and it is perhaps significant that the account of Robert Adams senior's goods drawn up after his death refers to £10 of debts incurred 'for provision & other necessaries that in the sickness of the said deceased & his family being visited with the plague for the space of 12 weeks together'.

If quarantine was attempted, it proved unsuccessful. By 3 February 1604, when the last plague burial occurred, the vicar had recorded a further thirty-eight dead from the plague, among them his own wife, Alice, his sons, Henry and Thomas, and his daughter, Anne. We do not know how the parish reacted to this scourge, whether it encouraged social atomization as the ties of friendship and sociability dissolved under fear of infection, or whether the plague engendered that desperate sense of solidarity that has been traced in some of the other afflicted locations in early modern England. We know that in the year before Brian

Gunter launched his witchcraft-accusations North Moreton had suffered the worst trauma in recent history. No Gunters died in this plague outbreak: as was usual with the wealthy, they probably moved out of the affected area as soon as the plague was known to have arrived.

There appears to have been no comparable disaster, and indeed nothing other than the standard recording of baptisms, burials and marriages, in the years before 1603 — until we come to 1598, with the entry recording the fatal injuries inflicted by Brian Gunter at the village football match, where our story really begins. Which leads us to a vital question: who was Brian Gunter?

The Gunter family was a widespread gentry clan with branches in a number of counties, although in the decades around 1600 they seem to have been especially prolific in Berkshire. The anti-quarian Elias Ashmole (1617–92), a native of that county, noted the family tree in his *Antiquities of Berkshire*. The Gunters proba-bly had their origins in Abergavenny in Wales, had moved to Wiltshire in the generation before Brian was born, and thence to Kintbury in Berkshire. There George Gunter, and his wife, Agnes, the daughter of a Wiltshire gentleman named Simon Yate, settled and brought nine children into the world, five sons and four daughters, with Brian as the fourth son and the fifth child (Ashmole, unfortunately, does not supply any dates of birth). Tracing all the branches of the Gunters is a task that might daunt even the most assiduous of family historians: it is enough to know that they were widespread and locally influential in Berkshire in the late sixteenth and early seventeenth centuries, perhaps typical of many county gentry who never achieved national importance but who were influential in their own areas. The Berkshire Gunters seemed to have died out or moved on by 1700, by which date references to them in the county records become infrequent. In their heyday, however, they constituted a locally significant, if generally unremarkable, gentry family.

Brian Gunter himself, on the estimate of his age that he gave during the Star Chamber investigations, was born about 1540. As a young man he settled in Hungerford. He evidently achieved some prominence in that township, for local government records reveal that he was elected churchwarden in 1582. Gunter refused to take the post, as did several other men, presumably because he wished to avoid its responsibilities, and, like them, was fined 6s.8d. In the legal year 1568–9, however, he had already been involved in litigation against the inhabitants of the town over rights to pasture in Freeman's Marsh, and this litigation was renewed in 1573. In 1581 he leased Charlton Manor in Hungerford, again a sign of local importance. The parish register of the town records the baptism of several of his children, among them a daughter, Anne, baptized on 10 May 1584.

Brian Gunter's first known connection with North Moreton is documented in 1579, when he was involved in litigation in a Chancery suit, in alliance with Edward and John Gunter, over possession of the rectory of the parish. It seems likely that he was still resident at Hungerford at that point, because he was offered a local government office in 1582 and Anne was born there in 1584. By 1587, however, he had moved to North Moreton. The subsidy roll for that year shows him assessed for £7.6s.8d. on his goods, making him the wealthiest man in the parish. From then until 1624 the subsidy rolls regularly reveal Gunter as being assessed more highly than any other taxpayer in the village. And it is noteworthy that he was always taxed on his goods. The parliamentary subsidy was assessed either on lands or goods, and the fact that Gunter, a gentleman living in a farming community, was invariably assessed on the latter is interesting. He did not, as was common for men of his status, invest his wealth (and presumably as the son of a gentleman he would at least have inherited some) in land, and live off rents or the profits of agriculture. He seems to have been happy to derive his income from other sources.

Some of these sources are revealed by details of the house where Brian Gunter and his family lived. One of Brian Gunter's few appearances in the manorial court rolls came in 1592. In that year North Moreton's vicar, Thomas Heard, was involved in the deliberations of the court. Heard, who pleaded that as vicar he did not owe suit to the lord of the manor, was presented for letting a cow stray on the common and, more importantly, was involved in a dispute with the lord of the manor over the rectory, which was called the Park. What seems to have precipitated this problem was action by John Stampe, gentleman (presumably a relative of the lord's steward, Thomas Stampe), who was farmer of the rectory of North Moreton. Farming the rectory meant, among other things, that John Stampe had rights to the tithes of the rectory. He had now, apparently without licence and against the will of the lord of the manor, William Dunch, let the Park to Brian Gunter, his wife and family. Thus the Gunter family was occupying the rectory of North Moreton, presumably one of the most substantial buildings in the parish.

John Stampe had in 1579 been involved as plaintiff in a dispute with Edward, John and Brian Gunter over ownership of North Moreton rectory, and further research demonstrates an earlier connection between the Gunter family and the village. Among the wills proved before the Prerogative Court of Canterbury there survives that of Edward Gunter, Brian's brother, who was involved in the dispute over the rectory and who was evidently resident there. In his will of 1585 he described himself as coming from North Moreton, although he also owned land at Chilton in Wiltshire. Edward was obviously a wealthy man, and he was anxious to leave part of his wealth to as many of his relatives as possible. He also left 20s. to All Saints', the North Moreton parish church, and, interestingly, a reference in the will to 'my sister Dunch' suggests that the Gunters had married into the family of the lord of the manor. Brian Gunter and his elder son, Harvey, received Edward's second-best bed and its furnishings, and he also left Harvey his second-best 'bell silver salt' and his second-best set of silver spoons and silver bowls. Most importantly, he left Brian Gunter his interest in the rectory at North Moreton. It was thus as a result of his brother's bequest that Brian Gunter came to North Moreton, lived in its rectory and enjoyed the profits of the associated tithes. Somebody else who benefited from the will was John Gregory, aged less than twenty-one, who was left £3 in money and a quarter of barley. We have no way of proving that this was the John Gregory who died as a result of Brian Gunter's violence in 1598, but it is interesting to see the connection between the two families.

Further evidence both of Brian Gunter's involvement in tithe collection and of his personality comes from 1620. In that year Gunter, now aged about eighty, was the principal defendant in yet more Star Chamber litigation. This time the plaintiff was the vicar, Gilbert Bradshaw, who launched a suit against Brian Gunter, Edward Leaver, Nicholas Kirfoote and Henry Townsend. At the centre of the suit lay a dispute over tithe corn, a dispute that, according to Bradshaw, had involved Gunter fomenting and participating in two riots against him, on one occasion in collusion with the gentleman's grandson, William Holland. Tithes may well have been one of the points at issue in the 1579 Chancery suit over possession of North Moreton's rec-tory, while Gunter was also involved in disputes over tithes at

Hungerford and other places in 1581, at Shrivenham in 1584 and at Kintbury, along with a John Gunter, in 1607. Litigation was a major cultural phenomenon in early modern England, but Brian Gunter's regular involvement in tithe disputes is striking.

The tithe is one of those subjects whose history, although hardly glamorous, is absolutely essential to understanding life in rural England from the early medieval period to the twentieth century. The tithe had its origins in the early church, when the payment of one tenth of all produce for the support of the parish clergyman became an established practice. By the sixteenth century this early simplicity had been lost, and tithe law and tithe collection were convoluted. There are two points that need to be grasped in reconstructing Brian Gunter's economic affairs. The first is that by the sixteenth century, in an increasingly commercial society, the initial practice of payment in kind was being replaced by cash commutations: a farmer would not necessarily give up his tenth sheep to the church but might pay an agreed sum of money instead. Second, after the Reformation, and especially after the Dissolution of the Monasteries and the sales of former monastic lands from the 1530s, many laymen gained the right to tithes. Those purchasing monastic lands frequently also obtained the rights to the tithes due to the monastery in question. Thus in many parishes after the Reformation the local clergyman did not collect the tithes himself, but received an allowance for his keep from a lay impropriator. A body of laymen now had an interest in tithe collection, and the tithe in many villages changed from being a straightforward mechanism for supporting the parish priest to a form of property or set of rights owned by a layman. And, like other forms of property or sets of rights, the tithe could be leased out, whether by clerical or lay impropriators, to laymen who acquired a keen interest in tithe collection. The tithe became a source of profit to lay owners and lessees, and Brian Gunter was a living demonstration of this. It is also worth noting that Gunter was chosen as escheator (a royal financial official) for Oxfordshire and Berkshire in 1596, which suggests a general recognition of his competence in money matters.

It is difficult to reconstruct Gunter's personality from the records, but a strong impression comes through. There is the constant involvement in tithe disputes, the launching of those apparently trumped-up charges of witchcraft that form the subject matter of this book, and the statement of Gilbert Bradshaw in the Star Chamber case of 1621 in which the vicar alleged that Gunter held 'hatred and malice' against him, 'never ceased to stir up many causes and unnecessary and trivial suits' against him and threatened to vex Bradshaw 'until he hath driven your said subject out of the town'. It would be a lucky gentleman of any status in this period who would not find himself involved in litigation at some point in his life, while the allegations of a plaintiff at the Star Chamber should not be accepted at their face value. Yet with Brian Gunter we are dealing with a man who obviously had a reputation for being contentious, who had committed a homicidal assault in his fifties, and who could plausibly be accused of leading a couple of riotous assaults as an octogenarian. Anne's statement to the Star Chamber suggests the pressures that came from having such a man as this as her father.

The most important light on Gunter's personality comes from another body of Star Chamber documents, in this instance recording proceedings launched against him by his fellow villagers in 1601, three years before his daughter fell ill. This litigation was set off by the problems that had led to Brian Gunter being presented at the manorial court for letting his horses graze on the common. According to these Star Chamber proceedings, Gunter, his son Harvey and a number of others (some at least of whom were Gunter's servants) became involved in a confrontation with Robert Adams and John Baker, who were then serving as the manorial officials responsible for impounding stray animals. The details of what happened are unclear (as so often in Star Chamber depositions, a number of versions were told), but at the very least there appears to have been a scuffle between Harvey Gunter and the manorial officers after they had impounded some of his father's horses. Further problems were averted when the parish constables, William Leaver and Richard Field, disarmed and pacified Gunter and his party, threatening to call the village out against them if they did not co-operate. The subsequent Star Chamber investigations took in this incident, asked questions about the fatal football match of May 1598, and recorded another affray involving John Sudbury and Brian Gunter's other son, William, where once again tithe collection was the basis of the problem. William Gunter and John Sudbury had an argument about the collection of tithe barley, as a result of which, as Sudbury put it, 'words were multiplied in so much as they fell by the ears'.

The more general allegations made in the bill of complaint against Gunter are the most remarkable aspects of this litigation. The bill was brought by William Leaver, John Mayne and Richard Field, and was obviously the outcome of decisions made by some of the more important people in North Moreton. Apart from the specific issues, the bill claimed that Gunter's servants Simon Watts and John Tailor were 'men trained up and brought up by the said Brian in fighting and quarrelling with the neighbours thereabouts, and thereby being fit executioners of any mischief whatever the said Brian should devise', and also claimed that they were involved in the assault on the Gregory brothers at the football match. The bill asserted that people went in constant fear of Gunter, his sons and his servants, that he was hostile to the parish officers, and that he was a disloyal subject because he refused to pay taxes. The relevant interrogatories also alluded to the possible involvement of Edmund Dunch, the lord of North Moreton manor after his father William's death in 1597, in attempts to indict Gunter for homicide after the football match, and the involvement of Edmund and his wife Mary in financing the current Star Chamber proceedings. Brian Gunter had offended many of his more influential neighbours, and was a contentious and violent man.

For most of his more substantial neighbours, involved as they were in agriculture, Gunter's position as a tithe farmer must have seemed inherently parasitic: he was seen as an interloper who was creaming off wealth from the local farmers, and would have been regarded with greater bitterness in the late 1590s, when a run of three bad harvests exercised terrible pressure on the rural world. And for final evidence of Brian Gunter's contentiousness, which can only have intensified any widespread dislike felt towards him, we can return to the rumours of dispute between him and the Dunch family. In 1595 Edmund Dunch launched a suit at Chancery against Brian Gunter. The suit had its origins in that dispute, noted in the manorial rolls, over the Gunter family taking up residence in North Moreton's rectory. Dunch claimed in 1595 that he had tried to sue Brian Gunter at the local assizes for trespass in a close near the rectory, but that Gunter had deployed delaying tactics so effectively that Dunch had been unable to obtain a judgement. He was therefore turning to Chancery to overcome the deficiencies of common law, claiming ingenuously that most of the witnesses he had gathered to give evidence on his behalf were elderly and likely to die if proceed-ings were not speeded up. This sounds unconvincing: the impression of Brian Gunter as a man who understood the tactics of litigation, conversely, is one that rings very true.

It is significant that Nicholas and Alice Kirfoote, who were allied to Brian Gunter in his accusations of witchcraft, were also newcomers to the village. They had lived previously at Little Wittenham, where the Dunch family had their main residence, and had married there (Alice's maiden name was Keyes) just after Christmas 1586. They were living in North Moreton by February 1593, for in that month the parish recorded the baptism of Mary Kirfoote, the first of four children of Nicholas and Alice to be born in the parish (Mary was to demonstrate the links between North Moreton's oligarchy of yeomen families by marrying a William Leaver in 1619). So there is the impression of an incoming family, successfully integrating themselves with the local farming elite, falling out with the Gregorys.

And what of the Gregorys, two of whom Brian Gunter had allegedly killed in 1598, and one of whom was to stand accused by him in 1604 of bewitching his daughter? They were one of the main yeomen families of the parish, although they were a little less wealthy than some: the family produced a cobbler and a bargeman as well as yeomen farmers. But William Gregory held part of former chantry lands in the parish in 1575, while a year earlier his kinsman Thomas Gregory had bequeathed him copy-hold lands. They were a family of long residence in the parish, and if their fortunes were not equal to those of the other established families, they may have been all the more likely to resent the wealthy and aggressive newcomer Brian Gunter and his family. That there was no representative of the Gregorys on the manorial jury after 1600 following the death of Robert Gregory reinforces the suspicion that their power within the village was growing uncertain.

The Gregorys also had their share of involvement in legal disputes. In 1584 Exchequer records reveal William and Richard Gregory litigating between themselves over the chantry lands, and over payment for thirty-two quarters of corn. In 1600 Robert Gregory litigated against William Field over possession of a messuage and land at North Moreton called the Chantry Land. In 1609 Walter Gregory, husband of the suspected witch Elizabeth, himself launched a Chancery suit against Edmund Dunch relating to a dispute over a business deal that had been made more than a decade previously: William Field, William Leaver and John Sudbury were also involved. And in 1595 the vicar Thomas Heard was locked in a suit against William Gregory at the archdeaconry court. Depositions survive relating to this dispute, which was over tithes. It may not be fanciful to see here a source of possible conflict between William Gregory and that man with such an interest in tithe matters, Brian Gunter. At the very least, it is clear that the Gregorys were no strangers to contention, especially as Walter Gregory had the distinction of being the only person in the recent history of the parish to have been presented before the manorial jury for breach of the peace.

So North Moreton in 1604 was small and prosperous, with its stratum of rich yeomen farmers, its young vicar and its lone gentry family. It had its share of disputes, and was recovering from a serious plague epidemic. But the village seems to have been a normal sort of place, its inhabitants going about their business and ordering their personal lives in conventional ways. At first sight, there seems to be no reason why this small Berkshire settlement should be riven by a witchcraft-dispute.

But perhaps some broad clues to the context of the witch-craft-accusation can be inferred from the manorial records. These suggest that in the late sixteenth century the affairs of North Moreton were still largely open to communal regulation, even if the 'community' doing the regulating was formed by the village's leading yeomen farmers. But if we can trust these records, early in the seventeenth century that traditional form of organization was breaking up. The meeting of the court of 1605 dealt with less business than those of previous years, the meeting of 1610 was recorded only in very brief documentation, the record of the meeting of 1613 was kept in a very scrappy fashion. There was a relatively well-written, if brief, court roll for 1616, but the following roll, that of 1621, is the last record of the court having met, and is very short, listing a jury of only seven men and containing no details of either presentments or orders. Perhaps too much should not be read into this documentation. Yet it seems to show a change in communal attitudes, a move to a world where families like the Gregorys, a little on the rough side, perhaps, but with their place in the community, were being eased out of local power and local status by really successful yeomen like William Leaver or Nicholas Kirfoote. Or, indeed, a world where economically and socially aggressive gentlemen like Brian Gunter might thrive.

chapter *three*

MANY STRANGE
TORTURES

ANNE GUNTER'S afflictions first beset her around
midsummer 1604, while her father himself was ill at
Oxford. We know little of the details of this first bout of Anne's
sufferings, but it is certain that witchcraft was not yet being discussed as a cause. As Brian Gunter testified, his daughter was
thought to be afflicted by 'the mother', or hysteria, at this stage. It
was when the illness recurred on 23 October, and continued over
the following weeks, that people began to take more note of the
symptoms. Even then, however, a natural malady was assumed,
although, as Brian Gunter put it, the disease now seemed to
resemble the 'falling sickness', epilepsy, rather than 'the mother'.
But Brian was again absent at this point, serving on a jury in
London, and it was his wife, Anne, who was responsible for
coping with their daughter's strange sickness. She called in a
number of doctors. The first to see Anne, a Dr Cheyney of
Wallingford, 'was of the opinion that the said Anne was not sick
of any natural cause or infirmity yet did minister a purge unto
her. And that time notwithstanding her fits continued & grew to
be worse & worse'. Bartholomew Warner, an Oxford-based

doctor, confirmed that the Gunters had called in several men of his profession, and that they 'were of opinion that the said Anne was not sick of any natural cause or infirmity'.

Anne's illness developed rapidly into a series of fits that, despite some variations, corresponded perfectly to the general pattern so frequently manifested in cases of supposed demonic possession. William Sawyer, a North Moreton yeoman who was one of many from the village to give evidence about Anne's illness, told how it began as a type of swooning, and then developed into severe fits, often characterized by the vomiting of pins. In her fits, she underwent various contortions. Mary Thornebury, a girl of about Anne's age, told of 'the turning of her hands back, strange juggling & turning of her eyes, going upon her ankles in a very strange and stiff manner'. Her body became heavier, so that she was, as William Sawyer put it, 'much weightier in her fits, than she was out of them'. She also, as the vicar Gilbert Bradshaw said, was able in her fits to 'declare and tell matters & speeches done & spoken privately & further did disclose & describe divers persons with their several habits and apparel which were to come unto her before they came or were seen of any'. Several witnesses also told how Anne's clothing would move mysteriously of its own accord as she suffered: her stockings came down, her garters unravelled, and the bodice of her petticoat unlaced itself. The girl's condition, Gilbert Bradshaw commented, became worse whenever she was offered food.

One aspect of the fits that attracted considerable attention, and that was to figure prominently when witnesses to the Star Chamber began to discuss whether Anne's sufferings were simulated, was her capacity to void pins from various bodily orifices. The vomiting of foreign bodies was one of the major symptoms of possession, and in Anne's case the foreign bodies most frequently referred to were pins. She vomited these up in the standard fashion, but also expelled them from her nose with violent sneezing: Gilbert Bradshaw, indeed, graphically described Anne's sneezing while expelling pins as so violent that 'it was thought her very heart strings would have broken'. Benedict Allen, a gentleman of Calne in Wiltshire, who was present during Anne's fits, told how pins were 'wrung out of her breast, some with the head & some with the points forward' and also that 'she had voided some pins downwards as well by her water or otherwise'.

That such evidence should be given by a gentleman resident in a township separated by some distance from North Moreton demonstrates that Anne's sufferings, as was common in posses‚ sion cases, were witnessed by a large number of people. From the beginning, as Margaret Bartholomew, a sixty‚year‚old widow living in North Moreton put it, 'the said Brian Gunter did very often send for this deponent and most of the neighbours to behold his said daughter in her fits'. Nicholas Kirfoote testified that Brian Gunter 'sent for most of the parish of Moreton to see and behold his daughter Anne in her fits', and that Gunter came so often to his house to ask him to see Anne's sufferings that 'he this deponent grew very weary of him and did of purpose shut up himself in his house that the said Brian Gunter might not speak with him'. Despite Kirfoote's reaction, news of the girl's bewitchment was eagerly passed on, and attracted observers from circles far beyond the Gunters' neighbours. Gifford Longe, a Bedfordshire gentleman, said how he and other gentlemen went to Brian Gunter's house to see Anne, 'of whom this deponent had heard very strange things'. He saw Anne 'by a poor fellow brought into the parlour of her father's house from the house of one of the neighbours of that town'; she was then sat in a chair, where she fell into 'a very strange agony of quivering & shaking'. Thomas Hinton, another Wiltshire gentleman who witnessed

Anne's fits and who was to become sceptical of their reality, said that 'men of all sorts and from all parts of the country thereabouts repaired unto North Moreton to behold the strange fits and trances of the said Brian Gunter's daughter, then reported by all men to be bewitched or possessed'.

Indeed, as Anne's sufferings progressed, witchcraft became identified as the cause. Attempts to diagnose her illness as natural broke down at a fairly early point. Roger Bracegirdle, a medical doctor of Brasenose College, Oxford, played an important part in identifying witchcraft as the cause of Anne's fits. Aged about eighty when he deposed to the Star Chamber in 1606, Bracegirdle told how he had known Brian Gunter for about a decade, and was asked to go to North Moreton to examine his sick daughter by Anne's sister, Mistress Holland, and Mary and Anne Dunch; the fact that two of the Dunches, lords of the manor, were taking an active interest in Anne's illness is signifi-cant. Bracegirdle recalled that he found Anne 'in an extreme fit or shaking & that the bed wherein she lay did shake by means of her shaking'. He saw the girl's condition improve when thatch from the roof of one of the suspected women's houses was burned, and 'was then persuaded that the said Anne Gunter was bewitched so he having no skill to redress it went his way'. Bracegirdle advised that she should be given no more physic, but that the girl's parents should look for 'some cunning men [that is, good witches] to do the deponent good'.

By this time, a few weeks into her illness, Anne, as was usual in these cases, was herself confirming the growing suspicions of witchcraft by seeing the spectres of her tormentors in her fits. According to one witness, when Anne suffered from her fits she apparently suffered from 'many strange tortures', and at the end of them named three women who afflicted her by witchcraft: 'the first was Goodwife Gregory, against whom she bitterly complained. The second was Mary Pepwell, of whom she spoke indifferently. The third was Mother Pepwell, whom she commended for a very good witch, and one that did not so much torment her as the other two did.' She also saw the familiars of the three witches. William Leaver told how in her torments the girl sensed the three women coming towards her father's house, and called out against them, 'saying that they and their spirits did torment her & called those spirits by names'. Brian Gunter, after confirming that she cried out against Elizabeth Gregory and the two Pepwells in her fits, gave details of the familiars his daughter saw in her afflictions. Elizabeth Gregory's was like a black rat with a swine's face and boar's tusks. Agnes Pepwell's was like a mouse with a man's face and a long beard. Mary Pepwell's was like 'a whitish toad, & was called Vizit'. Anne also, according to her father, saw other shapes, 'namely, the shape of a bull, a bear, & a black swan'. Several witnesses were able to refer to a remark-able instance of sympathetic magic that again pointed to Elizabeth Gregory's power over Anne. The girl's mother was one of several observers who told how at the time when Elizabeth Gregory was 'in labour & travail of childbirth' Anne 'had a swelling in her belly as big as a great household loaf & cried out exceedingly with the extremity of the pain of that swelling'. The mother recounted how before that incident the girl had told her 'that when Elizabeth Gregory was sick she the said Anne should also be sick, & sick after the same manner as the said Elizabeth was'.

The reactions of the various parties in the growing tangle of witchcraft suspicions were predictable. A number of witnesses told how Brian Gunter was 'greatly broken with the strangeness & suddenness of ye accident', that he was, in the words of Gilbert Bradshaw, frequently found bemoaning his daughter's condition, and that he tried to improve it by 'physic as by all other

lawful ways and means'. These 'lawful ways and means' included the input of clergymen. Three, Mr Chetwyn, Mr Whetcombe
and Mr West, came to help Anne 'by fasting & prayer'.
Attempting to win the goodwill of the supposed witches proved
less fruitful. According to William Field, when Elizabeth
Gregory heard that Anne Gunter was afflicted by fits, in which
she was accusing the older woman of bewitching her, she
declared that the girl was going to get worse. Gilbert Bradshaw
told how he had tried to engineer a meeting between Gregory and
Anne, one of those confrontations that were so often used in an
attempt to clear the air when witchcraft suspicions were growing,
which in this instance resulted merely in the suspected witch rail-
ing against both the girl and the minister.

Although Elizabeth Gregory appears to have had at most only a
slight reputation for witchcraft, it is clear that she was very badly
thought of among her neighbours. William Leaver, that representative of North Moreton's solid yeomen farmers, said that
Elizabeth Gregory was 'taken amongst all or most of her
neighbours to be a most notorious scold and a maker of great
debate & falling out amongst her said neighbours'. Martha, the
wife of Richard Baker, another North Moreton resident, thought
her 'a notorious scolding body & a vile curser & blasphemer',
and also declared that he had seen her familiar spirit. To another
villager, Elizabeth Baker, Gregory was 'a very devilish scold & a
horrible curser & swearer', while another of the parish's
yeomen, William Field, thought her 'a very unquiet person &
one that many times upon very small occasions doth use to curse
& threaten her neighbours, & is a common disturber of them & a
stirrer up of debate & strife amongst them'. The fullest and most

damning evidence about Gregory's character, however, came from Gilbert Bradshaw. He confirmed that the woman was 'accounted a scold & an unquiet body amongst her neighbours & a great curser & swearer & such an one as the women of the town where she dwelleth will not accept of her company at church-ings, weddings or at the labours or child births of women'. Indeed, according to the vicar, she was so disliked by her neighbours that they had 'forborne to accompany her in receiving the holy sacrament', and that she was unable to endure being in church at the time of 'the saying of the peace of God'. This last, declared Bradshaw in an interesting reference to the folklore of the period, was something that 'some hath observed as a note or mark of a witch'. She had, moreover, two years previously voluntarily confessed to him that her mother-in-law had been a witch, and that in consequence of this a familiar spirit infested Elizabeth Gregory's house. Thus suspicions of witchcraft were attached to a woman who was obviously seen as troublesome by a wide range of her neighbours.

Agnes Pepwell, conversely, had a long-standing and well-established reputation for witchcraft. To William Leaver, whose opinions on Elizabeth Gregory we have already heard, Agnes Pepwell was a bad lot, who had wandered up and down the country and become pregnant with Mary by a lame vagrant. Both the women, he declared in the standard terminology of the time, 'were reported and suspected to be persons of little credit before the sickness of the said Anne', 'credit' in this context referring to the symbolic capital of personal reputation rather than financial viability. Others, while confirming this generally poor reputation, focused on the Pepwell women's status as witches, especially Agnes's. John Leaver, a husbandman of South Moreton, neatly ran the two together by declaring that long before Anne's afflictions Agnes Pepwell was thought of as 'a person of very lewd & ungodly life & accounted for a witch', while Elizabeth Baker noted that 'long before the sickness of the said Anne Gunter' Agnes Pepwell was 'suspected to be a witch', although she admitted that she had heard no such reports about her daughter Mary or Elizabeth Gregory. William Sawyer said that he had heard rumours of Agnes Pepwell bewitching Anne Gunter with Elizabeth Gregory's assistance, and also that Pepwell had a reputation for bewitching men's cattle. This last point was confirmed by Gilbert Bradshaw. He said that Agnes had a general reputation for witchcraft, and that he 'hath been credibly told by his neighbours she did heretofore bewitch the horses of one Adams & was much talked of ... for the same'; she had also bewitched the horse of John Mayne, both of these men, it will be recalled, were members of the parish's yeomen elite. Bradshaw claimed that Pepwell had confessed to these harmful acts, 'as will be proved'. Another witness reported how when the bell tolled for Anne Gunter as she was felt to be moving towards death, Agnes Pepwell said, 'The Lord receive the soul of the gentlewoman Mistress Anne, but for her friends God reward them as they would reward me.' As so often, we find a witch speaking in ambivalent tones.

A number of witnesses, in response to the Star Chamber's schedule of questions, also offered their opinions about Brian Gunter. Mainly they appeared, contrary to that quality of contentiousness that we have traced about the man, to have taken a favourable view of him. Robert Tadmarten said that he had known Gunter 'since the time of Tilbury Camp' (an interesting allusion to the concentration of English land forces at that Essex location in response to the Armada and fears of invasion in 1588), from which point he had 'known & dwelt near' Gunter and 'never knew nor heard but that the said Mr Gunter was a very honest gentleman & well regarded & esteemed amongst all

men that know him'. Gunter's children, according to
Tadmarten, were 'of civil carriage & good education'. John
Hobgood of South Moreton, a yeoman, said that he had known
the Gunters for eighteen years. He declared Brian Gunter to be a
man of good reputation, who 'was noted to have brought up all
his children in the knowledge & fear of God'. This opinion was
confirmed in general terms by William Nicholas, a weaver of
North Moreton. A somewhat different note was struck by
Gilbert Bradshaw. Bradshaw, as we have seen, gave damning
character evidence against Elizabeth Gregory, and, as Anne's
sufferings continued, was to become very supportive to the
afflicted family. Yet, in his deposition, he recounted that he did
not visit the Gunter household at the beginning of Anne's
sickness, as there was 'some unkindness' between him and her
father.

There was, perhaps more surprisingly, some ambivalence
among the witnesses about Brian Gunter's relations with the
Gregory family. A number of witnesses, of course, remembered
the deaths after the football game in 1598. Alice Kirfoote told
how there was 'a great ill-will and displeasure between Brian
Gunter and William Gregory, father-in-law to Elizabeth
Gregory, by reason of the death of his 2 sons Richard and John
Gregory, imputed to the said Brian'. John Sudbury, described as
a Chipping Norton innkeeper, although almost certainly the
same John Sudbury who had previously been described as a
husbandman living at North Moreton, confirmed this. He stated
that the enmity stretched back to 'a match or play at football many
years past', although he was unable to say if either Richard or
John Gregory had said anything against Gunter on their
deathbeds (this might indicate a convenient lapse of memory:
John Sudbury was one of those who had tried to indict Brian
Gunter for homicide after the deaths of the two young Gregorys).

More specifically, Nicholas Kirfoote, involved with Gunter in the witchcraft accusations but by the time of the Star Chamber investigations clearly retreating from his earlier alliance, declared that after Anne was thought to be bewitched her father accused Elizabeth Gregory and the Pepwells, 'and that he rather named those than any other unto him because upon his hatred conceived against them he meant to bring them in danger of their lives'.

If this hatred existed, it was certainly reciprocated by Elizabeth Gregory. One witness, a member of the small party of men who went to bring the woman to Gunter's house for a confrontation between witch and victim, reported that Gregory reacted to the invitation by saying that Gunter 'was a murdering bloodsucker & that the blood of the Gregorys should be revenged upon the blood of the Gunters, & she would have blood for blood'. When further urged to go and see Anne Gunter, Gregory continued, 'I care not for her, let her live or die, I will not come at her.'

Another section of local opinion, however, seemed willing to declare that relations between Brian Gunter and the three women had been more amicable. William Leaver, along with one or two other witnesses, claimed that the deaths after the football match had happened too long ago to be of any consequence, and that there was no enmity between the Gunters and the Gregorys. William Sawyer, described at this point as a North Moreton yeoman, although possibly the man of that name who was referred to elsewhere in the depositions as a servant of Gunter, said that there was no ill-will between Brian Gunter and Elizabeth Gregory before Anne fell ill, and that Brian Gunter 'did very neighbourly & charitably help & relieve the said Elizabeth Gregory & Walter Gregory her husband by ploughing & manuring their land & by doing them other good turns'. According to this witness, Gunter had also helped Agnes and

Mary Pepwell 'with meat, drink & otherwise', and there had been no reports of malice or quarrels between him and the two women. Another witness confirmed that Brian Gunter helped the Gregorys and did them 'friendly & neighbourly good turns and benefits as namely fodder for their cattle, ploughing & manuring their land & straw for their cattle'. Martha Baker confirmed the stories of Brian Gunter performing acts of charity and helpfulness towards the three women, and said that he got on with them as well as anybody before Anne's illness began.

Evidence was also given about another relationship that was to become of vital importance in North Moreton in late 1604, that between Brian Gunter and Nicholas Kirfoote. Although the two men were jointly to accuse the witches, there appears to have been no long-standing friendship between them and, indeed, there had been some friction. John Hobgood told how Kirfoote had previously kept an alehouse, but, because of complaints made by Brian Gunter about some misdemeanours there (the disorderly alehouse was the bane both of local authorities and respectable elements in village society in this period), Kirfoote was banned from selling ale, and that it was at this point he became a bailiff. William Nicholas confirmed this story, while another witness referred to 'some unkindness & discontentments' between Gunter and Kirfoote, although he also commented that they had become more friendly of late.

This rapprochement may have been the result of the two men identifying a common enemy in Elizabeth Gregory. Alice Kirfoote did not, according to a number of fellow parishioners, get on very well with Elizabeth. Anne Gunter, indeed, declared that 'there was malice & enmity betwixt Nicholas Kirfoote and his wife & the said Elizabeth Gregory', and that the two women 'seldom met together but they railed one at the other & sometimes fell to blows'. Gilbert Bradshaw testified that the two women first fell out when they were both living at Reading 'in the time of the sickness at North Moreton', evidence of how even yeomen farmers' families were able to flee a plague outbreak and to take up temporary residence elsewhere. Certainly by the following autumn Elizabeth Gregory was still immensely hostile to the Kirfootes. William Leaver had heard Gregory say 'she would root Kirfoote out of North Moreton'. William Sawyer confirmed this, claiming that Gregory had said 'and for Nicholas Kirfoote I say that I will root him & his out of the town', adding that it was at about this time that Alice Kirfoote fell ill. The Star Chamber investigations thus unearthed a wealth of evidence about tensions and frictions in the village of the sort that so rarely enter the historical record directly, yet that were vital in the background to a witchcraft case.

For fears of witchcraft were spreading as Anne Gunter continued to suffer her fits. Her father, according to Nicholas Kirfoote, thought he was himself bewitched, 'by reason of a pain he had in his neck'. Gunter cured this by direct action, adopting the traditional remedy of scratching Elizabeth Gregory's face 'until the blood flowed', the relief he gained by this expedient, according to Kirfoote, making the woman 'more undoubtedly to be accounted a witch'. It was shortly after this that Alice Kirfoote fell ill, showing the same kind of symptoms that Anne Gunter was displaying, and complaining to one witness 'that her sight was darkened through the extremity she was in'. Edward Sampson, a clergyman from Kingston near Lewes in Sussex, gave details of Alice's fits, by which 'her husband & others in the house were much troubled'. He saw the woman suffering from 'a great rising or swelling in her belly, her neck & mouth also drawn awry, her eyes fixed in her head ... her body lying straight along in ye bed as if it had been drawn out', her body being stiff '& her joints like iron & she could not be made to bend or move any way'. As with Anne Gunter, doctors were called in to attend Alice Kirfoote, but here too they felt that the illness 'was not natural but supernatural, & that therefore physic was to no purpose'. And, again as with Anne Gunter, Alice Kirfoote began to call out in her fits against Elizabeth Gregory and Agnes Pepwell, claiming that 'those two women did vex her'.

On one reading, then, we can begin to trace what must have been a common situation when witchcraft fears began to overrun the early modern village. One illness, in this case that of the young woman Anne Gunter, was diagnosed as bewitchment, and a combination of pre-existing enmity, tension and a reputa-tion for witchcraft led to the first accusations. Then another person, in this case Alice Kirfoote, fell ill, and by the same processes witchcraft was again diagnosed as the problem, and the same women were accused. There are some signs that after Alice Kirfoote fell ill fear of witchcraft in the area began to develop its own dynamic. John Leaver, a South Moreton husbandman, aged thirty-one and clearly related to the North Moreton Leavers, was one of those who one Friday accompanied Richard Spooner, the constable of North Moreton, when he went to arrest Elizabeth Gregory and to take her to the justice of the peace, Sir Richard Lovelace, for questioning. He found the expe-rience a traumatic one. The party crossed a stile as they walked from Gregory's house to that of the justice, and Leaver suffered what appears to have been a panic attack when he tried to follow the suspected witch over it. Subsequently, 'every Friday after almost for a long time this deponent was somewhat troubled & had points [i.e. laces] of his hose tied in knots and his shirt string tied in knots likewise'; similar things had happened to Anne Gunter's clothing during her fits. His wife heard him say in bed (and presumably in his sleep), 'Pepwell and Gregory will you make a puppet of my shirt', 'puppet' being one of the terms used to describe the models or tokens witches used when performing image-magic, that form of witchcraft of damaging an effigy of the witch's intended victim in hopes that harm would consequently befall the person in question. In his dreams Leaver saw the two women, along with their familiars, things in the shape of a rat or a toad, and he was also enticed by them 'to receive the sacrament of the devil'. John Leaver may have been more imaginative or suggestible than other farmers in the area, but his testimony does show how fears of witchcraft could operate within the psyche. It also demonstrates how the popular view of witchcraft was already associating the witch with the devil.

Suspicions of witchcraft were clearly spreading, then, and one wonders how many others in North Moreton and the surrounding villages were, like John Leaver, becoming oppressed by fears of witchcraft, or found themselves wondering if misfortunes they had suffered might be attributed to that malign force. It is important to remember, however, that reactions to Anne Gunter's sufferings and to the allegations of witchcraft were not universally credulous. Even at this stage (or at least they were going to claim as much before the Star Chamber a year and a half later) a number of people were convinced that Anne Gunter was simulating her fits, and that her father was masterminding the whole affair. In particular, several witnesses remembered, and gave evidence about, the incident at Anthony Ruffin's house when Brian Gunter apparently used physical violence on his daughter to force her to maintain the pretence of bewitchment. But the suspicions of possession and witchcraft predominated at this stage, and accordingly we must stay with the narrative of their unfolding.

If the doctors failed, a number of alternative ways of helping the bewitched were available. The most obvious of these was to have recourse to 'cunning' men and women, those good witches who were the bane of contemporary demonologists and a source of constant and varied assistance to the inhabitants of early modern England. Soon after the second bout of Anne's illness began in late October, her father began to contact cunning men. One of his servants, William Sawyer, told how he was sent on 5 November 1604 to John Wendore of Newbury, 'being a person supposed to be cunning in matters concerning witch-craft'. Sawyer brought Wendore back with him and, on seeing Anne Gunter, the good witch declared that she 'was not sick, but rather … bewitched by some evil neighbour', although he added encouragingly that he had no doubt that the girl should 'with God's help be well again'. But after treatment from Wendore, according to Sawyer, Anne once more fell sick on 18 November. She was so afflicted that her father and others thought she was going to die, and they 'caused the passing bell to be tolled for her' (it was at this point, indeed, that Gilbert Bradshaw forgot the ill feelings between himself and Brian Gunter, and visited the gen-tleman's household). Sawyer was sent to Newbury to bring Wendore back again, but was informed that he had gone to London. Soon after this Gunter wanted to send another of his servants to find Wendore, but the servant, being unwilling to travel to Newbury on what might have been a fruitless errand, recommended another cunning man, named Blackwall. He, so the servant assured his master, was as competent as Wendore. Blackwall came, stayed overnight to observe Anne's fits, and then said he would go to Oxford to obtain 'things to minister to her'.

What is obvious from this testimony is that the reputation and identity of cunning folk was widespread. Gunter was able to bring one to mind readily, and one of his servants was apparently acquainted with another, if only by reputation. Other cunning men were consulted as the tale of possession and witchcraft progressed. Gilbert Bradshaw himself, apparently, discussed the witchcraft in the village with 'one Palliser', who was 'a man professing skill about matters of witchery', who told the vicar that Anne Gunter and Alice Kirfoote were bewitched, but that he would help them. It is remarkable that a clergyman should be able to enter into a discussion with a cunning man, while, as we have seen, the doctor Roger Bracegirdle, when he realized that what might be termed the 'official' medicine of the period would not help the girl, positively recommended to her parents that they should consult cunning folk. Evidently these magical practition/ers and charmers were taken seriously not just by the peasantry but also by the educated and affluent of rural and small town society.

Even so, the most detailed narrative of seeking assistance from cunning folk comes from Anne Gunter's farming neighbours. Robert Tadmarten, a sixty/year/old husbandman from North Moreton, described how he was walking in a wood at Ashampstead the day after the passing bell was tolled for that other sufferer from witchcraft, Alice Kirfoote. Tadmarten encountered an acquaintance named Browne, who asked him 'why he … was so sad'. The husbandman replied that Alice Kirfoote 'as the report went was bewitched & that the bell had tolled twice for her the evening & night before and that she was like to die being one that the deponent did wish well unto with all his heart & would travel forty miles to do her any good he could'. Browne answered helpfully that 'there was a thing in the country that had done good unto cattle that were supposed to be bewitched & that one Goodwife Higgs of Ashampstead afore-said would help this deponent unto it'. So Tadmarten went to Higgs, who said she would borrow the charm for him, and the day after their first meeting she gave him 'a little bag' done up with string and told him that it should be hung around the neck of Alice Kirfoote. The cunning woman also gave Tadmarten 'a little green vial glass with about two spoonfuls of water in it', and told the husbandman to make Alice Kirfoote drink it, saying that it would do her good, '& especially help her eyes, saying she would lend these things unto this deponent for five days'. He took the charm and the drink to Alice Kirfoote's house, where the sister of Goodwife Bartholomew, who was helping the afflicted women, suggested that some of the water might be ministered to Anne Gunter.

Goodwife Bartholomew was presumably the widow Margaret Bartholomew, who gave evidence about Anne's sufferings and treatment and who also specifically mentioned the 'little glass with water in it' that Tadmarten (or, on her evidence, his wife) brought to the Kirfoote household; this was subsequently given to Anne, although with little effect. Nicholas Kirfoote gave more evidence about this drink, saying that it came in a 'double vial glass' and that 'either the colour of the glass or the water was green'. He confirmed that Anne was 'troubled and displeased at the taking of it' (the reader will recall Anne's comments on the effects of this liquid), and also that its taste was such that his wife 'could take but a little of it down into her stomach'.

Whatever the actual nature of this concoction, and of the charm Tadmarten brought for Alice Kirfoote, when giving evidence to the Star Chamber the husbandman was anxious to distance himself from any direct involvement in magical practices; however widespread recourse to cunning folk may have been, most people realized that the attitude of higher authority towards them, and towards those who went to them, was likely to be hostile. Tadmarten assured his questioners that he himself had no knowledge of how to make the drink he had got from Goodwife Higgs, that he had not taught Brian Gunter how to make it, and that he earned his living by 'husbandry and tillage' and had no knowledge of 'physic or surgery'.

Cunning folk were only one way to counter the effects of witchcraft: there were a number of practices that, although disliked by officialdom, were used regularly by the population at large. Anne Gunter's bewitchment prompted those around her to try some of these. As we have already noted, her father scratched Elizabeth Gregory's face, a standard means of obtaining relief from witchcraft. Another technique, burning the witch's hair, was also tried. Gilbert Bradshaw, apparently as accepting of this type of counter-magic as he was of cunning folk, told how the Gunters confronted Elizabeth Gregory and 'for their better satisfaction and for their daughter's ease desired to have a little hair of her head to burn'. Elizabeth at first refused on the grounds that 'they should have none of her hair for that might be a means or an occasion to detect her', but eventually, and presumably while under heavy pressure, she consented. Her hair was burned on three or four occasions, and it was remarked that each time Anne Gunter seemed to get some relief. All three of the women were regularly brought before Anne, in hopes of either reaching a reconciliation or, as things worsened, conjuring the spirits out of her, but the most common outcome of such meetings was that the girl's fits became even more intense. There was also a tradition that moving the afflicted person away from her residence brought relief. Anne seems to have been moved to a number of locations in and around the village, perhaps most notably to her brother Harvey Gunter's house at Stanton St John in Oxfordshire. This tactic, so a number of witnesses said, did seem to prove beneficial.

The form of counter-magic most frequently mentioned, however, was burning some of the thatch from Elizabeth Gregory's and Mary Pepwell's houses. Again, the practice seems to have been firmly rooted in the folklore of the period. A number of Brian Gunter's neighbours, notably William, the son of Peter Field, a young man from one of the village's solid yeomen families, told Gunter 'that if the thatch, straw, or reed of the house wherein a witch dwelleth which hast bewitched any persons be burnt that there during the burning thereof the party bewitched should have ease or else the witch would come to the house where the party bewitched remaineth'. Gunter asked William Field to burn some of Elizabeth Gregory's thatch. This was done, and the practice was repeated on both her roofing and that of Agnes Pepwell on a number of occasions. The thatch was burned outside the chamber of Anne Gunter, and a number of witnesses, among them Gilbert Bradshaw and the substantial yeoman William Leaver, testified that she derived ease from this. Nicholas Kirfoote, however, added one of those discordant notes that were fairly common in the Star Chamber depositions. Anne, he recounted, seemed to benefit from the burning of the thatch when she had been informed that it was being burned: when this information had not been passed to her, she seemed to remain in her fits. Yet, for most of those observing her afflictions, her apparent recovery when Gregory's or Pepwell's thatch was burned served as a confirmation that her sufferings were inflicted on her through the witchcraft of the two women.

This battery of folkloric remedies – the resort to cunning folk, the scratching of the witch, the burning of the witch's hair or thatch – are all frequently mentioned in the witchcraft narratives of the period. What was more remarkable in the Gunter case was the way in which several people gave or loaned Gunter books on witchcraft to help him become better informed about such matters. A number of works, ranging from full-scale demonological tracts to slighter trial pamphlets, had been pub-lished in England on the subject of witchcraft by 1604, yet it remains unclear how wide the readership or ownership of such works was, especially readership outside scholarly circles or the upper reaches of the clergy. Anne Gunter's case provides rare information on this point. Anne herself, as we have seen, told how an interested party brought her father 'the book of the witches of Warboys', and Nicholas Kirfoote confirmed that 'a book written of the witches of Warboys touching the bewitching of Mr Throckmorton's children' was in Gunter's house. Shortly afterwards, 'Darrell's book concerning some that were bewitched', one of the flurry of publications printed at the very end of the sixteenth century in the controversy provoked by the career of John Darrell, the Puritan exorcist, was brought to Brian Gunter by a William Carter. Gunter also obtained a book describing people 'said to be possessed with wicked spirits at Denham', a work to whose significance we shall return at a later point. The purpose of bringing these books, according to Anne, was so that her father 'should see in what manner the parties named in those books were tormented & afflicted', and she testified that he did indeed 'read & consider of them'. As already mentioned, she admitted that her simulations were very heavily based on the descriptions of the sufferings of the Throckmorton girls in the tract dealing with the Warboys case. Print culture was joining with popular beliefs, helping to define witchcraft and to inform opinion on how both witches and those they bewitched acted, and on what could be done about such matters.

Witchcraft and possession were live issues that were very widely known about, talked about, and seen as being of general interest. And this knowledge, discussion and interest were not confined to simple villagers. Gilbert Bradshaw, the vicar, was living in a world where witchcraft was operating in much the same way as it was in the minds of the more lowly members of his flock, while medical doctors, including those who moved in educated circles in Oxford, were happy to ascribe illnesses that defied diagnosis and treatment to supernatural causes or, more specifically, witchcraft. And, as the number of witnesses before the Star Chamber who were gentlemen from neighbouring counties suggests, tales of cases such as Anne Gunter's would spread, become newsworthy over a wide region; interested parties would either make a special visit to the home of the sufferer, or make sure that they went to his or her home if other business brought them into the area.

But the experience of Anne Gunter herself lay at the centre of North Moreton's witchcraft fears. On her later evidence, the girl simulated possession under her father's instructions, although she did so sufficiently well to convince the crowds that thronged to see her in her fits, and at least some of the witnesses who gave evidence a year and a half after those fits commenced. Both her own evidence and the statements of yet other witnesses give us an indication of the pressures she was under as she contorted, or voided pins, or went into trances. But her sufferings at North Moreton were only the beginning: her case was already attracting the attention not only of a wide range of people in her area but also those in a higher sphere.

chapter *four*

WITCHCRAFT

O F   C O U R S E , we all 'know' about the witches the villagers of North Moreton feared so much: the old women in the pointed sugar-loaf hats, dressed in the long skirts and shawls that are in fact, along with the hat, a stylized version of female peasant dress of around 1700, riding on broomsticks, perhaps with cats perched precariously upon them. Most educated Europeans and North Americans have, since about 1800, learned to recognize this iconographic representation of the witch through children's literature and folk-tales. A few of those educated Europeans and North Americans have, on reaching adulthood, become sufficiently intrigued by the problem of witchcraft to study it on a scholarly or academic level, and developed rather complex sets of ideas about its significance. But it has proved very difficult to escape from the view that would see belief in witchcraft as something that differentiates 'modern', 'advanced' or 'rational' societies from those of the 'superstitious' or 'backward' past. As one aspect of this, the willingness to persecute witches has become symbolic of intolerance and mindless persecution (note how the term 'witch-hunt' has entered our vocabulary and consider the ahistorical ways in which it is used).

Numerous historians and others have tried to 'explain' the witch-persecutions. How and why was it that between about 1450 and 1750 maybe 40,000 of Europe's inhabitants, most of them women, were executed, many of them by burning at the stake, as witches? How and why was it that the legal systems of the period were able to entertain accusations of witchcraft? How and why were the clergy able to endorse these accusations and the beliefs and fears that led to them? And how and why were some of the best brains in Europe able to write long books supporting the witch-burnings? The historians and others who have turned their minds to this most peculiar of phenomena have come up with a formidable range of explanations for it: the European witch-craze, to use a well-known if somewhat hyperbolic term, has been attributed variously to the Protestant Reformation, to the Catholic Counter-Reformation or, more generally, to a desire by official Christianity to root out and destroy believers in an earlier, pre-Christian religion. It has also been ascribed to the rise of capitalism, to the break-up of the traditional village community and the emergence of the modern state, to male hatred of women; with perhaps less certainty, it has also been attributed to the shock caused by the arrival of syphilis as an epidemic disease or to the use of hallucinogenic drugs. Psychiatry (once Freudian, now often Kleinian) has been brought in to help us explain witch-accusations, as have social anthropology and gender theory. The subject, however, remains elusive.

At the core of this elusiveness (setting aside the sheer range and complexity of the explanations on offer) is, perhaps, the fact that witchcraft as a historical phenomenon poses a severe challenge both to the historical imagination and to the common notion of what historians are meant to be doing. Generally, study and writing about history involves the critical reading of as many documents or other source materials about a subject as possible, looking at what other people have written about that subject to see how far the undergrowth has been cleared, and then reflecting on the results of these two exercises until enough clarity of thought and intellectual self-confidence have been acquired to write about the subject. This writing should encapsulate an attempt to give an accurate representation of the 'reality' of the subject in question, although most historians have long recognized that what they are doing in effect is writing provisional reports, the best version that they can reconstruct of what happened. With witchcraft the exercise encounters considerable problems at the last hurdle: most modern historians do not believe in the 'reality' of witchcraft in the way that they believe, for example, in the reality of Henry VIII. Obviously, most people living in North Moreton in 1604 did believe that certain of their neighbours could inflict harm by occult means, and that Brian Gunter's daughter was suffering from such harm – but getting to grips with how they were able to do so demands a considerable imaginative leap on the part of the modern observer.

What did witchcraft mean to the inhabitants of England, and, more narrowly, North Moreton, at the beginning of the seventeenth century? Or, to put the matter slightly differently, when Anne Gunter fell ill and that illness was diagnosed as being caused by witchcraft, what presuppositions and mental equipment did those who came to take an interest in her suffer-ings, from the humble villagers among whom she lived to the clerical intellectuals and skilled medical doctors who were to become involved in her case, have at their disposal?

For most English villagers and, indeed, for most of the inhabitants of peasant or small-town Europe, the key issue in witchcraft was *maleficium*, the ability to do harm or to inflict damage by witchcraft. Most witchcraft cases that reached the English assize courts (and it was the assizes, where most serious crimes were tried, that usually dealt with accusations of malefic witch-craft) were concerned with the infliction of concrete harm: killing humans, whether adults or children, by witchcraft, or (as in Anne Gunter's case) making them ill, or killing livestock. When we have richer documentation than the rather terse trial indictments, we discover witches interfering with such domestic operations as churning butter or brewing beer, although it seems that this type of activity was rarely thought serious enough to justify taking a suspected witch to court. For the most part, English witches do not seem to have been suspected of causing large-scale damage, such as raising storms or blasting crops, nor were they thought to have interfered with female fertility or male potency. Insofar as we can reconstruct beliefs on the matter, most people seem to have thought that the witch inherited her powers, most often from her mother or some other female relative, or had learned how to use them, again normally from female relatives. The clergy, of course, were attempting to inculcate the notion that the witch's powers were derived from a pact between the witch and the devil.

The English malefic witch was also typically thought of as female: in the largest sample of court cases for which we have evidence, those tried by the south-eastern assizes in the late sixteenth and seventeenth centuries, over 90 per cent of the 574 accused were women. Explaining this sex ratio has been the source of considerable controversy in recent years. Few serious scholars, even those writing from an avowedly feminist position, would attribute it to straightforward woman-hating, although England around 1600 was a patriarchal society in which religious, scientific and medical thinking all took the moral, intellectual and physical inferiority of women for granted. The key, however, seems to lie not in simple misogyny but rather in the ways in which witchcraft was seen as something that operated in the female sphere. Women had no inhibitions about accusing other women of being witches, about witnessing against other women in witchcraft-trials at the assizes, or about serving in the more or less official female juries that searched women suspects for the witch's mark. Close reading of some of the better-documented cases shows witchcraft-accusations arising from disputes between women over access to domestic space, over the interruption of domestic chores or domestic regimes and, above all, over harm thought to have been inflicted on children. Indeed, the frequency with which a witchcraft-charge involved a mother accusing an older, post-menopausal woman of bewitching her child has fed into psychological explanations of witchcraft, with the witch being recast as the 'bad' mother.

For it was not just any woman who was likely to be accused of witchcraft. More commonly it was women like Agnes Pepwell, poor, elderly, with a bad moral reputation, living outside the constraints or protection of the patriarchal household, or women like Elizabeth Gregory, with a local reputation as a troublemaker. Witchcraft operates in different ways in different societies, but in Tudor and Stuart England it was characteristically a matter of richer villagers accusing poorer, and normally female, ones. The accusations usually arose after a misfortune befell a household: a child fell ill, or the head of the household was blasted by a strange disease, or cattle or pigs began to die inexplicably. This misfortune defied explanation in natural terms, and came to be attributed to witchcraft. The 'witch' was usually identified by an existing reputation for *maleficium*, this reputation having been honed for her accuser by a recent dispute or argument between the witch and a member or members of the afflicted household. These disputes ('fallings-out', as they were frequently described at the time) could take a variety of forms, but the most common, especially in the economically advanced zones of southern England, arose from a refusal of charity or favours by a richer villager to a poorer one. An old woman came to the door and begged alms: a little money, or some food or drink, or perhaps the chance of doing some work. She was refused and went away displeased, possibly muttering threats or even hurling imprecations as she went, worrying enough if she were already thought to be a witch. A little later a child sickened or cattle died, and the link was made between the old woman's hostility and the misfortune. The transition was made between the generalized fear of the person with a reputation for being a witch and the focused accusation of *maleficium*.

This recurring motif has encouraged an interpretation that connects these accusations between villagers to the broader socio-economic changes of the period. The population of England rose from maybe two and a half million in 1530 to maybe five million in 1630. This doubling, although modest enough in both its rate and its outcome by modern standards, had massive implications. Employment prospects, the extent of cultivated land and agrarian production, especially of grain, could not keep up with this increase, and one of the consequences of this was the creation of a large number of poor people whose lives were becoming increasingly precarious. There were simply more poor people around, and in towns and villages the attitudes towards the poor of their more comfortable neighbours was at best ambivalent or at worst hardening. Until the Poor Law became fully established around the middle of the seventeenth century, people confronted by the neighbour begging at their door were caught between old traditions of communal charity and the harder attitudes engendered by the economic realities of an increasingly capitalistic, market-orientated economy.

Many must have felt guilty about turning away the poor, yet the very act of subsequently accusing them of witchcraft subconsciously transferred that guilt: it was now not the refuser of charity but rather the witch who was the transgressor of community values. Wider studies (not least those directed at areas other than the economically advanced south-east of England) indicate that this pattern was not as pervasive as some of the pioneer studies of the sociology of English witchcraft accusations may have suggested. It is clear, none the less, that witchcraft-accusations were usually made between people among whom there were existing grudges, feuds or rivalries, with richer villagers directing these accusations against poorer ones. Witchcraft involved power, and one way of understanding it at the level of the local community is to see it as a way in which the relatively powerless were thought to be able to gain access to power. A poor old widow with a grudge against a yeoman farmer was ill placed to use physical violence or litigation against him: she could, according to the logic of the times, use witchcraft to harm him or his family, or to kill his cattle.

Witches, in English popular beliefs of around 1600, were not very often thought of primarily as agents of the devil; this notion was to become more entrenched during the seventeenth century, as the population at large became more aware of educated thinking on the subject. Yet one of the peculiarities of English witchcraft beliefs was the centrality of the familiar spirit. The familiar, which usually took the form of an animal, was a domesticated demon, which might be used by the witch to do harm on her behalf, and which might also stand in for the devil proper by making a pact with the witch. The bargain that lay behind this pact was a simple one: the witch renounced Christ and gave the familiar her soul in return for the power, with or without the familiar's assistance, to do harm to her enemies. Even witches who were thought to have inherited their power to perform evil were often held to possess a familiar spirit or two, and accounts of witchcraft cases in late Elizabethan England frequently record the presence of these animal demons. The lore about familiars added an additional complication: either when the pact was first made or shortly afterwards the familiar was thought to suck blood from the witch, normally from a protuberance on her body like a supernumerary nipple. Thus the existence of such a protuberance, the English version of the witch's mark, came to be seen as a legal proof that a suspect was a witch. The location of the mark varied, but by the mid seventeenth century it was thought to be placed on the genitals or near the anus of the witch.

What could you do if you thought yourself bewitched? It was possible to take a witch to court, but this took time and, perhaps surprisingly to the modern reader, money: in witchcraft cases, as with the prosecution of other serious crimes, it was the accuser who was expected to pay the costs of prosecution, expressed in fees to the court's clerical staff, and who was by custom expected to help witnesses with their expenses. Other remedies existed. The clergy recommended prayer, but only a small proportion of the population were willing to take this line, which, although theologically sound, excluded the possibility of immediate gratification or relief. Those seeking a more direct solution had at their disposal a whole repertoire of informal counter-measures, practices held by the godly to be as devilish as the *maleficium* they were thought to counteract. These counter-measures (several of which were familiar to the residents of North Moreton) included scratching the witch's face until blood was drawn, burning thatch from her roof or hair from her head, burning one of a flock of bewitched animals in order to save the rest, or plunging a red-hot spit into milk that was inhibited by witchcraft from turning into butter. As these folkloric remedies

remind us, witchcraft did not exist in an ideological or cultural
vacuum: it was one element of a much wider set of beliefs that
took in ghosts, portents, poltergeists, prodigies, fairies, sympathetic magic, popular astrology, fortune-telling and all of those
popular re-fashionings of Christian belief that so outraged
educated Reformers. The acceptance of witchcraft was thus an
aspect of a much wider mental world that would be regarded by
most modern observers, and was indeed regarded by many
educated and theologically precise people at the time, as
superstitious.

A key component of this mental world were the practitioners
of good witchcraft, most commonly known as 'cunning' men or
women. We have already seen that many of the parishioners of
North Moreton, among them Brian Gunter's servants, were
aware of the existence of such people in the vicinity of their
village, and in this respect they were probably typical of their
period: few settlements could have lain more than five miles from
the residence of one of these good witches. Cunning folk were
very useful people. They provided you with remedies against
malefic witchcraft or helped you to identify the culprit if you
thought yourself bewitched; they supplied help in finding stolen
goods, made charms and herbal remedies for the sick, told fortunes and revealed to servant girls the identity of their future hus-
bands. Indeed, surviving documentation has left us roughly as
much evidence about these good witches as the malefic ones.
This documentation also suggests that whereas the malefic witch
was very likely to be a woman, cunning folk were drawn equally
from both sexes, or maybe enjoyed a slight majority of men.
Attitudes towards cunning folk were one of the main points of
divergence between popular views on witchcraft and those of the
trained theologian. The population as a whole obviously found
the services of cunning folk indispensable, and were to do so until

well into the nineteenth century. English demonologists, anxious to eradicate popular superstitions and implant correct religious values, decried the cunning folk as great deluders of the people: the good witches derived their powers from the devil as surely as did the bad ones, and ought to be punished accordingly.

We need to extend our discussion of beliefs about witchcraft beyond the world of village *maleficium* and local cunning folk, and consider what witchcraft might look like to the representatives of a more educated culture. Among them, too, ideas about witchcraft and magic were widespread. In general the Reformation, by stressing the depravity of humankind and creating a tension over the need to inculcate correct religion, had created a greater sensitivity towards the devil and all his works. Concern over witchcraft was one aspect of this sensitivity. There were a number of major English books dealing with witchcraft, but the topic also received regular mention in a wide range of contemporary devotional and theological works. Tracts on idolatry, for example, and the relevant sections of commentaries on the Ten Commandments seem to have been especially fruitful in this respect, while the visitation articles of sixteenth-century archbishops and bishops often included witchcraft and sorcery among the undesirable practices to be sought out and corrected. Belief in witchcraft was widely diffused socially, and the Reformation, by emphasizing the need to combat sin and hence to struggle with the devil, did help to define educated or theologically informed opinion on the subject.

From the fifteenth century onwards the printing presses of Europe poured forth a steady stream of large works on demonology that sought to convince their readers both of the reality of diabolic witchcraft and of the threat it offered to the Christian state. Some of these, at least, were known in England by the end of Elizabeth's reign. The demonological tract that has become most notorious in the twentieth century, the *Malleus Maleficarum* of 1487, was little regarded by English writers: Protestant and Catholic commentators on witchcraft shared much theological common ground, but English Protestant writers were unlikely to buttress their arguments with a work written by two Dominican Inquisitors. Probably the most influential work on witchcraft by a foreign writer in late sixteenth-century England was Jean Bodin's *De la Demonamanie des Sorciers*, published in 1580. Bodin based the book on his experiences of trying witches while he was a royal judge in France, and hence servant of a Catholic monarch, but his intellectual stature (he was one of the leading political theorists of the era) and his reputation for being relatively free-thinking in religious matters made his work acceptable to Protestants. English writers on witchcraft also depended heavily on the translation of a tract by one of the major Calvinist intellectuals of the day, the French theologian Lambert Daneau, published in English in 1575 as *A Dialogue of Witches in Foretime named Lot-Tellers and now commonly called Sorcerers*. What was to become one of the most influential works of demonology in the seventeenth century, the Jesuit Martin Del Rio's *Disquisitionum Magicarum Libris Sex*, had appeared in 1599, although it is doubtful if it had much impact in England by the time Anne Gunter fell ill.

Drawing on these and other Continental works, on scripture, on the writings of the church fathers, on tales of magic found in Greek and Latin literature, and on their perceptions of peasant beliefs and practices, educated English writers were in a position to construct large, densely argued and well-documented demonological works. Yet only one such had been published by an English author by the time of Anne's illness, Henry Holland's *A Treatise against Witchcraft* of 1590. Holland, who died in 1604, the year when Anne was first afflicted by her mysterious illness, was a Cambridge-educated Puritan divine, and also author of a tract on the spiritual lessons to be derived from the bubonic plague and of a digest of that key Reformation text, Jean Calvin's *Institutes*. His book on witchcraft drew heavily on Daneau and Bodin, while he also made use of a demonological tract by the Danish Protestant theologian Neils Hemmingsen, the *Admonitio de Superstitionibus Magicis Vitandis*, published at Copenhagen in 1575. Another English work that demonstrates what theological ideas on witchcraft were current at the time of the Gunter case was William Perkins's *A Discourse of the damned Art of Witchcraft*, which originated as a series of sermons and was published posthumously in 1608 (its author died in 1602). Perkins was the leading English Protestant theologian of his age, with an international reputation that led to the publication of his works in Latin and most European languages. The adherence to witch-hunting of such an important and influential figure was to provide succour for English demonological writers until the early eighteenth century: the New England divine Cotton Mather, for example, was to cite Perkins's work in his *Wonders of the Invisible World* (1692), a defence of the witch-prosecutions at Salem. And, of course, English witchcraft writers rapidly became familiar with the *Daemonologie* of 1597 written by James VI of Scotland, later James I of England.

Consulting the demonological works of Henry Holland and William Perkins leaves the reader with a very different impression of the nature of witchcraft from that provided by accounts of village accusations. The concerns of these two

writers were predominantly theological. They agreed with earlier
Continental writers in that for witchcraft to operate, three elements needed to be present: divine permission, satanic power and
human agency in the form of the witch. Following a logic that
sometimes seems strained, the demonologists argued that the
devil could function only within limits set by the Almighty; the
notion that the devil could operate as freely as God was too
terrifying to contemplate, and was in any case heretical. Yet
the devil was constantly at war with God, and his legions with
good Christians. Witches were, therefore, humans who had
renounced their maker and fallen for the devil's temptations.
Holland and Perkins, like later English demonologists, agreed
that the crucial step in this process was the satanic pact. God, to
that English Protestant mind, had made a covenant with his
people, and it was logical that the devil should make one with
his. Thus if *maleficium* was the crucial element in witchcraft for
the villager of the period, it was the pact between the witch and
the devil that was of central importance to the demonological
writer.

Yet there was another major emphasis in Holland's and
Perkins's demonology, and one that was again to remain of
considerable importance to later English writers. The English
Reformers wanted to erect a Christian Commonwealth in
England and to plant true religion among their compatriots. This
meant that these compatriots should be weaned away from what
the Reformers regarded as superstitious excrescences that could
be interpreted either as the remnants of popery or as the leftovers
of pre-Christian beliefs (the Reformers often conflated the two:
the rituals of the Catholic Mass were frequently equated with the
practices of village sorcerers). Roughly as much space is devoted
in Holland's and Perkins's works to attacking counter-magic
and cunning folk as to lamenting the presence and activities of

malefic witches. Folkloric counter-measures against witches
(Perkins seems to have been particularly upset by the practice of
scratching) were denounced as superstitious, unchristian, devoid
of scriptural basis, and thus inspired by the devil. Cunning folk
attracted special opprobrium. The standard theological line was
that the devil empowered cunning folk as well as malefic witches,
but that the cunning folk, by deluding the populace into thinking
that their activities were beneficial, were worse than the 'hurting'
witches. Perkins, therefore, ended his 257-page tract on witchcraft by concluding that death was 'the just and deserved portion
of the good witch'.

The publication of full-scale demonological tracts came late
to England, and not many literate people in late Elizabethan or
early Jacobean England would want to read a 257-page technical
tract on witchcraft like Perkins's. But there was another, and for
the most part less demanding, source of printed information on
the subject. From the mid sixteenth century England had enjoyed
a growing print literature of shorter works, tracts and pamphlets
aimed at a more popular audience than that likely to immerse
itself regularly in the large theological treatise. Among this
literature were a number of publications describing not the
theological framework of witch beliefs, but rather specific
instances of witchcraft or specific witch-trials. The first of these
had appeared in 1566, describing the trial and execution of three
witches at Essex (the relevant court archives corroborate that
these trials and executions did indeed take place). By 1600 a
number of such tracts had appeared, covering incidents of
witchcraft over much of southern England. Although the
narratives of witchcraft provided by these tracts and pamphlets
were mainly concerned with *maleficium*, many of them were
prefaced with admonitions to the reader that drew theological
lessons from the incidents described in the main body of the

work, placing these incidents firmly in the context of the cosmic battle between good and evil, God and the devil. And although these tracts are often described as popular or ephemeral, some of them were weighty, detailed and as much as a hundred pages in length. One such was published in 1582, describing a bundle of accusations from St Osyth in Essex. Another was that work recounting the story of the demonic possession by witchcraft of several children of the Throckmorton family at Warboys in Huntingdonshire.

The literate Englishman or woman of the early seventeenth century could, therefore, learn about witchcraft from a variety of printed sources, and it is the knowledge of this literature that has seduced many later observers, as they considered the European witch-craze, into thinking that there was a single view on witch-craft, and that the educated European of around 1600 was thoroughly inculcated with a theologically driven desire to hunt and burn witches. This was not the case. It is, indeed, one of the peculiarities of the history of English witchcraft that the first major book on the subject written by an Englishman, Reginald Scot's *Discoverie of Witchcraft* of 1584, was unrelentingly sceptical. Scot was an obscure Kentish gentleman, whose only other known publication was a book on hop cultivation. His total rejection of the possibility of witchcraft has led to his being hailed as an early prophet of 'modern', 'enlightened' or 'rational' thinking about the phenomenon, but close inspection of his book proves this to be a gross oversimplification. Scot was certainly informed by a rough common sense, which led him to reject much of what witches were supposed to do as patently absurd. But the arguments on which he based his rejection of existing notions of witchcraft were firmly grounded in contemporary theology. For Scot, to ascribe too much power to witches, and thus to the devil, was to downgrade the importance of God.

Moreover, much of what popular traditions supposed witches to do reflected popish superstitions, which all right-thinking Christians ought to reject. And, in any case, the scriptural references to witchcraft upon which the demonologists depended so heavily were usually rendered irrelevant by the mistranslation of Hebrew terms. Scot should not be regarded as a premature rationalist: his importance lies in showing how any thinking Christian of his day could construct a theologically based objection to witch-hunting within the existing intellectual framework.

Further evidence on this point is provided by the writings of George Gifford, author of two tracts on witchcraft. Gifford was a Puritan clergyman, from 1582 the vicar of Maldon, a small port on the coast of Essex, a county that was experiencing high levels of witchcraft-prosecutions. He was a fairly extreme Puritan, so much so that he was deprived of his living by the church authorities (his parishioners at Maldon were so impressed by his preaching that they persuaded him to stay in the town, and he died there in 1620). There is an understandable tendency among modern observers to equate Puritanism with an enthusiasm for witch-persecution, but with Gifford we discover something more complex. His books on witchcraft were not in the standard demonological pattern. He had a comprehensive knowledge of the popular witch beliefs of the Maldon area, but was hostile to heavy persecution. This has led modern writers to regard him as some sort of Tudor anthropologist, and to portray him, like Scot, as a proto-rationalist rising above the mental limitations of his period. Once more, close reading of his works reveals how erroneous it is to try to fit sixteenth-century people's thinking into modern categories. Perhaps his approach, which explored the dynamics of witch-hunting and the popular dependence on cunning folk and counter-measures, could be described as anthropological. But his reasons for urging caution in matters of

witchcraft are similar to those theological ones adopted by
Reginald Scot. Witches existed, Gifford conceded, but the real
problem was to eradicate popular superstitions that, by imputing
too much power to witches, led to an overestimation of the devil's
powers. Moreover, Gifford's close observation of attitudes to
witches in southern Essex had made him all too aware of the
interpersonal tensions and neighbourly disputes that so often
underlay accusations. Gifford's writings on witchcraft, of which
modern scholars have made considerable use, reinforce the
argument that it was possible in the late sixteenth century for
educated Christians to take a sceptical or cautious line about
witchcraft without their having to imbibe modern rationality.
There was no single view of witchcraft, no mindless intolerance.
Some people were rabidly against it, some were very sceptical,
but most people's thinking on the subject was somewhere in
between: unable to reject the notion of witchcraft entirely, they
were none the less ready to evaluate each supposed instance of it
on its own merits. This will become clear as our story unfolds.

The people involved in Anne Gunter's case displayed a range
of reactions to what they saw, or thought they saw, and their
statements testify to the pervasive and widespread nature of the
witchcraft beliefs of the culture they inhabited. More specifically,
we must speculate on how far the thinking about witchcraft of
many of these witnesses had been sharpened and focused by a
case occurring in Berkshire, at Windsor, in 1579. Taking place a
quarter of a century before Anne's sufferings, this incident,
which resulted in the trial and execution of four witches at
Abingdon, formed the basis of a pamphlet that gives fascinating
insights into the nature of the witch beliefs in the county. Most of

the pamphlet consists of a statement allegedly made by one of
those accused and hanged, Elizabeth Stile, a widow aged sixty-
five or so. Stile had been brought before a local justice of the
peace, Sir Henry Neville, who had accepted her neighbours'
evidence that she was a witch as well as a lewd, malicious and
hurtful woman; he had therefore committed her to Reading Gaol
to await trial. Apparently while she was in prison the gaoler,
Thomas Rowe, persuaded Stile to confess her misdeeds as a token
of repentance, hoping that she would return to God and prepare
herself spiritually for the fate that awaited her. Accordingly, she
told Rowe and three other men about her witchcraft.

The witches and what they were meant to have done fitted the
popular stereotypes. Stile herself was an elderly woman. She
described Mother Devell, another of those hanged, as a very poor
woman. A third witch, Mother Margaret, lived in the almshouse
at Windsor and walked on crutches. We have little information
on the fourth witch to be hanged, Mother Dutten, but there is no
indication that she was anything other than poor. Stile also stated
that another inmate of the Windsor almshouse, Mother Seder,
now deceased, had been the chief witch in this small group. The
witchcraft these women indulged in, on the strength of Stile's
statement, was essentially straightforward *maleficium*. They
killed a farmer from Windsor called Langford. They killed
Richard Galis, a former mayor of Windsor, who had published a
tract describing his sufferings. They also killed a maid of
Langford's, a butcher named Switcher and another butcher
called Mastlin. According to Stile, they bewitched some seven
other people, all of whom lay sick for a long time but did not die,
although she did confess to killing a man called Saddock by a
clap on the shoulder (he went home and died), because he did not
keep his promise to make her a 'safeguard', or overgarment. She
also referred to lesser acts of witchcraft, such as killing a cow, and

generally claimed that all the witches would send their spirits to harm those who had offended them, giving the familiars a drop of their blood by way of payment before they went off to wreak havoc.

All of the women, Stile said, kept familiars, although ideas on how they were fed had not yet been formalized into sucking from a teat in the witch's private parts. Thus Mother Dutten had a familiar in the shape of a toad and fed it blood that she made come from her thigh (the toad, a homely touch this, lived in a border of green herbs in Dutten's garden). Mother Devell kept a spirit in the shape of a cat, which aided her in her witchcraft. It was called Jill and was fed on milk mixed with Mother Devell's blood. Mother Margaret kept a kitten called Jenny and fed it with drops of her blood and bread. Stile herself kept a familiar in the shape of a rat called Phillip, which she fed with blood from her right wrist (the pamphlet records there was a mark there) or, as all of these Windsor witches did, from her right side.

This pamphlet account of a witch's confession does provide clues to a wider body of witch beliefs that take us beyond the usual stories of *maleficium* and familiar spirits. The key element in this instance seems to have been Father Rosimond, a male witch living at Farnham Royal in Buckinghamshire. He reputedly had the ability to change himself into any shape he desired, and presided over meetings with his daughter (also a witch) and the four Windsor witches in the 'pits' (presumably sawpits) that lay behind the house of a Windsor resident named Dodge. There the witches gathered to plan and discuss what harm they were going to inflict on their neighbours, and it was at one such meeting, so Stile claimed, that Dutten and Devell enticed her to renounce God and give herself to the devil. Shape-changing, of the type at which Rosimond apparently excelled, was central to witchcraft beliefs in subsequent periods, although references to it are comparatively rare in the formal court documentation of the late sixteenth century. Although the idea of the witches' sabbat, so essential to the thinking of many Continental demonologists, did not really take hold in England, in the meetings of the witches in Dodge's sawpits we see some sort of folkloric notion of the witches coming together to learn their trade, plot evil and induct new recruits. And old Mother Dutten was said to have another talent: she could tell people's business as soon as she set eyes on them, adding telepathy to the witch's powers.

There was one other somewhat unusual element in Elizabeth Stile's account of the doings of herself and her fellow witches. They made considerable use of image-magic. This was a very widespread witchcraft technique, albeit one rarely referred to in English sources of the period, in which an image, typically of wax, is made of the person against whom witchcraft is intended. The image is then harmed, most often by sticking pins or other sharp objects into it, or perhaps by melting and, by a process of sympathetic magic, harm is inflicted on the object of the witch's malice. Mother Dutten was the expert here, making four images of wax a hand span long and two or three fingers broad, to represent Langford, his maid, Galis and Switcher. The left-hand sides of these images were pricked, and the four people represent-ed by these wax models all died.

The Windsor witches were unfortunate because the accusations against them came a few months after a scare in London involving image-magic against Queen Elizabeth. In August 1578 three wax figures thought to represent Queen Elizabeth and two of her privy councillors, all of them with bristles implanted in the left side of their bodies, were discovered in a dunghill. On hearing of the Windsor case, the Privy Council (essentially the body that ran England) intervened, and it was probably a degree of central government concern and

intervention, in the wake of the occult threat to the Queen, which
led to these local practitioners of image-magic being sentenced to
death and hanged. Yet the text of the pamphlet is concerned
mainly with village-level beliefs. We do not know what induced
Stile to tell her story: the 'confessing' witch is a problematic figure, especially in England where torture was not a normal part of
trial process. What we have here is an insight into village witchcraft in the part of the world where Brian Gunter lived and where
his daughter was born. We cannot be certain if the account of
what Stile said is accurate, although there is plenty of circum-
stantial detail there, and little that seems to owe anything to the
inventions of the pamphlet writer. So we are left with a core of
maleficium and familiars, with shape-changing, image-magic and
telepathy added, along with a prototype sabbat. There is also
mention in the pamphlet of going to cunning folk for medical
advice or help in finding stolen goods. Berkshire is one of those
counties for which we have little evidence about witchcraft, but,
when such evidence entered the historical record in the form of
the 1579 pamphlet, it demonstrates that witchcraft beliefs were
complex, developing and widely held.

The same impression is conveyed by the Gunter case, both in
general terms and in the more focused form of another witch's
confession. For, if Elizabeth Stile was telling tales of witchcraft
in Reading Gaol early in 1579, so was Agnes Pepwell at
Windsor and London in late 1605. Agnes had escaped trial at
Abingdon in March 1605, but had subsequently been apprehended and was by the autumn of that year being held in custody
in London. She was also brought to Windsor, presumably to be
interrogated afresh by King James. In both these places she seems
to have had few inhibitions when telling her own personal tale of
witchcraft. At one point she was placed in the custody of
William Gwillyam of King Street in Westminster, described as

a 'citizen and merchant', and he, his wife, Anne, and his servant all gave evidence to the Star Chamber in which they related Pepwell's confession. Much the same story was told at Windsor to two royal servants, Richard Hawkins and William Turnor, both of whom worked in the King's stables. And, perhaps most remarkably, Pepwell also confessed to Nicholas Gunter, a gentleman of Reading, obviously a kinsman of Anne and Brian Gunter and presumably the same Nicholas Gunter who was mayor of Reading at roughly this time. The accounts these various witnesses gave of Agnes Pepwell's career as a witch make fascinating reading.

Like Elizabeth Stile a quarter century before her, Agnes Pepwell owed at least part of her initiation into witchcraft to a woman who was dead by the time she told her story, in this case a Goodwife Bishop. This woman, according to Pepwell, had bequeathed a familiar, in the shape of a black rat, to her. Pepwell told how Elizabeth Gregory also had a familiar, in the form of a ragged colt, which had been bequeathed to her by another woman, Goodwife Gregory, presumably a relative. And like the Windsor witches (and we can only speculate if this detail came into Pepwell's head through knowledge of the earlier incident) these later Berkshire witches met together, in their case 'upon the heath & at the four ashes near to North Moreton'. Witchcraft was planned at these meetings, and it was also there that it was agreed that the two older women should pass their familiars on to Agnes Pepwell and Elizabeth Gregory at their deaths.

As was entirely conventional in the folklore of English witchcraft of the period, Agnes Pepwell used her familiar (to which, like Elizabeth Stile before her, she sometimes referred, in what may have been peculiar local terminology, as her 'bun') to perform *maleficium*. One of her first acts was to use it to bewitch two horses, a sow and some pigs belonging to her neighbours, with the result that, in her own words, 'the young pigs did split asunder by means thereof'. As a reward, she had 'at one time given her said spirit a live dog & at another time a live cat' to eat. Pepwell claimed that Elizabeth Gregory on one occasion came to her home to bake bread, declaring that 'it were a good deed to make him and his lame', her curious comment that 'she could do nothing at home but her mother-in-law carried it to Gunter's' providing a tantalizing clue of an ongoing relationship between the Gunter and Gregory families of which Elizabeth Gregory disapproved. Pepwell replied that 'it were a great pity to make them all lame', but that she was happy to send her familiar to hurt Anne. It was William Gwillyam who was giving evidence here, and he claimed that at this point he interrupted Pepwell, and reminded her that the general opinion was that Anne's fits were feigned. Pepwell insisted that she was responsible for the girl's fits, adding that she repented for what she had done, declaring that 'I would to God it were in my power to help her as it is not, & I would that her afflictions & extremities were laid upon myself so she were eased'. Pepwell also commented that Elizabeth Gregory's heart was so hardened against the Gunters that she was unable to repent.

William Gwillyam's evidence was backed by his wife. She described Pepwell's response to the information that Elizabeth Gregory was hotly denying Pepwell's story. Sitting 'at the table with this deponent & her husband', Pepwell took 'bread, meat & salt & desired of God that the same which she purposed to eat might not pass through her if the said Elizabeth Gregory were not guilty of the fact of bewitching of the said Anne Gunter', adding that she would 'evermore justify the same whether she were hanged or burnt or whatsoever became of her'. Throughout, all of the five relevant witnesses insisted, Pepwell was emphatic that she was a witch, that she had been one for fourteen years, and that she and Gregory (interestingly, her daughter Mary did not figure in her story) had bewitched Anne Gunter.

As might be expected, most detail on this point was provided by Nicholas Gunter's account of his conversation with the suspected witch. Nicholas had seen Anne in her fits, and was obviously anxious to talk to one of the supposed authors of his young kinswoman's vexations. Agnes told him of one of those trivial incidents of tension that so frequently occur in narratives of witchcraft. There was a belief that the witch could work her evil on people from whom they had obtained some property, most often articles of clothing. In this instance, however, it was a small sum of money. Pepwell told the Reading gentleman that she had no power to harm Anne 'until Mrs Anne Gunter [i.e., the girl's mother] had given her twopence for the pot she broke of the said Agnes Pepwell's when the said Agnes came to Mr Gunter's for porridge'. This is an interesting variation on the theme of charity and witchcraft suspicions: the old woman coming to the gentle/ man's house for food ('porridge' in the England of this period normally referred to a vegetable/based stew) and receiving a couple of pennies recompense when the wife of the house broke the vessel in which the woman intended to carry away the gift. Agnes also told Nicholas Gunter that her familiar 'would do nothing for her unless he had a drop of her blood, or some live thing as a cat or dog', and also told him that 'the devil [as she allegedly termed her familiar at this point: or was the word that of the testifying gentleman?] did use to suck her blood in her back & that the place was sore & to be seen'. She added that the spirit 'would speak big unto her like a man'.

There are always problems in interpreting evidence like Pepwell's confessions, but it should be noted that they were not forced: the impression one gets, on the contrary, is that by late

1605 Pepwell was happy to tell her tale of witchcraft to anybody who would listen. Indeed, a passage struck out in a letter from James I to his chief minister, the earl of Salisbury, suggests that Pepwell had been promised an indemnity if she confessed fully. James had initially drafted a request that Pepwell should be re-examined, 'considering the danger wherein she stands, having lost now the benefit of our royal word, which was conditional, if the truth had been rehearsed by her, which was not, as is now otherwise discovered'. Sceptical writers like Scot might dismiss such confessions as the product of 'melancholy' or other forms of mental confusion. Perhaps a more accurate interpretation would be that, especially given her long-standing reputation for being a witch, Pepwell felt that she had been cast in a role, and that the logic of her situation persuaded her to play that role to the best of her ability. She was enjoying her moment in the limelight: being a witch, which brought her from her home parish to both London and the royal court at Windsor, gave the poor old woman a certain status, one that was risky but none the less undeniable. And the tale she had to tell was composed of witch beliefs that were firmly embedded in the culture in which she had grown up. She had taken the main elements of those beliefs, and fashioned them into a personal witchcraft narrative. The supposed witch had fully internalized popular contemporary notions of witch-craft and, briefly, in the unfamiliar environment of a London merchant's house or the royal court, was able to relate the results of her refashioning of beliefs to her keepers, to royal servants, even to a relative of the girl she had supposedly afflicted.

There was little by way of a satanic cult in Agnes Pepwell's confession, just the usual notions about familiar spirits, these being, in all conscience, remarkable enough in themselves. There is no evidence that Agnes Pepwell was either a believer in some early, pre-Christian, religion or that she was a female healer being victimized by a male-dominated, misogynist clerical or legal establishment. What her narrative does show was that, for most of England's population, witchcraft was part of the fabric of everyday life, maybe something that you came across very rarely, but that was a known and recognized quantity when it did crop up.

chapter *five*

The OXFORD

CONNECTION

THE STORY now moves about twelve miles from North
Moreton to Oxford. In the early seventeenth century
Oxford was a very different place from the city with which the
modern tourist or student will be familiar. The distinctive complex of university buildings that now fills its centre was largely
incomplete in 1600; Oxford was still a medieval city. Most of its
inhabitants, of whom there were maybe 4,000 by 1600, lived in
the area of ninety acres or so enclosed by the city walls, although
suburbs were beginning to open up to the south, along the road to
Abingdon, to the north, an area of university expansion, and to
the west, where there was a well-founded settlement at Osney.
Inside the walls there was some social zoning, with the area to the
east of Carfax dominated by the university, that to the west by
Oxford's citizens. By 1600, however, general population pressure
and the expansion of the student body meant that there was
extensive building within the city, mainly dwellings thrown up in
courts and alleys off the main roads. Some central areas, for
example around the university church of St Mary the Virgin,
were kept swept and clean, but most of the city was characterized

by the squalor generally associated with urban life of the period, with the ditches on the city's peripheries resembling open sewers. There was little industry in Oxford. Tax returns of 1534 revealed a situation that was unchanged in 1600: 75 per cent of taxpayers (in effect, economically substantial males) worked in the victualling, clothing or service trades, obviously largely depend-ent on the university for employment, while a further 10 per cent of taxpayers worked directly for the university. Despite the odd friction, the sometimes homicidal medieval confrontations between town and gown were a thing of the past: the relation between the university and Oxford was, by now, an essentially symbiotic one.

Oxford was a town with which North Moreton's inhabitants would have had frequent contacts. It was a market for local grain production, and there is no doubt that the village's farming families would have sold produce in the city. There were also social connections. North Moreton's vicar, Gilbert Bradshaw, was a native of Oxford and maintained family contacts there: thus on 21 September 1605 Margaret Bradshaw of Headington, just outside Oxford, was married in All Saints' Church, as was Amy Bradshaw of the same parish on 29 July 1606: these two brides were presumably sisters of the vicar, who had come to be married by their clergyman brother in the parish where he was minister. The Gunters had connections with Oxford too: Harvey Gunter, then aged sixteen, had matriculated at Brasenose College in 1589, although there is no record of his having taken a degree, while Brian Gunter had been seriously ill in Oxford when his daughter Anne had the first symptoms of her mysterious malady around midsummer 1604.

By far the strongest connection between the Gunters and Oxford was forged by the marriage, celebrated in All Saints' Church on 22 July 1593, between Brian Gunter's daughter

Susan and Thomas Holland. Holland was born in Ludlow in
Shropshire around 1550, which would make him at least twenty
years Susan's senior. He had taken his BA at Balliol in 1570, and
had then gone on to take his MA, BD and, in 1584, DD. He had
become chaplain and fellow of Balliol in 1573, but had managed
to combine his college responsibilities with being chaplain to the
earl of Leicester, the most important nobleman in the early years
of Elizabeth's reign and, from 1564, chancellor of Oxford
University. Holland, who had accompanied Leicester on his
military expedition in support of the Dutch Revolt in 1585, had
impressed his patron, who had probably eased his early steps up
the professional ladder in Oxford. But Holland was a man of
considerable talent and deep scholarship. In 1589 he had become
regius professor of divinity at Oxford, in early 1592 a fellow and
later that year rector of Exeter College. His elevation to head of
house was made under the influence of the Queen, and it is
noteworthy that his only known major publication was a revised
version of a sermon in which Holland defended the practice of
celebrating Elizabeth's accession day as a national holiday against
the criticisms of papists and over-precise Protestants alike.

As regius professor of divinity at Oxford, Holland had an
important role both in teaching and administration within the
university, and in the religious politics of the period. Indeed, his
appointment as rector of Exeter was based partly on central
government's desire to have a doctrinally reliable head of house
presiding over a college that was thought to be tainted with
Roman Catholicism. Holland was also involved in public
displays of theological learning. In 1592, shortly after becoming
rector of Exeter, he had to preside over a disputation in divinity
held before the Queen, a role he was to repeat when James I
visited the university in 1605, at the same time as the King had
his first meeting with the professor's allegedly bewitched

sister-in-law. He evidently impressed the new monarch with his abilities, for he was later to be one of the team of academic theologians selected by James to work on what was to become the Authorized Version of the Bible. Holland also performed another public function on behalf of the Church of England. Matters of controversy or importance, on which the church wished to promote a particular line, were regularly made the subject of sermons delivered by preachers of known competence at St Paul's Cross in London. In 1602 Thomas Holland delivered such a sermon: ironically, it was in support of the church's sceptical position on possession, witchcraft and exorcism. It is a matter of note that although Susan Holland was called on to give evidence at the Star Chamber and was involved with her sister's sufferings from an early stage, Thomas Holland was not questioned and seems to have adopted a more detached attitude to the whole business.

We have no materials, apart from rather stereotyped contemporary comments on his godliness and learning, for assessing Holland's character. The most noteworthy of these comments came after his death in 1612, when on 6 March of that year a funeral sermon was preached in his honour at St Mary the Virgin in Oxford by a somewhat obscure clergyman, Richard Kilby. The sermon was a standard and conventional encomium on the admirable qualities of the deceased, and included a description of a classic good death: Holland, no longer able to pray as his voice failed him, lifted 'his hands unto heaven, and his eyes unto the hills from whence cometh salvation ... he shortly thereafter died a most sweet and a quiet death'. Kilby reminded his audience that Holland was a learned man, that he had served faithfully and effectively as regius professor, and that both the then archbishop of Canterbury and the bishop of London had studied under him. These were only the two most distinguished of the many pupils Holland had taught who had gone on to hold positions in the church, for he had been, in Kilby's words, 'a father of many sons, by a scholastical creation of them in the highest degrees of learning'. He was also, Kilby informed the congregation, 'blameless from all great enormous and scandalous offences; being full of the works of the spirit, as love, peace, gentleness, meekness, temperance ... full of alms, deeds and mercifulness unto the poor: so that as he was a shining bright lamp for his learning & lighting others with the knowledge of the truth; so was he a shining bright star too in his life, enlightening others in the pathway to heaven'.

Unfortunately Kilby made no more than conventional references to Holland's personality, and no mention at all of his qualities as a husband or a father. A better-known figure than Kilby, Thomas Fuller, writing half a century after Holland's death, suggested that such was the regius professor's dedication to scholarship that he would have had little time for such matters. 'He did not with some only sip of learning, or at the best but drink thereof,' wrote Fuller, 'but he was *mersius in libris*, drowned in his books, so that the scholar in him almost devoured all other relations.' This opinion is, however, challenged, and something of the quality of Thomas and Susan Holland's family life revealed, by the North Moreton parish register. A series of entries there recorded the baptism of five children of Dr Thomas Holland in a period of six years immediately after his marriage to Susan Gunter, who was herself obviously happy to bear her children in the comforting surroundings of her parents' home. One of the sons was named Brian, and one of the daughters Anne, suggesting that Thomas Holland had a proper sense of respect for his father- and mother-in-law.

The university where Thomas Holland pursued his career was an expanding and dynamic institution. Its traditional medieval functions had been to conserve learning and educate young men who were to enter the priesthood. But Oxford had been shaken by the religious and cultural changes that accompanied the English Reformation, and it was probably the uncertainty of the priesthood as a career that caused student numbers to drop to their lowest level for many years in the 1550s. But from the time of the accession of Queen Elizabeth I in 1558, Oxford, like Cambridge, experienced a boom in undergraduate admissions. Estimated annual freshman admissions rise from 157 for the years 1553–9 to 231 in the 1560s, 413 in the 1570s, and 445 in the 1580s. Economic hard times in the 1590s probably account for a diminution away from this peak, but annual admissions remained at more than twice their nadir of the 1550s, and were to pick up again dramatically from 1630.

Oxford's traditional function had been to supply clergymen, and this function continued over the late sixteenth and seven-teenth centuries: England's 10,000 or so parishes needed the type of educated and theologically equipped ministers now considered essential for implanting and maintaining right religion, and the combined efforts of Oxford and Cambridge meant that by the outbreak of the Civil Wars in 1642 the English clergy was more or less a graduate profession. But from the mid sixteenth century a new trend developed. Changing cultural standards among the nobility and gentry, and possibly a perception of career prospects for educated laymen in the royal administration, meant that the youths described as 'plebeians' in the college records, who were mainly destined to become clergy-men, were joined by the sons of peers, esquires and mere gentry. Thus at the beginning of the seventeenth century about 3 per cent of Oxford freshmen were the sons of peers, knights or baronets, 19 per cent the sons of esquires and 31 per cent the sons of gentle-men, which meant that just over half the undergraduate intake came from well-heeled backgrounds. Some of these well-born students, in the best traditions of Renaissance nobility, went on to become very learned men. But many, like Harvey Gunter, simply matriculated without taking a degree. For such students, university exercised something of the function of a finishing school: they picked up a little learning and a little social polish, availed themselves of the dancing-masters and modern language tutors who added their services to those of the teachers of the official curriculum, and made useful social contacts. Such young men obviously needed control and guidance through the dangerous years of adolescence, so the system of college tutors was developed to reassure gentry parents that their sons were being kept from youthful debauches. And, of course, accommo-dation had to be found for the student influx. Few new colleges were built during this period of expansion, but those in existence grew as new buildings were added and cock-lofts opened up to make room for the expanding undergraduate body.

This broadening of the student body to include a substantial proportion of England's future ruling class made it all the more vital that the instruction they received at Oxford, and especially the religious teachings they might be exposed to, should be thoroughly orthodox. The Reformation had introduced rival religious ideologies into England, and after 1558 the Protestant regime headed by Elizabeth was extremely anxious to eradicate any vestiges of Roman Catholicism at both the universities. One immediate consequence of this was that the chancellorship of Oxford University became in effect a political appointment. From 1564 until his death in 1588 the chancellor was Robert Dudley, earl of Leicester. Leicester was extremely influential in the early part of Elizabeth's reign, and it was probably no detri-ment to Thomas Holland's career that his patron was chancellor for such a lengthy period. For Leicester, despite his many other concerns, was to prove a hands-on chancellor, taking an interest in university regulations, as well as university and college appointments; he was also, here as elsewhere, a keen adherent of the Protestant cause. Leicester ensured that popery was banished from Oxford, although his tendency to favour further reformation meant that by the end of his chancellorship nests of relatively advanced Puritans, some leaning to Presbyterianism, existed in the university. Leicester was succeeded on his death by Sir Christopher Hatton, lord chancellor of England, a man much favoured by Queen Elizabeth and an opponent of Puritanism. Under his chancellorship, and that of Thomas Sackville, Lord Buckhurst, who followed after Hatton's death in 1591, the prevailing ethos affecting appointments and promotions at Oxford favoured middle-of-the-road Protestants. Buckhurst's was an overtly political appointment, made under intense royal pressure in the face of the dons gathered in convocation, the body which in theory elected the chancellor: they preferred the current favourite of the Puritans, Robert Devereux, earl of Essex. Thomas Holland's appointments as regius professor of divinity and as rector of Exeter College took place in a period when the politics, and especially the religious politics, of Oxford were in a state of flux and a matter of considerable interest to central government.

Exeter College, over which Holland presided as rector at the time of Anne Gunter's sufferings, was a microcosm of the broader developments in the life of the university. It had been founded in 1314, but extensive benefactions made by Sir William Petre in 1566 had amounted to a virtual refoundation. Petre, a Devon man, was one of the more successful administrators of early Tudor England, secretary of state to every monarch from Henry VIII to Elizabeth I, and hence clearly a man who, despite his Catholic sympathies, was able to ride out the religious

changes of the period successfully enough. The new regulations
he instituted modernized both the government of the college and
its teaching regime, and left it well equipped to take part in the
changes of the late sixteenth century. But Petre's Catholicism,
and that of his son, Sir John, who took an active role in the
nomination of scholars to the college, meant that Exeter came to
be regarded as a hotbed of popery. The Privy Council at
Westminster was expressing its concerns about the college's
doctrinal orthodoxy in 1577, and there was something of a purge
in 1578. Thomas Holland's appointment to the rectorship in
1592 owed much to the conviction that this very able and ideolog-
ically reliable cleric would continue the struggle against the
Romanists. By that date, however, Catholicism within the
college had waned: the steady protestantization of English life
that had followed Elizabeth's accession was having its effect both
in Oxford and in the West Country, from which Exeter College
drew many of its undergraduates and fellows.

Through Thomas Holland, Brian Gunter had access to the
upper reaches of academic society in Oxford, and one of the
more remarkable aspects of his daughter's bewitching is the way
in which he managed to mobilize a powerful body of support
among the Oxford dons of his day for the reality of his daughter's
sufferings, and hence for the need to convict her tormentors. To
the modern reader, the Oxford men who gave evidence on behalf
of Gunter in the Star Chamber proceedings of 1606 may seem
no less obscure than the villagers of North Moreton. In their own
world, however, many of them were figures of some importance.

Those who Gunter called upon for help included a number

of medical experts. The most significant of these, in terms of his position, was Bartholomew Warner, aged forty-nine when he and the others gave their evidence in 1606, and regius professor of medicine at Oxford from 1597. Warner, who had known Brian Gunter for seven or eight years before he gave his evidence, and Anne for about three, was not a dazzling presence on the stage of international medicine, and his career was an undistinguished one that left few traces in the university records of the period. Yet Warner, who was to serve as professor until 1612, held the key medical post in Oxford, and his marriage to a stepdaughter of John Case, doctor of medicine, former fellow of St John's College and a major university figure, ensured that he was well connected in university circles. It is therefore significant that he was one of the medical men to whom Gunter, assuming on an established acquaintanceship, sent a sample of his daughter Anne's urine when her mysterious illness resumed in October 1604, and it is noteworthy that in his evidence to the Star Chamber he was able to state that it was the general opinion of the doctors involved in the early stages of the case that 'the said Anne was not sick of any natural cause or infirmity'.

Another recipient of a sample of Anne's urine was Roger Bracegirdle, the physician who first gave a definite diagnosis of witchcraft as the cause of Anne's sufferings. Bracegirdle, an octo-generian when he gave evidence to the Star Chamber, was a fellow of Brasenose College, and a veteran medical practitioner who had taken his BM in 1569 and his DM a decade later. Bracegirdle had known Brian Gunter for about ten years when he gave his evidence, and he was acquainted both with Susan Holland and with members of the Dunch family. The other medical experts were less distinguished. Robert Vilvaine, aged thirty and a fellow of Exeter College when he gave his evidence, had taken his MA in 1600, but was not to take his BM and DM (which he did together) until 1611. He was subsequently to return to his native Devon and become a successful physician in Exeter, being buried in the choir of Exeter Cathedral in 1663 when he died at the age of eighty-seven. John Hall, another MA, aged thirty, was probably that John Hall who married a daughter of William Shakespeare in 1607, and thereafter lived in Stratford-on-Avon, where his skills as a doctor gave him considerable local eminence.

Those giving evidence who did not have medical expertise included some impressive figures. Perhaps the most important of them, although most of that importance lay in the future, was John Prideaux. Prideaux, then aged twenty-seven, was a fellow of Exeter College and man of West Country origins, coming, like Vilvaine, from Devon. Prideaux had taken his BA in 1600, his MA in 1603, and was to proceed to a BD in 1611 and a DD the year after. He followed Thomas Holland as rector of Exeter College on Holland's death in 1612, and then became regius professor of divinity in 1615. He subsequently rose to considerable eminence, becoming vice-chancellor of the university three times before his death in 1642. Holding the post of chaplain to young Prince Henry and, after the prince's untimely death in 1614, to his father, James I, gave him ready access to preferment, and he picked up a number of clerical livings in Oxfordshire. He was unavoidably involved in the religious politics of the period, for his professorship meant that he had to preside over theological disputations, as differences in religion were becoming more marked and bitter. Even so, he retained a reputation as a moderate and impartial divine. He was unfortunate enough to be appointed bishop of Worcester in December 1641, a few months before the Civil Wars broke out and Parliament abolished episcopacy. Prideaux consequently spent the last years of his life (he died in 1650) in comparative poverty, selling his books to help support his family and living with his son-in-law, the rector of Bredon in Worcestershire.

Others giving evidence for Gunter included another future bishop, Thomas Winniffe, also a member of Exeter College. Winniffe, who was to become a friend of the poet John Donne later in life, came from Dorset, and was to found his professional fortunes on sound learning and being a royal chaplain, in this case to Prince Henry and then his younger brother Charles, the future Charles I. Winniffe gained brief political notoriety, and a spell of imprisonment in the Tower of London, when in 1622 he delivered a political sermon whose anti-Spanish content included some offensive criticisms of the Spanish ambassador to England, Gondomar, and compared Spinola, the leading Spanish general of the time, to the devil. Like Prideaux, he was made a bishop, of Lincoln, at an inauspicious moment, in his case in 1642, and died in 1654. Another distinguished university figure to give evidence for Gunter was John Harding, regius professor of Hebrew, fellow of Magdalen College from 1583, president of the college from 1608 to his death in 1610, and chaplain to James I.

Some of the other Oxford men involved, although less distinguished, were all to enjoy respectable careers as clergymen after their time at the university. William Helme, BD, fellow of Exeter College, a Wiltshire man aged thirty-eight when he gave evidence, was one such. He was a fellow of the college between 1587 and 1615, and was probably a senior figure there. As such, he obviously knew the rector's family, and declared that he had been acquainted with Brian and Anne Gunter for about eight years. In 1615 he was to leave his college fellowship and become vicar of Bishopstone in his native county until his death in 1639. William Harvey of Exeter College (not to be confused with the eminent physician of that name) was another Devonian, the son

of a clergyman, who was to become vicar of Burrington in
Devon in 1612. John Whetcombe, son of a Dorset gentleman,
fellow of Exeter college and aged twenty-six when he gave his
evidence, was to enjoy a couple of clerical livings in his native
county. A more noteworthy clergyman was Thomas James, an
MA who was described as parson of 'St Tolles', Oxford, in the
Star Chamber record. St Tolles was apparently a synonym for St
Aldates, which suggests that this was another major university
figure of the period, the Thomas James who was to become the
first librarian of the Bodleian Library.

The biographical details for this group of witnesses illustrate
the strength of the support that Gunter had managed to build in
Oxford for his campaign against the North Moreton witches.
Gaining solid backing from his fellow villagers was essential, but
now he was able to reinforce this with the opinions of some of the
educational elite, many of them skilled or on their way to being
skilled in medical and theological matters, men whose evidence
and opinions on the nature of Anne Gunter's sufferings were
likely to be taken seriously. Although some of their testimonies
dealt with what happened while she was staying at Thomas
Holland's lodgings at Exeter College immediately before the trial
of the suspected witches at Abingdon, most of these Oxford
witnesses told of what they had seen at the Gunter house at
North Moreton, or at the home of Anne's brother Harvey at
Stanton St John. Brian Gunter had obviously been trying to
involve his Oxford contacts from the very start. And, as might be
expected, these Oxford dons were to provide us with many of the
longest and most detailed accounts of Anne's sufferings; for they
were all convinced that the sufferings were genuine, that their
origins were supernatural and, for some of these academic
observers at least, that they were caused by the malice of
Elizabeth Gregory, and Agnes and Mary Pepwell.

At the core of their descriptions of Anne's sufferings were details of strange afflictions that were commonplace in contemporary descriptions of cases of demonic possession or other maladies of a supernatural nature. Anne writhed and contorted, and then passed into trances. Her feet twisted away from her legs, so that she would walk on her ankles. She suffered from what William Helme described as 'a strange kind of swelling of her body', a swelling that, according to John Prideaux, was the size of a man's head. Another physical peculiarity that was frequently found in such cases was the sufferer's body becoming unusually heavy. Thomas Winniffe told how, during one of Anne's fits, he and Robert Vilvaine attempted to lift her head from the pillow on which it lay in hopes of getting her to sit up in bed, but he found that they 'could with all their strength & force hardly move her head from the pillow'. She was unable to take food, explaining on one occasion that 'the witches would not suffer her to receive or eat any meats'. Even more alarmingly, Robert Vilvaine told how in one fit Anne seemed to stretch, and that he and Susan Holland 'found her to be almost 12 inches longer than usually she was'. She called out against the witches in her torments, naming them or their familiars: John Prideaux, for example, told how Anne declared that Elizabeth Gregory's familiar was called Catch, Mary Pepwell's Vizitt and Agnes Pepwell's Sweat.

Pins figured prominently in the evidence of this group of witnesses. John Prideaux said she had pins buried in her breast, but that she did not bleed when they were pulled out. William Helme saw pins in the ends of Anne's toes and so many in her breast that it was 'as if it had been a pinpillow'; he agreed that Anne did not bleed when these pins were removed. This lack of bleeding was further attested to by William Harvey, who also recounted how numerous pins were found in Anne's mouth, and that, despite some worrying over the point, it was generally accepted that she had not put them there, an opinion that was seconded by John Hall. Robert Vilvaine told how pins were found in Anne's nostrils, which gave further weight to the state‚ ments that removing pins from the girl did not cause bleeding.

Several of these Oxford witnesses attested to Anne's apparent second sight, to her ability to report on conversations or tell of happenings that she had not witnessed, or to sense the coming of strangers or the suspected witches to her house. John Hall told how, while at Stanton St John, a Mrs White and her son entered the chamber where Anne lay. Anne promptly sat up in bed and tried to beat White's son, berating him for refusing to get his hair cut. Mrs White had indeed had an altercation with her son about his hair at dinner and had used language very like that which Anne was using, the sick girl being well out of earshot when the family squabble occurred. John Prideaux related how Anne had reported on a private conversation between him and a Mr Stoner, 'nobody revealing the same to her'. Similarly Robert Vilvaine told how while Anne was lodged at Stanton St John she was able to repeat a conversation that her brother Harvey had conducted in the buttery, well out of her hearing, with a visiting gentleman. Several accounts told how Anne sensed the presence of the suspected witches in or near her father's house; on one occasion, as Mary Pepwell stood in the porch, Anne declared that she 'smelt a savour like the smell of the burning of an old thatch house', and then fell into a trance (thatch from the supposed witches' houses had, of course, previously been burned as one of the standard counter‚measures against witchcraft).

One very unusual feature of Anne's supernatural afflictions was the way in which her clothes, according to nearly all of this group of witnesses, seemed to develop a life of their own. The garments most affected were her shoes, stockings and garters. William Helme gave a typical account: Anne 'did cast and throw off her shoes and hose being straight [i.e., securely] fastened, tied and gartered to her feet & about her legs for a pretty good distance from her as if the same had not been tied, fastened or gartered at all'. The stockings, shoes and garters were described by Helme as 'lying in the room where she supped towards the lower end of the table having one bow knot in the middle thereof & that garter lying there'. Suddenly the garter began to tie itself 'without the hands or art or other help of any living creature that could be perceived & they tied (how or by what means he cannot say) all along (saving about the middest thereof) in fashion of a chitterling, whereat this deponent did much marvel'. Robert Vilvaine filled in more details, telling how a garter about a yard and a quarter in length apparently tied itself into fifteen knots.

Helme also told how Anne's petticoat showed a disturbing tendency to unlace itself. Once while Anne was in her fits he heard 'the lace of her petticoat' making 'a little kind of noise as though it did slide & untie & afterwards this deponent did plainly see that it was unlaced and he saith that the said petticoat lace did untie without the hands or help of any living creature that this deponent could perceive'. William Harvey remembered how Anne's petticoat unlaced itself despite 'her gown being buttoned close up to her petticoat'. Bartholomew Warner remembered how 'the petticoats of the said Anne untied and fell from her somewhat strangely'. A rather closer observer was Robert Vilvaine. He, during one of Anne's fits, 'putting his hand on her breast felt & heard as it were plucking at the lace of the petticoat under her gown. And her gown being a little unbuttoned the petticoat was unlaced in a very strange manner', again apparently without the intervention of any visible creature.

These witnesses were convinced that Anne's sufferings were not counterfeited, and that she was not being forced into simulating bewitchment by her father, or that he was supplying her with intoxicating drinks or other forms of medication to help such simulation. Prideaux, for example, was insistent that Gunter did not 'at any time abuse, threaten or beat the said Anne his daughter', and that he did not 'give or minister any drink or other means unto her to show any strange fits'. This witness, indeed, was one of a number of these Oxford dons who remembered occasions when Anne's maladies had occurred in her father's absence, in this instance when she went into 'a very extreme fit' at her brother Harvey's house.

The concomitant of all this was a clear belief that Brian Gunter and his daughter were genuine victims of supernatural malevolence. Thomas Winniffe, indeed, gave a graphic portrayal of the effect of the affair on Brian Gunter, declaring that 'he hath often heard the said Brian Gunter much complain of the visitation of his daughter & of the great charge her sickness had been unto him, desiring her release from that visitation'. On one occasion, when he was at Harvey Gunter's house, 'the said Brian Gunter coming thither & then finding Anne his daughter in a fit did with tears much bewail her present grief'. Anne's pain could have a similar impact on the spectators: John Prideaux told how Anne suffered an unusually bad fit, 'wherein she wept very bitterly & caused this deponent & all or most of the standers by to weep likewise, her torments being so great that they thought her bones would have been disjointed'. The impression is that this influential group of academics was convinced that Anne's sufferings were genuine, and that they had their origins in the supernatural.

Although the Star Chamber interrogatories did not invite a straight answer on the issue, there can equally be little doubt that the evidence of these university witnesses focused the blame for Anne's sufferings very directly on the three alleged witches. All of the witnesses confirmed that Anne called out against the women in her fits, and several of them agreed that Mary Pepwell's coming to the Gunter residence in North Moreton tended to send Anne into fits and convulsions. John Prideaux, moreover, reported an incident in which Mary was subjected to a test that, in effect, proved she was a witch. After Anne had noted Mary's arrival at the Gunter residence by saying that she could smell burning thatch, the supposed witch was brought into Anne's chamber, and there made to repeat a charm that ran: 'In the name of the Son and of the Holy Ghost I charge thee, white toad [Mary Pepwell's familiar was thought to take this form], to come out of thee, Anne Gunter, daughter of Brian Gunter.' Anne promptly recovered, and the implication was that Mary Pepwell was a witch, able to direct her familiar at will. Many of the same techniques had been used by the family and friends of the Throckmorton children, supposedly bewitched at Warboys in Huntingdon a few years earlier, although in that case the academic advice came from Cambridge. The alleged bewitchment and possession of the Throckmorton children led to the conviction and execution of three witches. Given the reactions that Anne's sufferings were provoking among his Oxford contacts in the period before the trial of Elizabeth Gregory and Mary Pepwell, Brian Gunter must have been confident of a similar outcome.

Ironically, the most forceful exponent of scepticism about Anne's plight at this point was not a proto-rationalist philosopher or a subtle theologian, but rather a country gentle-

man almost as obscure as Brian Gunter, named Thomas Hinton.
The Hintons, like the Gunters, appear to have been a widespread
if not particularly well-documented gentry clan with members
living in Wiltshire and Berkshire. There is a near certainty that
the Thomas Hinton in this instance, aged about thirty when he
was questioned by the Star Chamber and described variously as
living at Chilton Park or Marlborough in Wiltshire, was the
same Thomas Hinton who had matriculated at Queen's College,
Oxford, in 1591, was a justice of the peace and a militia captain
in his native county by 1608, knighted in 1619, and the MP for
Downton in Wiltshire in 1621. Certainly the ease with which he
was to approach important people, and the apparent seriousness
with which these important people treated what he had to say,
suggests that he was a well-connected man of considerable local
reputation.

Hinton's family connections included Brian Gunter,
although we do not have details of the exact relationship, and it
was the news that a kinsman was in trouble that first interested
him in Anne's bewitchment. About three weeks before the trial
of Elizabeth Gregory and Mary Pepwell, early in February 1605,
Hinton went to Gunter's home; he was intrigued to hear 'that
men of all sorts and from all parts of the country thereabout
repaired unto North Moreton to behold the strange fits and
trances of the said Brian Gunter's daughter, then generally by all
men reputed to be bewitched or possessed' and 'that the said
Brian Gunter, a man allied unto this deponent, was greatly
broken with the strangeness and suddenness of accidents
himself'. Hinton therefore 'resolved to be an eyewitness of these
things which were related to him by others'. Hinton was clearly a
concerned kinsman, but his evidence demonstrates how a witchcraft or possession case might be a subject of gossip and
discussion throughout a region.

On arrival at the Park in North Moreton, Hinton was met by Anne's mother, who told him that Anne was away receiving sustenance, as she was unable to eat or drink unless she was taken 'a certain number of miles from the house'. A little later Anne, in a fit, was brought back by her father. She was sat in a chair, 'where she made show of many strange tortures', and at the end of her fit 'made mention of the three women that she said had bewitched her'. Brian Gunter (and this may be further evidence that Hinton was a man of some influence) then asked his kinsman for his 'assistance in prosecuting the matter against the women, and to yield his best help for the procuring of a session to be held before the assizes for the arraignment and execution' of the witches. Hinton, at this point convinced of the reality of Anne's sufferings, agreed to lend such assistance: 'whereunto this deponent willingly assented, and forthwith concluded with one Mr Bird, a neighbour of Brian Gunter [in fact Thomas Bird, vicar of the nearby parish of Brightwell], to ride speedily towards London, and to meet the said Mr Bird at an appointed place in London to effect the said business'.

This agreement made, and Anne temporarily out of her fits, the company sat down to supper. As they ate, Anne, apart from the others by the fire, made off on her own, accompanied only by a serving maid. A quarter of an hour later she returned, and promptly went into a fit, crying out that Goodwife Gregory had come to her, and had bitten her garter in three places. Those present examined her garter: they found it to be loose and looking indeed as if it had been bitten or cut at three points. But Hinton was suspicious: Anne had gone out of the room accompanied by only a maidservant, and hence, in Hinton's opinion, without being properly observed or supervised; he also noted that Anne had a knife in her hands when she returned. He therefore suspected that the girl had cut the garter herself, and told the Star Chamber how 'this suspicion was an inducement to move this deponent to make further trial'.

The opportunity to do so was soon forthcoming. That evening Alexander Jermin of Exeter College arrived at the Gunter residence. Jermin was one of the younger Oxford scholars involved: he had matriculated at Exeter in December 1602, and had not yet taken his BA when he became concerned with the Gunter case at the age of twenty-two or so. The son of a gentleman from Exeter in Devon, Jermin was a young man of promise, and was shortly to become a fellow of Exeter College, a position he held until his early death in 1614. He conversed with Hinton about Anne Gunter's 'strange fits and trances', and told Hinton that if he had been there the previous night 'he might have been the beholder of a very strange matter that then happened'. He and several others had watched Anne while she was in her fits, and had come to her 'with a certain sentence which they had written in paper' and had laid it down on her bed. She picked up the paper, tore it and 'not looking at it as she tore it ... told them every word that was contained in it'. Hinton repeated this experiment with Jermin. According to his account to the Star Chamber, he watched Anne wriggling and contorting so that she might read the paper unobserved before tearing it up, and telling him and the others present what was written on it. He also noticed how her ability to describe who had come to the house and what they were wearing was simply the result of her being able to see newcomers, without others knowing, as she contorted her head in her supposed fits. What is surprising, as with the business of the cut garter, is that Hinton was the only person able to interpret what was going on in a sceptical way: as so often in cases of witchcraft and possession, most of those attending the afflicted had made up their minds about what was happening at an early point and were unwilling to change their opinions.

A fortnight after his stay at North Moreton, a few days before the witchcraft trial at Abingdon, Hinton went to Oxford to place his younger brother as a student at Queen's College, which he had attended himself: in fact, a Giles Hinton, Esquire, of Wiltshire, is recorded as having matriculated at Queen's on 22 March 1605, which is perfectly in line with his having taken up residence in late February. His brother's affairs put in order, Hinton went to Exeter College, where Anne was staying in the lodgings of Thomas Holland. There he found Brian Gunter and Anne's brothers Harvey and William. He told them of his suspicion that Anne was feigning bewitchment 'which they by all possible means laboured to persuade him from, procuring diverse scholars of that house to produce many arguments which they had framed and matters to prove unto this deponent the certain bewitching of the said Anne Gunter'. Neither side was willing to give way in this argument, but Hinton was invited to come back later, which he did, finding that Anne was in her chamber. It was generally held by the dons attending Anne that she, as in her parent's house, knew 'any stranger standing out of her sight, and that if a stranger came next [to] her she should be grievously tormented'. Hinton and the others decided to try some experiments based on this assumption.

They approached Anne's chamber, but as they did so they heard a great noise from within, with Anne screaming and crying out. Somebody inside the chamber attending to her called out that the girl knew that there were strangers outside, 'and entreated them for God's sake to be gone'. She proved uncontrollable, so the party felt obliged to go down to a lower room. William Helme, who must have been among those with Anne in her chamber, came and told Hinton that Anne knew that he was there, to which the gentleman replied 'that she might imagine so much: for that he said in the morning, he would come again at night'. Hinton recalled being told that Anne 'would not endure a stranger', but that she had 'made choice of some four gentlemen of the college (as this deponent now remembreth) whom she esteemed for her best friends, and whose presence she could well endure', among whom was Helme, who was now insisting to Hinton that Anne was bewitched. Hinton 'entreated the said Mr Helme to join with him in an experiment for both their satisfactions'. Helme agreed, and Hinton asked him to go alone up the stairs, making him promise that 'he should make himself as like unto a stranger as he could' by whispering to himself or by making some small noise.

Helme went up, carrying out Hinton's instructions on the way, whereupon Anne went into a fit, and those with her in the chamber asked whoever it was outside to leave. Helme stayed outside the chamber, and Anne's fit grew worse, the girl, in Hinton's words, 'taking the said Mr Helme her friend as it seemed for a stranger'. Helme came away from the door, and Hinton went up very quietly, so that although Anne could hear Helme go, she 'could not hear the coming of the deponent to the door, going very softly'. Hinton then stood at the door for longer than Helme had done without Anne showing any reaction at all: her apparent sensitivity to the coming of strangers seemed to have left her. Hinton descended the stairs, and talked to Helme about what had happened. Helme, according to Hinton, 'shook his head, and confessed that they thought they were deceived, and that he did now think she did not know one man from another standing out of her sight'. But despite such doubts, and despite Hinton's renewed discussion of his suspicions with Brian Gunter, it was decided (not least by Gunter) that the prosecution of the three women should go ahead. Helme, was, of course to give unequivocal evidence in favour of Gunter in the later Star Chamber investigations.

Although it was Hinton's scepticism that was to be most important, others at Oxford were not convinced by Anne's sufferings. One observer giving evidence was Francis Stewart, second son of John Stewart, the earl of Moray, who had been murdered by the earl of Huntly in 1592 in the course of Scottish faction politics. Stewart, an undergraduate at Christ Church, aged about sixteen or seventeen when he met Anne Gunter at Oxford, was obviously very taken by the girl. He claimed that he had won her trust, and that he had not voiced his doubts about the reality of her sufferings because he had hoped to persuade her to confess the matter herself. Stewart's evidence is especially enlightening on the mysterious undoings and knottings of Anne's garters and hose. He described a number of occasions in which Anne, for example while standing in a dark doorway, would cry out and beat the wall or doorframe with her head or hand to create a distraction while she secretly undid her garters and loosened her hose. He also recounted one incident in which Anne was sitting at a table, pretending to be in a fit, crying out and writing the names of Elizabeth Gregory and the Pepwells on scraps of paper. While she was doing this, she was fiddling with her garters and hose under the table. One of her brothers took a candle and tried to get under the table to see what Anne was doing, whereupon she picked up a ruler that was lying on the table and struck him over the head with it. Again, one wonders why others present did not choose to recognize what were so obviously signs of fakery. Stewart noted that his doubts were shared by another Christ Church man, George Hamden, a few years Francis Stewart's senior and a future rector of Chelsea.

But it was Thomas Hinton who was determined to make his scepticism public. As he explained to the Star Chamber, he was worried that an injustice should be done to the women. He was fully conscious of the weight of opinion Gunter had gathered in Oxford: there was a 'multitude of witnesses' against the three witches, 'most of them men of worth'. He had also sensed 'with what violence the matter was carried against them, in so much that nothing but the lives of the women, especially Goodwife Gregory, would satisfy them'. But he knew that the women 'had not deserved to die' and was anxious that those who were seeking their deaths, not least his kinsman Brian Gunter, should be preserved 'from the guilt of innocent blood'. Accordingly, he decided to voice his doubts about the accusations to officialdom.

At Oxford, he consulted with Sir Francis Knollys. Knollys was the sixth son of his namesake, a major statesman of the Elizabethan period, and 'young Sir Francis', as he was known in his area, was a powerful man, resident at Reading, who had been MP for Oxford City from 1572 until 1589, and for Berkshire in 1597. He was, in fact, one of those minor figures of the period who seem to encapsulate the spirit of the Elizabethan age. He had served in various privateering expeditions, been knighted by the earl of Leicester while on service at Flushing in the Low Countries, was active in the Armada campaign, and was implicated in the rebellion of the earl of Essex (it is a sign of his family's importance that he was related by marriage to both of these noblemen). By 1605 these adventures were well behind him, and Knollys was a settled man of considerable local influence. He heard Hinton out, and appeared to be sympathetic to the accused women. Having raised his doubts with Knollys, and evidently encouraged by the response he received, Hinton decided to return home via Abingdon, where the trial of the three witches was to be held, and to do what he could there to turn opinion in their favour. The accusations against Elizabeth Gregory and the Pepwells would not be uncontested.

chapter *six*

The WITCH-TRIAL *at* ABINGDON

WHATEVER DOUBTS may have developed at Oxford about the reality of Anne's sufferings, Brian Gunter was still intent on prosecuting the women he held responsible for bewitching his daughter. Witchcraft was taken seriously by the village culture, by the theologians and by the government of the age, for it was, in England as on the Continent, a crime that could be tried at the secular courts and was punishable by death.

How frequently witchcraft was tried in the courts of England before the sixteenth century remains a largely unexplored question. Such information as we have suggests that references to relatively infrequent trials are scattered through the court archives that survive from the Middle Ages, these trials in most instances being held before the ecclesiastical courts, which could inflict only minor punishments. And, of course, English monarchs, like other European rulers of the fourteenth, fifteenth and six-teenth centuries, were troubled by treason plots against themselves and the royal family, in which sorcery allegedly played a major role. The first statute to be passed against witchcraft in England, making witchcraft a felony punishable by death, was not enacted until 1542, fairly late in the reign of Henry VIII. This Act, along with other legislation passed under that monarch, lapsed in the reign of his son, the young and short-lived Edward VI, but a new law against witchcraft, albeit a less harsh one than her father's, was passed in the fifth year of Elizabeth I's reign, 1563. This Act was in turn superseded by a further statute of 1604, passed just over a year after James VI of Scotland had come to the throne of England as James I.

Given James's reputation as a witch-hunter, there has been a tradition that the 1604 Act was largely the creation of the newly arrived royal demonologist. We will delay discussion of James's standing as a persecutor of witches until a later point; but there is little evidence for his direct involvement in the drafting or progress through Parliament of the 1604 Act, which in many respects did little more than build on the earlier legislation of 1563. Intent to injure people by witchcraft, kill them, provoke them to 'unlawful love' or to find stolen goods was, under both Acts, punishable by a year's imprisonment and four sessions on the pillory for a first offence; death was the penalty for a second offence of injuring someone by *maleficium.* Causing the death of a human being or conversing with or trying to raise evil spirits were capital offences under the 1604 Act. The main innovation of the Jacobean Act was that it made actually causing injury to human beings or damage to property a capital offence, as was the newly defined and rather odd crime of using a dead body for occult pur-poses. Thus if they had been convicted, Elizabeth Gregory and Mary Pepwell would have faced the death penalty for harming Anne Gunter, and also, if it could be proved that they had famil-iars, for consorting with evil spirits.

England, like most other European states, by 1600 possessed a complex and well-established court system, and there were a number of tribunals before which a suspected witch might find herself. But by the late sixteenth century most cases of malefic witchcraft, along with most other felonies, were tried by the assize courts. Established in the late twelfth century and abolished in 1971, the assizes were to be one of the longest-running legal or administrative institutions in English history. Twice annually (early in the year and around midsummer) two judges were appointed at Westminster to ride each of the six circuits (that is groupings of counties) into which England was divided for this purpose. Berkshire was on the Oxford Circuit, which comprised, along with Berkshire and Oxfordshire, the counties of Gloucestershire, Herefordshire, Shropshire, Staffordshire, Worcestershire and Monmouthshire. No other circuit included so many counties, and riding the Oxford Circuit was a lengthy process: the business of this circuit normally took twenty-eight days from the opening of the first court on the circuit to the end of the last, and the judges who set out on horseback from London to ride the Oxford Circuit would cover some 400 miles before their return. The annual fee for this work was only £20, although the judges on the Oxford Circuit might also expect some £170 in expenses. It was through these that they made their profit: much of the accommodation and subsistence that this sum was meant to cover was met by the gifts and hospitality that the judges received from gentry and other local notables.

The men presiding over assize trials were usually very senior judges, professionals of considerable experience and learning. This was in contrast to the situation that obtained over much of the Continent, where witchcraft-trials were sometimes conducted in local or even village courts presided over by local judges with little or no legal training. English assize judges were able to bring intellectual rigour to the accusations of witchcraft that came before them, while their high position in the social hierarchy meant that they were distanced from the village squabbles and neighbourly disputes which, as in Anne Gunter's case, so often lay at the heart of a witchcraft accusation. This distancing was reinforced by a convention that assize judges should not ride the circuit where their chief residence was, something that again helped them stay detached from the local issues at play when villagers accused one of their neighbours as a witch. To this judicial professionalism and detachment was added another factor: a further peculiarity of the English criminal justice system was that the English common law, unlike the Roman law system that operated over most of western and central Europe, did not countenance torture as a means of extracting confessions to establish guilt and implicate accomplices in criminal cases. Thus, English witches were spared the rack and the thumbscrews; and the tendency for tortured suspects to create large-scale panics as they named ever widening circles of fellow witches in hopes of placating their torturers was largely absent.

One outcome of these peculiarities of the English criminal justice system was that England experienced an acquittal rate in witch-trials that was, by the standards of many contemporary Continental courts, surprisingly high. Infuriatingly, the records of the Oxford Circuit simply do not exist for the relevant period, but we know that on the south-eastern or Home Circuit (Essex, Hertfordshire, Kent, Surrey and Sussex), witchcraft-prosecutions, which had been at their heaviest in the 1580s and 1590s, were beginning to decline in number by the opening years of the seventeenth century. Calculations made by one of the pioneers of English witchcraft history, Cecil L'Estrange Ewen, show that there were 156 indictments involving 87 witches at the south-eastern assizes in the period 1588–97, compared to 73 indictments involving 39 witches in the years 1598–1607, and totals both of accusations and accused were to fall until a new wave of prosecutions came in the 1640s. Only a small proportion of those tried were hanged. In 1588–97 only 18 of the 87 accused were executed, in 1598–1607 only 16 of 39 accused. Thus when Brian Gunter took Elizabeth Gregory and Mary Pepwell to court, not only were English witch-trials declining in number, but there was a low capital conviction rate that must in part have been a reflection of the caution and scepti- cism exercised by judges.

So Brian Gunter, in launching legal proceedings for witchcraft against Elizabeth Gregory and Mary Pepwell, was embarking on a very uncertain undertaking. Given the rate of convictions in witchcraft cases at the beginning of the seven- teenth century, he stood rather less than a 50 per cent chance of convicting the two women he had accused. His chances were lessened by another development that must have been both unexpected and unwelcome: Nicholas and Alice Kirfoote had refused to join him in prosecuting the North Moreton witches. Despite Nicholas Kirfoote's earlier co-operation with Gunter, and despite his wife's enmity towards Elizabeth Gregory and her claims that she too had been bewitched by Gregory and the Pepwells, the couple had no stomach for taking the supposed witches to court. Gunter may have orchestrated a considerable and potentially influential body of opinion in his favour in Oxford, but he suffered a serious setback in his efforts to maintain that coalition of interested parties in the local community that was usually crucial to the successful prosecution of witches. The trial of Elizabeth Gregory and Mary Pepwell was destined to take the form of a direct confrontation between them and Brian Gunter.

During the past thirty or so years research into the records that survive from the English court system of the sixteenth and seven-teenth centuries has revealed much of the operations of criminal justice in the era. It has not, unfortunately, told us a great deal about the actual running of the period's criminal trials: the documentation produced by the courts was not designed to furnish historians operating at a distance of three or four centuries with details of what happened in the courtroom. What we know is that, certainly in the south-eastern counties in the closing years of the sixteenth century, trial of felony was usually a speedy and rather haphazard affair. There was little by way of formal rules of evidence, and hearsay evidence and evidence derived from the reputation of the accused or the accuser (both of these very important in witchcraft cases) were acceptable, as was the testimony of children. The basic notion was that the trial should give weight to an existing presumption of guilt rather than establish the specific details of a charge through the application of formally defined rules of evidence. Lawyers were largely absent from criminal trials, and defence lawyers were unheard of. Indeed, whereas witnesses for the prosecution gave sworn evidence, defence witnesses were unsworn, making their statements intrinsically less trustworthy in an age that took oaths very seriously.

The classic description of a criminal trial in this period is given in the *De Republica Anglorum* by Sir Thomas Smith, first published in 1583 but written in the 1560s while he was Queen Elizabeth's ambassador in France. According to Smith, the accused would be called into court and have the charge read to them in English. They would then make a plea, normally of not guilty, and, after a few further preliminaries, trial would com-mence. On Smith's account, the judge

Asketh first the party robbed [the same would apply for other offences] if he know the prisoner, and biddeth him look upon him: he saith yea, the prisoner sometime saith nay ... [the accuser says] I know thee well enough, thou robbest me in such a place, thou beatest me, thou tookest my horse from me, and my purse, thou hadst then such a coat and such a man in thy company: the thief will say no, and so they stand a while in altercation, he telleth all he can say: after him likewise all those who were at the apprehension of the prisoner, or who can give any *indices* or tokens which we call in our language evidence against the malefactor.

Here is the essence of the criminal trial of the period: the direct confrontation between the accuser and the accused; the way in which the two, in a trial devoid of either defence or prosecution lawyers, would stand 'in altercation'; and the assumption that those giving what 'we call in our language' evidence should be doing so against the accused. The judge, Smith continued, when he had heard enough, would ask the witnesses if they had any more to say. If the reply was no (Smith obviously assumed that it would be), the judge would then turn to the trial jury and direct them to give their verdict.

In fact, most of the relevant scraps of evidence indicate that the judge played a key role in directing the assize trial. Despite the eulogies that writers in the English common law tradition were already lavishing on the jury system, and despite those occasional episodes in which juries made, and were disciplined for making, displays of independence, in the majority of trials at the assizes the juries were expected to follow a strong lead given by the presiding judge, and were generally willing to do so. Juries in any case usually tried offenders in batches of six or so, and it is improbable that they retired from the courtroom to reflect on their verdict, or, indeed, that they could have kept many of the details of each trial they were meant to be considering in their heads. The judge questioned the accused, the accuser and witnesses in open court, and his role in thus eliciting evidence, and the interpreta-tion that he placed on the evidence, was crucial. Moreover, the sheer speed with which cases were dispatched militated against reflection on the part of juries. The issue may have been less acute in a relatively sparsely populated county like Berkshire, but in some of the heavily populated counties on the Home Circuit, when bad harvests in the late 1590s resulted in a massive increase in the number of property offences being tried, it seems probable that trials for felony, many of them resulting in hanging, were completed on average in twenty minutes.

The judge's input was as important in the trial of witchcraft as it was with any other offence. The earliest pamphlet we have describing an English witchcraft-trial, dating from 1566, shows the judge directing the proceedings, cross-examining the suspects and, in particular, getting one of them to give details to the court of where her familiar had sucked blood from her. A trial from 1602, three years before the trial of Anne Gunter's supposed tormenters, provides insights into a judge's way with defence witnesses. This case involved the bewitchment of Mary Glover, a girl of about fourteen, by a woman called Elizabeth Jackson. The physician Edward Jorden, who also appears in the Gunter case, was giving evidence for the defence, claiming that Mary was suffering from hysteria and was not bewitched. The judge, Sir Edmund Anderson, was unconvinced by the doctor, who was declaring that 'for these causes [of Mary Glover's sufferings], I think it may be natural' and ' these accidents and symptoms for aught I see be natural'. When pressed for a more direct answer (and there was equivocation in his opinions), Jorden replied that, in his conscience, the illness was 'altogether natural'. The judge asked what the illness was called: 'Passio hysterica,' replied the doctor. The judge asked if Jorden could cure it: 'I cannot tell; I

will not undertake it, but I think fit trial should be made thereof,'
he replied. After some further questions, the judge declared, 'In
my conscience, it is not natural; for if you tell me neither a natural
cause for it, nor a natural remedy, I will tell you it is not natural.'
Anderson, after 'pausing awhile', then harangued the jury. 'The
land,' he informed them, 'is full of witches; they abound in all
places. I have hanged five or six and twenty of them; there is no
man here can speak more of them than myself ... they have on
their bodies diverse strange marks at which (as some confessed)
the devil sucks their blood, for they have forsaken God,
renounced their baptism, and vowed their service to the devil,
and so the sacrifice which they offer him is their blood.' Elizabeth
Jackson, he reminded the jury, had such marks on her, and he
also dwelt on the way in which the woman was 'full of cursing,
she threatens and prophesies and still it takes effect'. Jackson was
convicted, although, as she had only allegedly injured Mary
Glover and was being tried under the 1563 statute, she was sentenced to imprisonment and the pillory rather than to hanging.

The personality of the judge presiding over the trial of Elizabeth Gregory and Mary Pepwell was, therefore, crucial. They were
tried by the experienced and learned Sir David Williams. Born
around 1536, Williams was the son of a substantial yeoman
farmer in Brecknockshire. His father must have been a wealthy
man for his social class, for he was able to afford a legal education
for his son: Williams entered the Middle Temple in 1568 and was
called to the bar in 1576. He pursued a successful career in which
a steady rise in the legal profession was accompanied by a gradual
accretion of wealth and land. Between 1581 and 1595 he was the
Queen's attorney-general for a circuit of five Welsh counties, and
was also recorder (senior legal official) for Brecknock between
1587 and 1604. He served as an MP, representing Brecknock four
times between 1584 and 1598. His first marriage, to a Brecknock

girl, was followed by the birth of nine sons and two daughters, and, after the death of his first wife in 1597, he married a widow named Dorothy Latton, and settled at Kingston Bagpuize in Berkshire. Williams was knighted in 1603, and in the following year, despite his residence in Berkshire, was chosen to ride the Oxford Circuit. James Whitelock, a judge who served extensively on that circuit in the first half of the seventeenth century, remembered how Williams had taken him under his wing when he was an inexperienced barrister and given him much useful advice. Williams was, therefore, a man who had done well out of the law, with his knighthood and his extensive estates, but he was a kindly man. And by 1605 he was an extremely experienced judge.

Two judges were appointed to each assize circuit. It was the custom, at each assize, for one of them to hear criminal cases, while the other dealt with civil disputes. It is a sign that Anne Gunter's case was regarded as somewhat unusual that the other judge riding the Oxford Circuit in 1605, Sir Christopher Yelverton, was also present at the trial. Yelverton was almost exactly the same age as Williams, but, unlike him, had been born into a legal dynasty. He was the third son of William Yelverton of Rougham, in Norfolk, a reader at Gray's Inn, which Christopher entered in 1552. Yelverton also enjoyed a successful career, and in 1601 took a leading role in the most important political trial of the late Elizabethan period, the one that resulted in the execution for treason of the earl of Essex. Again like Williams, he served as an MP, in his case for Northamptonshire. He was another recent arrival on the Oxford Circuit, which he rode for the first time in 1602. He had previously served on the Northern Circuit, but had become involved in a dispute over precedence with the lord keeper of the Council of the North at York. The Council of the North was an instrument of royal prerogative power, and Yelverton, obviously a keen defender of the rights of the common law (he also had the reputation of being a Puritan), became involved in friction between the Council and the Northern Circuit assize judges. More specifically, at the York Summer Assizes of 1600 he delivered a public snub to the lord president of the Council of the North. This led to his being reprimanded by the Star Chamber, and forced to change circuits.

Evidence for Mary Pepwell does not survive, but we know that Elizabeth Gregory had been brought into the criminal justice system through the normal processes of the period. As suspicions of witchcraft against Gregory grew, Brian Gunter obtained warrants from a justice of the peace for her to be arrested and examined. Accordingly, Richard Spooner, the constable of North Moreton, set out with a group of other men to arrest Elizabeth Gregory and take her before a local justice of the peace (it will be remembered that the experience of participating in this arrest left the evidently impressionable John Leaver with night-mares about witches and receiving the sacrament from the devil). The justice in question was Sir Richard Lovelace, aged just over thirty, resident at Hurley, where his family had acquired monastic lands after the Dissolution of 1536. Lovelace was another man who had enjoyed a colourful career before settling to the life of a country gentleman. He may have served at sea under Lord Howard of Effingham, and had certainly served in Elizabeth's Irish wars, being knighted at Dublin by the earl of Essex in 1599. Like so many others, Lovelace was implicated in Essex's rebellion of 1601, but managed to survive any of the conse-quences of his involvement, and was a justice of the peace for Berkshire by 1604 when he sat as MP for Abingdon, having already sat as MP for Berkshire in 1601. Lovelace would have taken down statements from the accuser, the accused and witness-es (these statements, known as examinations or depositions in the

terminology of the period, have long since been lost), and would
have then committed the suspected witch to the county gaol in
Reading, where she awaited trial at the next meeting of the
assizes. We may safely assume that Mary Pepwell, who was to
stand trial with Elizabeth Gregory, went through much the same
process.

County gaols at this time were not the most salubrious of
places. The lack of assize and quarter sessions records means that
we have scant information about Reading Gaol, but some
impression of conditions in such institutions can be formed from
the information that between 1558 and 1625 some 1,292 prisoners, nearly all of them being held before trial, are known to have
died, mainly through illness and malnutrition, in the gaols of the
five counties on the Home Circuit of the assizes. The gaols were
often insecure, half-ruinous structures: in 1625 the county gaoler
of Warwickshire complained that the gaol was so decrepit he was
forced to keep prisoners in his own house to prevent escapes; a few
years later prisoners were left standing up to their knees in water
after a heavy storm burst through the imperfect protection offered
by the ruined roof of Colchester Castle, site of Essex county
gaol. The parish registers of the church of St Mary the Virgin in
Reading note the occasional burial of prisoners from the
Berkshire county gaol, along with the baptism of the odd child
born in the gaol and, in 1683, the marriage of two prisoners in
custody there. Insights into life in the gaol are provided by
Reading borough archives. These record a complaint of 1630
from the gaoler that a quarter of mutton had been stolen from
him by a prisoner and passed out of the gaol to an accomplice
through an open window, and an incident of 1635, in which one
of the gaoler's servants helped prisoners escape. On another occasion, in 1652, the borough authorities were troubled by reports of
a 'great disorder in the gaol by reason of the gaoler's keeping a

common alehouse there'. We have no reason to believe that the gaol at Reading was either well regulated or healthy when Elizabeth Gregory and Mary Pepwell were held in it awaiting trial in the winter of 1604–5.

Mary's mother Agnes, as was perhaps appropriate for a woman with an existing reputation as a witch, had fled. Margaret Orpewood, the wife of a tanner in Abingdon, record-ed how Pepwell was in her house when one of Brian Gunter's servants came looking for her. Orpewood, fearing that if she revealed Pepwell's presence, the suspected witch would bewitch her three children, told him that Pepwell had gone to Reading and was intending to go from there to London. Pepwell was, understandably, 'in very great fear', and took Orpewood's advice to make off, which she did 'hastily and fearfully', without letting Orpewood know of her intended destination. Orpewood's brother, Robert Whisteler of Goring in Oxfordshire, told how he had been in the house at the time and had seen a strange woman, whom he later discovered to be Agnes Pepwell, disappear into some nearby woods. Agnes was apparently not apprehended in time for the trial, although she had been taken by the summer of 1605, for a number of witnesses in the Star Chamber investigation gave evidence of the confessions of witchcraft she made while in custody.

The trial of Elizabeth Gregory and Mary Pepwell, which took place at the assizes at Abingdon on 1 March 1605, was preceded by one of those personal interventions in witchcraft cases that occurred so frequently and that appear so irregular to the modern observer. The key figure here was Thomas Hinton, whom we last encountered when he was deciding to make public his conviction that Anne was simulating bewitchment, and that the accusations against Elizabeth Gregory and Mary Pepwell were false. At Abingdon he voiced his concerns to an

acquaintance of his, the Berkshire justice of the peace Alexander
Chocke. In Chocke's words, Hinton declared that he was
determined to 'make it plain and apparent to the jury that the said
Anne Gunter did counterfeit, and that all she did was but
counterfeiting'. Hinton had overcome some reservations about
speaking out, these reservations being founded, as he expressed it,
on an unwillingness 'to be the means of disgrace to his kinsman,
if otherwise a course might be taken for the women's safety'. But
Chocke and Sir Francis Knollys put him in touch with the
judges in order to make his opinion known to them (Sir Richard
Lovelace, the justice who had committed Gregory to prison and
was present in court, had refused to do so). David Williams
recognized Hinton, who was a kinsman of the judge as well as of
Brian Gunter, and, on hearing his views, ordered Chocke,
Lovelace and another justice of the peace, Edward Clarke, to
take down his statement in writing. But before that, he instructed
them, they were to go to the King's Head Inn in Abingdon,
where Anne Gunter was lodged, and interview her. Hinton was
to be kept away from this meeting, locked in a chamber, presumably so that he could not influence the three justices' opinion of
the nature of Anne's afflictions.

The gentlemen entered the inn and found Anne 'standing at
a cupboard or chair' (as Chocke explained, his memory of some
of the details of the incident was imperfect), supported on 'either
side and behind her with some of her friends', these friends, in
Chocke's opinion, being 'scholars of Oxford'. As the trio went
in, Anne came towards them, and after some initial pleasantries
Chocke, Lovelace and Clarke began to question her. They asked
her if it was true that she could smell witches who entered the
house she was in, to which Anne replied that 'I could so do, but
now I am told by the spirit, I shall so smell them no more'. On
being asked whose spirit, she said, 'Mother Gregory's spirit [i.e.,

her familiar] and Mary Pepwell's spirit', speaking (as Chocke commented) 'before but of one spirit'. She gave somewhat evasive answers when asked if these spirits always told her to speak the truth, but when asked by what smell she identified witches, she answered readily enough that it was an odour 'like the burnt thatch of an old house'. Memories of thatch from the alleged witch's houses being burned in the Gunter family home in North Moreton had not left her.

Chocke was a little vague on the details of this questioning, but his account reads as if Anne failed to put up a convincing show of being genuinely bewitched. But she was supported, both physically and morally, by a group of associates who, if we may trust Chocke, were not merely her neighbours from North Moreton but 'scholars of Oxford', people whose opinions officialdom would regard as rather weighty. After this short interview, the three gentlemen released Hinton from the chamber where they had left him, and returned to the courtroom. There they gave the judges a full account of their questioning of Anne, and relayed what Hinton had told them. We have no means of assessing the impact of this on Williams and Yelverton, although the reports that the three justices gave them of Anne's perform-ance would hardly have encouraged them to bring a verdict of guilty. But, with the two judges apprised of the three justices' information, proceedings began, and the witch-trial proper took its course.

The trial demonstrated two peculiarities. The first was its length. As already mentioned, assize trials in this period were normally short affairs, sometimes taking as little as twenty minutes. The trial of Anne Gunter's tormentors began, according to Chocke, with the jurors being sworn in between 2 and 3 p.m., after which 'they stood at the bar, hearing the evidence' for eight hours, at the end of which process 'they went from the court, to consider the issue, and the proofs, that were made of the evidence'. Thomas Hinton, likewise, was to comment that 'a great part of that whole day (as he remembreth) was spent by the judges with great diligence in the business'. Secondly, the social profile of the trial jury was unusually high. The jury at an assize trial was usually composed of men of middling property, typically drawn from those yeomen, husbandmen and tradesmen whose role as constable or other local officer had ensured that they were already at the assizes, and therefore might conveniently be empanelled as jurors. On this occasion, Alexander Chocke, gentleman and justice of the peace, was made foreman of the jury, two other justices, Edward Clarke and Thomas Dolman, were sworn in as jurors, while the remaining jurymen were, in Chocke's words, 'very sufficient jurors, and men of good quality and sufficiency for the trial of the said persons'. The judges, perhaps alert to the general difficulties involved in trying witchcraft, or perhaps conscious of the difficult circumstances surrounding this case, were evidently cautious to show as much care as possible in securing a fair trial.

This raises the intriguing possibility that the judges might have been briefed to expect a difficult witchcraft case at Abingdon. We know that Anne's alleged bewitchment had attracted official attention in London before the judges had set out. Early in 1605 the newly appointed bishop of London, Richard Vaughan, had asked the fellows of the College of Physicians to examine Anne to determine whether her sufferings were caused by witchcraft. We have already encountered Edward Jorden giving medical evidence in the case of Mary Glover, which occurred three years before Anne's, and trying unconvincingly to persuade the judge that in this instance the allegations of witchcraft were false. Jorden was, in fact, only one of a number of doctors involved in this case, for those anxious to secure a conviction, as well as those who thought the supposed bewitcher innocent, had gone to the College of Physicians in search of expert medical opinion to help bolster their position. The Glover case was one of a number of well-publicized incidents of bewitchment and possession that took place around 1600, and it is perhaps significant that the opinions of the College should once more be sought. The three members of the College appointed to examine Anne made their report on 4 March (that is, immediately after the trial at Abingdon), and in it they said that Anne was feigning possession. It is interesting to speculate as to whether the assize judges had been given advance warning of this opinion. It is also interesting to note that one of the three doctors making this report was John Argent, a rising star in the contemporary medical establishment who was to be president of the College of Physicians eight times in the 1620s and 1630s. Argent, already a medical man of some reputation, had been associated with Edward Jorden in providing evidence for the defence in the Mary Glover affair.

It is, moreover, significant that it was Richard Vaughan who was encouraging this high-level medical examination. Vaughan, born around 1550 in Caernarfonshire, was a kinsman of John Aylmer, an important figure in the English Reformation, bishop of London between 1587 and his death in 1594, and perhaps most remarkable for his observation that God is an Englishman. Under Aylmer's patronage, Vaughan had attended Cambridge and acquired a number of ecclesiastical livings. After his patron's death he had, like so many others, moved into the circle of that rising but doomed favourite, the earl of Essex, become bishop of Bangor in 1596, and then moved on to the more impor-tant see of Chester in the following year. While bishop of

Chester, Vaughan had made a decisive intervention in the case of Thomas Harrison, 'the boy of Northwich', who was the supposed victim of one of the flurry of possession cases that occurred around 1600. Harrison's fits, as was not uncommon, lasted for a year or two, and, again as was not uncommon, became a matter of dispute between those who held that he was genuinely demonically possessed and those who argued that he was suffering from a natural ailment. Vaughan and the other three clergymen appointed as commissioners to keep an eye on this case were convinced that young Thomas's sufferings were genuine, but that they had natural rather than demonic causes. Vaughan took the theologically correct line of allowing prayer and fasting as means of easing the lad's afflictions, and was also very careful to avoid unseemly displays of religious enthusiasm by precluding the gathering of those large crowds of spectators who usually surrounded the bed of the possessed (Anne Gunter's experience is an excellent example of this). Vaughan had good contacts with the upper reaches of the Church of England, and his involvement in Anne's case suggests strongly that the Berkshire girl's sufferings were coming to the attention of higher officialdom by early 1605, and to a segment of higher officialdom that was well informed about possession and witchcraft, and that regarded them with some scepticism.

Chocke's account of the trial does not touch on these broader matters, and he was not even, alas, asked to give the full story of the eight hours of proceedings. What his statement to the Star Chamber supplies is vivid evidence about Anne and Brian Gunter's contribution to the events in the courtroom. As was becoming usual in witchtrials, the allegedly bewitched party was brought into the court, although in this instance, according to Chocke, only after her father had 'made earnest suit by himself that his daughter might be brought into the court, in the face of the country [i.e., the jury] at the said trial, which with much ado was at length granted him'. Anne was carried in on a chair and placed before the judges, at which point she immediately went into a fit. Her father, who was standing near her, explained to the court 'that in her said fits she was senseless, and declared how she would pass from fit to fit', which the girl promptly did. On his mentioning rolling eyes as a symptom, Anne rolled her eyes, 'so as no part of them but the whites could be seen'. As a demonstra-tion of the insensitivity that her father then alluded to, the supposedly possessed Anne began to beat her knuckles against the chair she sat in, although Chocke, who was standing a mere two feet from where she was seated, noted that although she initially struck the chair with her knuckles, she then used 'the brawn of or lower part of her said hand', which suggested to this well-placed observer that 'she had sense and feeling in the saving of her knuckles'.

Anne, and again apparently in response to her father's listing her symptoms, began mumbling incoherently; then she passed into a trance and fell out of her chair, to sprawl directly in front of Chocke. The justice turned juryman 'took her by the left hand, and there held her, feeling her pulse', while 'Mr Fowler, the clerk of assize' held her by the right hand. The clerk of assize was responsible for the smooth running of the court, the organization of its paperwork and the keeping of its records, and 'Mr Fowler' was in fact Richard Fowler, educated at both Corpus Christi College, Cambridge, and Lincoln's Inn, the son of the William Fowler who had been clerk of assize on the Oxford Circuit a generation earlier. So Anne, after running through her repertoire of fits and symptoms of possession for the benefit of judges and jurymen, now found herself prostrate, feigning complete insensi-tivity as her hands were held by the foreman of the jury and the clerk of the court.

As if all this were not enough, Brian Gunter was by now attempting to give the judges advice on how to conduct the trial. According to Chocke, he was 'earnestly suing the judges that a spell which he had might be read to the said Elizabeth Gregory and that she might say it after the party that read it'. The judges were initially reluctant to comply with this request, 'but upon his importunacy, they granted it unto him'. In fact, Sir Richard Lovelace was asked to read something, although apparently the wording differed from the formula that Brian Gunter desired (once again, Chocke is unhelpful on the exact details here). After Lovelace read out the spell, and Gregory repeated it, Judge Williams turned to him and asked, 'What say you now Gunter to it, you have your request', to which Gunter responded, 'She [that is, Elizabeth Gregory] saith it not right.' This exchange cannot have endeared Gunter to the judges, and it may not be reading too much into the tone of Chocke's account (it was only after 'much ado' that they had agreed to have Anne in court in the first place) to suggest that he was doing his case little good.

Anne, meanwhile, was still lying prostrate on the floor of the courtroom, with Chocke taking her pulse. Emerging from her supposed trance, she added to the general confusion by beginning a conversation with him, telling him that 'the spirit [presumably Gregory's familiar] told her, that Mother Gregory would not say the spell right'. She told Chocke that Elizabeth Gregory had come into the court 'trickle and trim'; Anne 'recited and named all her apparel from the foot to the head, saying further that she smelt her well enough so soon as she came into court, and that she smelt the burnt thatch of an old house', looking the gentleman directly in the face as she spoke. The inference was obviously that she had detected the witch's presence and had been able to describe her clothing through second sight. Chocke was unconvinced: he thought that the girl had seen Gregory enter, and that she had been instructed on how to behave when she came in. It is, however, remarkable that Anne should be allowed to speak to the foreman of the jury in this fashion. More of the flavour of the trial is conveyed by Chocke's remembering that he was so near to Anne, her father and Elizabeth Gregory that he could have touched all of them. The encounter between the witches and their accusers in that Abingdon courtroom was a remarkably intimate one.

The trial was a confrontational and dramatic affair. But let us return to one of its elements that Chocke recalled so vividly: Brian Gunter's insistence, that Elizabeth Gregory be required, as part of the trial process, to repeat a charm or spell. When this charm, in Gunter's opinion, was not read correctly, and the judges refused to have it read again, Gunter, according to the sceptical Thomas Hinton, cried out to them that 'he had not that justice Mr Throckmorton had'. This, of course, was a reference to the trial of the witches of Warboys in Huntingdonshire, and the bewitchment and possession of several of the children of the Throckmorton family. The background to this incident displayed some surprising parallels with the Gunter case: the Throckmortons were a family of gentry newcomers to Warboys who had done well out of land sales after the Reformation, and their adversaries, the witches, were members of a long-established if slightly rough farming family. The presence in the Gunter household of a tract relating the story of the Warboys affair was a matter of concern in the Star Chamber investigations, and Anne confessed to having modelled many of her own fits and trances on this detailed account of the sufferings of the Throckmorton children.

The tract also describes numerous confrontations between the supposedly possessed children and their alleged tormentors, in which the latter were subjected to immense psychological pressure, what was virtually illegal arrest, and physical assaults, most frequently taking the form of that traditional remedy for witchcraft, scratching the face and drawing the blood of the supposed witch. But the children's torments could be guaranteed to terminate if the suspects repeated a charm that was, in effect, a confession that they were witches. On the evening before the trial of the Warboys witches, the judge, Edward Fenner, along with a large body of justices of the peace and other gentlemen, was treated to a remarkable display at the Crown Inn at Huntingdon. The Throckmortons, better connected and more powerful in their county than Brian Gunter was in his, were able to provide authority with a convincing display of their offsprings' anguish. One of the afflicted children, Joan Throckmorton, then aged about nineteen, went into a fit before Fenner and the others. She was brought out of her fit when one of the accused, Agnes Samuel, the daughter of Joan Samuel, the chief witch at Warboys, said, 'As I am a witch and a worse witch than my mother, and did consent to the death of Lady Cromwell [a member of another important local family, and step-grandmother of Oliver Cromwell], so I charge the devil to let Mistress Joan Throckmorton out of her fit at this present.' After this and similar conjurations, Joan was 'as well as ever she was in her life' and, indeed, underwent a complete recovery from her afflictions.

These proceedings could have done little but help convince Fenner and the others present of the witch's guilt, not only of injuring the girls, which, it will be remembered, was not a capital offence at this time, but of killing by witchcraft, which was. At the trial, another of the accused witches, Joan Samuel's husband John, under an illegal threat of immediate death if he failed to co-operate, had to repeat this formula, this time for the benefit of Jane Throckmorton, who was contorting before the court much as Anne was to do, and promptly came out of her fit when the charm was read. It was almost certainly something like this charm, a confession that ended the sufferings of the bewitched person, on whose use Gunter was insisting; if it had been used and repeated correctly, Anne would doubtless have come out of her fit as promptly as Joan and Jane Throckmorton had done, hence giving 'proof' of her bewitchment before the court. But Brian Gunter was right: he did not have that justice that Mr Throckmorton had. Joan, John and Agnes Samuel were hanged on 6 April 1593, the day after their trial. Elizabeth Gregory and Mary Pepwell, admittedly remanded after their trial for unspeci-fied reasons, were acquitted. Gunter's prosecution of them, for all his and his daughter's performances in the courtroom, had failed.

Elizabeth Gregory and Mary Pepwell were among the first people to be tried under the new witchcraft Act of 1604, which has generally been regarded as a harsher law than that previously obtaining. On 29 March of that year the bill from which the eventual Act resulted was referred to a parliamentary committee, on which sat six earls, sixteen other peers and twelve bishops (the bill had originated in the House of Lords). This committee called on a formidable array of legal experts to give it advice in drafting this new legislation against witches. Among the one ecclesiastical and six common lawyers asked to advise were the same David Williams and Christopher Yelverton who were to preside over the trial of the two North Moreton witches: the judges trying Elizabeth Gregory and Mary Pepwell were there-fore very skilled in the law relating to witchcraft. A few months after the Act was passed, they conducted a witchcraft-trial with considerable circumspection and in such a way as to make an acquittal likely. There could hardly be a better illustration of the contention that attitudes towards witchcraft in early modern England were not monolithic.

The acquittal of the two women thus redounded to the credit

of the trial judges and, more generally, to English judical attitudes towards witchcraft allegations, but it brought scant comfort to Brian Gunter. His plan had failed. A substantial part of village opinion might continue to accept that Elizabeth Gregory and the Pepwell women were witches, but the truth was that the richest man in North Moreton had proved himself unable to sustain a successful witchcraft prosecution against a member of the Gregory family. It is easy to speculate on how this could have affected the standing in the village of a man whose popularity might already have been uncertain. Brian Gunter's next move, designed to reverse any damage to his local standing, was a disastrous miscalculation that landed both himself and his daughter in considerable trouble.

chapter *seven*

DEMONIC POSSESSION

and the POLITICS *of*

EXORCISM

T HE ACCOUNTS that have come down to us of demonic
      possession in Europe in the sixteenth, seventeenth and
eighteenth centuries seem unbelievable, with their supposed victims of possession writhing, contorting, speaking in the voice of
the devil or vomiting foreign objects. Belief in demonic possession, like belief in witchcraft, can all too easily be interpreted as
one of those phenomena that separates early modern culture from
that of the modern world. Readers now are at a loss, for example,
when confronted with cases like that of the Viennese demoniac
Anna Schlutterbäurin, who in 1584 was allegedly possessed by
12,652 devils.

Yet the idea of spirits entering and taking possession of a
human body is a widespread one. It is commonly found by
anthropologists in Third World societies, where it is enmeshed in
the related phenomena of trance, spirit mediumship and
shamanism. Historically, its reality had been accepted for many
centuries by the time Anne Gunter went into her fits. Credence
in something very like possession by evil spirits existed in
Ancient Egypt, while, more importantly for early modern

writers, it was present in the belief systems of Greece and, perhaps more markedly, Rome. Writers on the occult in the sixteenth and seventeenth centuries could buttress their arguments by reference to the works of classical authors.

For most of these early modern writers, and for the population at large, the crucial factor was that they lived in a Christian culture, and that the spirits that entered the bodies of the possessed were demons doing the will of an anti-Christian master, the devil. As demonologists were fully aware, the Bible, and the New Testament in particular, was full of references to evil spirits, and to the capacity of Jesus Christ to cast them out of human bodies: 'then was brought unto him one possessed of a devil, blind and dumb: and he healed him, insomuch that he spake and saw' (Matthew 12:22); 'behold, they brought to him a dumb man, possessed with a devil, and after the devil was cast out the dumb man spake' (Matthew 9:32–33); 'they brought unto him such as were possessed by devils ... and he healed them' (Matthew 4:24); 'when the even was come, they brought unto him many that were possessed with devils; and he cast out the spirits with his word' (Matthew 8:16); 'And he preached in their synagogues throughout all Galilee, and cast out devils' (Mark 1:39). The New Testament also contained fuller narratives of possession, such as that of the man, dwelling in the land of the Gadarenes, who had been possessed by a devil for a long time, and tormented by so many unclean spirits that they proclaimed their name as legion. He, like many of the possessed, showed unusual physical strength, breaking the bonds and chains that were being used to restrain him. Yet the devils recognized Christ as their Lord and left the man, after which he recovered at once. These numerous biblical references helped convince Christians of the reality of demonic possession, and of their Saviour's ability to cast out devils. Moreover, Christ had evidently passed on the ability to exorcize to his followers: 'And when he had called unto him his twelve disciples, he gave them power against unclean spirits, to cast them out'(Matthew 10:1). It was this power that had been inherited by the exorcizing priests of Catholic Europe.

Despite the biblical references, the reality of demonic possession in early modern Europe was contentious; even if the general possibility of possession by demons was accepted, there was still room to disbelieve that demonic possession existed in specific instances. Such disputed cases might lead to detailed and lengthy pamphlet wars between rival groupings of clergymen and physicians, and a whole range of explanations could be offered for possession, including the simulation that appears to have accounted for Anne Gunter's sufferings. Even if downright pretence were precluded, demonic possession could be attributed to other, natural causes: thus it was accepted that the devil could really possess some people, but that other instances of what might be diagnosed as demonic possession were more properly attributable to that catchall mental disorder that the age labelled 'melancholy', or simply to delusions on the part of the supposed sufferer. Belief in demonic possession flourished in a time when religious convictions were deep, and could be enthusiastic: unusually religious individuals might undergo intense spiritual experiences that could induce an ecstatic state, one in which the spirit of godliness was thought to be filling the person as surely as the evil spirits sent by Satan filled the bodies of the demonically possessed. Yet the frequency with which the phenomenon occurred, and the publicity that was sometimes afforded to incidents of it, meant that it was widely recognized: people 'knew' what happened in cases of demonic possession, and demoniacs 'knew' how to behave if they thought they were possessed.

Demonic possession was a recognized phenomenon at the

end of the Middle Ages, but the Reformation, by unleashing religious controversy, shaking old certainties and engendering widespread heightened concern over matters religious, created a context in which possession, like witchcraft, might thrive and be more readily accepted. Many of the demonologists of the period, dismayed at the apparent pervasiveness of witchcraft and related phenomena, asked why the devil and his agents should be so active in their age. Answering this question helped put demonic possession in the context of broader ideas about theology, society and human history. Possession cases represented microcosms of the macrocosmic struggle between good and evil, with the body of the possessed person serving as the battlefield where priests and exorcists struggled with the unclean spirits that were the devil's servants. There was an additional edge to all this. Writers from all parts of Europe, Catholic and Protestant alike, were convinced that they lived in the 'last times', the time immediately preceding the Second Coming of Christ and the End of the World. If the world was to end, so also was the career of that most worldly of beings, the devil. Thus the knowledge that there seemed to be more human wickedness in general, and more witchcraft in particular, about was a sign that the devil, aware that the sands of time were running out for him, was becoming ever more active: the closer the last times came, the more Satan would rage. Cases of demonic possession, those dramatic demonstrations that the devil was going to desperate lengths to manifest his continued powers on earth, fitted neatly into, and helped reinforce, the apoc-alyptic thought of the period.

While Catholic and Protestant theologians differed in their views of possession, most of them, at least down to about 1600, accepted it as a possibility. They disagreed, however, on the most appropriate method of dealing with it. To the Protestant, the traditional Catholic rite of exorcism was just another piece of popish mummery, a ridiculous show of theatre rendered doubly laughable by the claims of Catholic priests that they could emulate Jesus Christ and cast out demons. And, in the sixteenth century at least, educated Protestants were a little more likely to argue for natural causes or fraud in possession cases. When confronted by what they considered to be a genuine instance of demonic possession, they recommended prayer and fasting as remedies, rather than what they considered to be the inanities of Catholic exorcism.

This, unless they were the most convinced of Protestants, offered little by way of satisfaction to those who thought that they, their children or their servants were suffering from demonic possession. The Catholics (despite the embryonic nervousness about the issue among some senior clergymen) realized that they were able, in exorcism, to offer a service for which there was a considerable demand, and that their religious rivals were in no position to provide. Every successful exorcism by a Catholic priest was a striking, dramatic and, in most instances, very public demonstration that theirs was the true faith. Although ignored, or at best given passing treatment, by mainstream ecclesiastical historians, cases of possession and exorcism could become matters of considerable import in the confessional strife of the late sixteenth and seventeenth centuries. Anybody doubting this should look at the example of the German city of Augsburg, where in the late sixteenth century the cause of Catholicism was advanced against a previously successful Protestantism by a series of well-publicized exorcisms.

Those cases of possession that are best known occur after Anne Gunter fell mysteriously ill in 1604. The most famous of all was in Salem, Massachusetts, in 1692, when a group of possessed girls was at the centre of an outbreak of witch-hunting that sent twenty people to their deaths. The Salem persecution, thanks to Arthur Miller and *The Crucible*, is one of those historical events that is better known through a fictional account than through history proper. Much the same can be said of that other well-known outbreak, the possession of a convent of Ursuline nuns at Loudun in France, which led to the torture, trial and burning of the local priest, Urbain Grandier, in 1634, an incident commemorated in a book by Aldous Huxley and a film by Ken Russell. Both these episodes, although occurring at opposite ends of the confessional spectrum, had girls and young women living in an environment of intense religiosity at their centre. The Loudun incident was one of a number involving the inmates of nunneries in France, perhaps the best known to contemporaries taking place at Marseilles and leading to the execution of another priest, Louis Gaufridy, in 1611. But the events at Loudun were especially remarkable in that they became enmeshed in high politics, as had another, slightly earlier French case. This concerned a young woman called Marthe Brossier, its major political import being the way in which the extreme Catholic faction in France (the country had just come to the end of a generation of religious warfare) used it to attack the religious policies of Henri IV, a recent, and many suspected still lukewarm, convert from Protestantism. The speed with which the royal regime sent in medical doctors to show that the girl was an impostor suggests a political dimension, one that supports the view that demonic possession was taken very seriously indeed in this period. The English knew of the Brossier case, not least because an English translation of a tract describing the incident, dedicated to Richard Bancroft, bishop of London, was published in 1599. And in that year the Church of England, and Bishop Bancroft, were facing some very vexing home-grown problems of demonic possession.

In England, as in much of western Europe, the years after the Reformation were accompanied by an upsurge in cases of possession. But the English examples seem to have exhibited a peculiarity: in a large number of instances, or, perhaps more accurately, in many of those that attracted enough attention to have been recorded in detail, demonic possession was attributed to witchcraft rather than to the direct action of Satan, and was frequently followed by the prosecution of supposed witches who sent unclean spirits into the bodies of the possessed. It remained, of course, perfectly possible for somebody to be possessed by demons sent directly by Satan rather than by his human agents. But in what might be termed the classic English possession cases witches were normally accused and sometimes executed. There was a certain logic to this. If you were convinced that witches were causing the problem, you could at least do something about it, by taking them to court, a remedy that was obviously not possible when dealing with the devil. So in England ideas about witchcraft and ideas about possession overlapped, and it was not unusual to find those undergoing supernatural sufferings being described (as Anne Gunter was) as 'bewitched or possessed'.

There were a number of instances of demonic possession during the reign of Elizabeth I, evidence that England had entered the European mainstream in such matters. One of the earliest cases to attract attention involved no less a cleric than John Foxe, whose *Acts and Monuments of the English Church*, more familiarly known as *The Book of Martyrs*, was one of the key texts of English Protestantism. In 1574 Foxe was involved in the dispossession of a law student called Briggs who was thought to be possessed by the devil. After a lengthy verbal struggle with the unclean spirit, punctuated by heartfelt prayer, Foxe managed to persuade the youth to tell the devil in God's name to leave his body, which promptly happened. Foxe's actions with Briggs influenced later advanced Protestant views of how to handle possession cases. There was another incident a year earlier, again without accusations of witchcraft, when a young man, Alexander Nyndge, had gone into fits and convulsions that were attributed to demonic causes. Again in 1574, in an episode exposed as a fraud, two London girls, Agnes Briggs and Rachel Pinder, simulated possession, showing all the usual symptoms and making an accusation of witchcraft against a woman. And, of course, there was that case at Warboys in which the possession of six children of a gentry family resulted in the execution of three alleged witches.

For informed Protestants in England, as for their Continental co-religionists, the traditional Catholic rite of exorcism was unacceptable. This left them groping for a means of coping with possession, a phenomenon that was believed to be becoming more frequent. Fortunately, they happened upon a distinctive form of counteraction with a sound scriptural basis. In Mark 9:14–29, Christ cures a young man afflicted with a 'dumb and deaf spirit'. The disciples had been unable to ease the young man's sufferings, and Christ explains his success to them by saying of the evil spirit in question that 'this kind can come forth by nothing but by prayer and fasting'. Thus English Protestants sought to succour the demonically possessed, and to persuade the demons to leave their bodies, through sometimes lengthy exercises of prayer and fasting. These exercises often attracted large and enthusiastic crowds who more or less literally cheered on the ministers gathered around the bed of the tormented demoniac; the onlookers spoke variously with the victim or with the supposed demons. To some of the more sober-minded contemporary observers, these performances seemed disturbingly similar to those popish exorcisms that they were meant to have superseded.

But the Catholic rite of exorcism, in England as elsewhere, served as an important means of propaganda for the old faith. The most celebrated, and to the Church of England most worrying, use of exorcism came in 1585–6, with the exorcizing of six possessed people in the homes of a number of leading English Catholics, among them the residences of Sir George Peckham at Denham in Buckinghamshire and that of Lord Vaux in Hackney. William Weston, a Jesuit priest, acted as master of ceremonies in these proceedings. Catholic exorcisms were to continue well into the seventeenth century. In 1620 Catholic priests had been heavily involved in another case of fraudulent demonic possession, involving William Perry, the 'Boy of Bilson'. The Catholics tried exorcism, the Protestants tried their own remedies, and both sides engaged in a propaganda war that ended when young Perry confessed that the whole business had been trickery. But Catholic involvement in such episodes continued, and in 1626 it was claimed that Catholic priests operating in England had performed sixty successful exorcisms that year. The propaganda value of these performances might be gauged from the comment by Samuel Harsnett, the Church of England's most scathing critic of the activities of the exorcists, that the exorcisms associated with Weston in the mid 1580s had attracted four or five thousand converts to Rome.

Catholic exorcisms remained a problem. By the late sixteenth century the Church of England was also aware of the need to combat the adherents of a hotter sort of Protestantism, who have passed into historical discourse as Puritans. These were, among many other things, thought to be developing a distinctive and unacceptable style of dispossession. The key figure here was a young preacher, John Darrell. Born in Mansfield around 1562, Darrell matriculated in 1575 at Queens' College, Cambridge, as a sizar, that is a student who was in effect working his way through college as a servant to the fellows and the better-heeled undergraduates. He took his BA in 1579, and seems to have studied the law for a while afterwards, but gave this up to return to Mansfield as a preacher (it remains uncertain whether he was actually ordained). In 1586 he began a remarkable career as a Protestant exorcist by dispossessing a Derbyshire girl called Katherine Wright; a woman called Margaret Roper had been accused of bewitching her. The case against Roper was quashed by a sceptical magistrate, and Darrell seems to have disappeared from history for a decade or so. He resurfaced in 1596 when he was involved in dispossessing a fourteen-year-old boy named Thomas Darling, of Burton-upon-Trent. A woman called Alice Gooderidge was accused, tried and convicted for bewitching Darling, who claimed he first attracted her malevolence by breaking wind in her presence. Then in March 1597 Darrell, who had gained something of a reputation in such matters, was asked to go to Leigh in Lancashire, where he helped dispossess seven people, most of them children or adolescents, in the house-hold of a gentleman named Nicholas Starkey. This case too was followed by the conviction of a witch, in this instance a man, who was executed.

The most dramatic of Darrell's dispossessions came after he was invited in November 1597 to go to Nottingham, to help an apprentice named William Somers. Such was Darrell's skill with Somers, and, indeed, his general reputation, that he was made preacher at one of Nottingham's churches, St Mary's, and attracted the support of a sizeable faction in the town. Somers, in his fits, accused a number of local women of bewitching him, and something verging on a major witch-panic ensued. But there was a rival faction in Nottingham who were sceptical about what was going on, and reports of these events led the archbishop of York, Matthew Hutton, to send a commission of inquiry to Nottingham and to ban Darrell from preaching. Subsequently the archbishop of Canterbury, John Whitgift, a man notable for his opposition to Puritanism, became interested and referred the affair to the like-minded Richard Bancroft, bishop of London. Darrell was hauled down to the archbishop of Canterbury's palace at Lambeth and interrogated. He was exposed as an impostor (William Somers had, by this time, confessed that he had been simulating possession under Darrell's guidance) and imprisoned for a year. The affair was accompanied by a pamphlet war that generated numerous publications, several of them penned by Darrell. The chief propagandist on the Church of England's behalf was Samuel Harsnett, chaplain to Bancroft.

Bancroft, the sceptical bishop who was to become involved in Anne Gunter's case, was a Lancashire man, born of gentry stock at Farnworth in 1544. He had, through his mother, connections with Hugh Curwen, bishop of Oxford, and it was under Curwen's patronage that he entered Christ Church, Oxford, taking his BA there in 1567. After serving in a number of minor clerical capacities, he was made rector of Teversham in Cambridgeshire. A few years later, while in Bury St Edmunds, Bancroft came across seditious writing, comparing Queen Elizabeth to Jezebel, hanging over the altar of one of the town's churches. Bancroft demonstrated his zeal for the Elizabethan regime by reporting this to the secular authorities, and as a result two Brownists, members of an extreme Protestant group, were executed. A few years later Bancroft was involved in the Marprelate Controversy, in which proponents of advanced Protestantism were again targets of governmental hostility. He played a leading part in detecting printers who had published anti-establishment tracts in the course of the controversy, and advised the Queen's Counsel when they were subsequently prosecuted at the Star Chamber. As might be expected, he had by this time attracted the attention of the Queen, who was a major force behind his appointment as bishop of London in 1597. The capital was regarded as a hotbed of Puritanism, and it was sound policy to have the see in reliable hands. Bancroft gave further proof of his loyalty in 1601 when, in the face of the attempted *coup d'état* by the earl of Essex, he raised a body of pikemen who defeated the insurgents in street fighting in Ludgate.

Bancroft's chaplain Samuel Harsnett was a younger man of humbler origins. He was born in Colchester in 1561 and, like John Darrell, worked his way through university as a sizar, gaining a BA and MA at Cambridge. He took holy orders shortly after receiving his BA in 1583, and slowly climbed the clerical career ladder, punctuating it with a brief, and unsuccessful, spell as a schoolmaster in his home town. He became Bancroft's chaplain, and in 1597 was given the living of Chigwell in Essex. His service on the commission that investigated John Darrell came a little later, and his major justification of the commission's handling of the Darrell affair, *A Discovery of the Fraudulent Practices of John Darrell*, was published in 1599.

The pamphlet war engendered by Darrell's official exposure as a fraud died down in 1601, only to be followed by another major case of disputed witchcraft and possession in early 1602. This was the incident involving Mary Glover, the fourteen-year-old daughter of a London shopkeeping family. Mary had fallen out with a neighbour called Elizabeth Jackson, became ill, and fell into the usual repertoire of fits, convulsions, trances and mysterious physical symptoms. Jackson was tried for witchcraft, convicted and sentenced to a year's imprisonment with four sessions on the pillory, although it is doubtful that this sentence was actually carried out. The Glover case attracted considerable attention at the time, because it took place in the capital, and involved a family that, although not in itself powerful, had strong connections with London's governing elite. The most remarkable feature of the affair was the way in which both the accusers of Elizabeth Jackson and the party that gathered in her defence called on medical advice to bolster their case, with the College of Physicians heavily involved. The fullest account we have of Mary Glover's sufferings was written by a doctor, Stephen Bradwell, who was convinced that the girl was bewitched. On the defence side evidence was offered in court by the physician Edward Jorden, who was three years later to be involved in the Anne Gunter case. His argument that Mary Glover was suffering not from witchcraft but from a natural illness, hysteria, was, it will be remembered, strenuously rejected by the trial judge, Sir Edmund Anderson. Browbeaten in court by Anderson, Jorden was later to justify his position in a tract, published in 1603, entitled *A Briefe Discourse of a Disease called the Suffocation of the Mother.*

With Mary Glover, Bancroft now had another well-publicized episode in his own diocese, characterized by an adolescent going into spectacular fits and trances, by accusations of witchcraft, by a dramatic trial that rapidly turned into a confrontation between the alleged witch and her supposed victim, and, as Mary Glover's sufferings continued after the trial, by an overly enthusiastic Puritan prayer meeting convened in hopes of dispossessing her. Bancroft was heavily involved in orchestrating the medical evidence for Jackson's defence, and Jorden's tract was almost certainly written and published with Bancroft's encouragement. A number of the clergymen involved in Mary Glover's dispossession were summoned by Bancroft, interrogated, imprisoned and suspended from their offices. Reliable preachers, Anne Gunter's brother-in-law Thomas Holland among them, were directed to preach sermons question-ing the reality of possession. And in a tangential but not totally unrelated case, Thomas Darling, whom John Darrell had tried to dispossess in 1597, was sentenced in February 1603 to have his ears cut off and a public whipping for a seditious libel against a number of the leading secular and ecclesiastical officials. In 1604 Bancroft's attitudes to exorcism and dispossession became enshrined in the canons of the Church of England: the prayer and fasting that ministers could resort to in hopes of aiding the afflicted was heavily circumscribed, and was permitted only when licensed by the local bishop.

Bancroft was mobilizing all his resources against the disturb-ing symptoms of Puritan zeal that the Mary Glover case had aroused, and it was perhaps inevitable that he would call again upon the polemical talents of his chaplain. In 1603 Samuel Harsnett published a major propaganda work, *A Declaration of Egregious Popish Impostures*. The seriousness with which this work was taken in governmental circles may be gauged from the fact that it was produced by order of the Privy Council, and reprint-ed in 1604 and 1605. Its major objective, as its title suggests, was the discrediting of the Catholic position on exorcism; its subject was the exorcisms performed by the Jesuit William Weston in 1585–6. A number of those involved in that affair had been re-examined in 1602, and their testimonies were published in Harsnett's tract. It was published while what was known as the Archpriest Controversy was raging among England's Roman Catholic community, and one of the aims of the work was to cause further divisions, notably between England's more traditionally minded Catholics and their would-be mentors, the Jesuits. But Harsnett also managed to take a swipe or two at John

Darrell and the Puritan clergymen who had so recently involved themselves in the dispossession of Mary Glover. The intention of the *Declaration* was to deny the reality of demonic possession. Indeed, at some points Harsnett came very close to denying the reality of witchcraft, at least as the phenomenon was understood by the bulk of his compariots.

Demonic possession and the witchcraft-induced diseases that so resembled it also had a cultural history. The behaviour of the possessed followed set patterns: it was known about, people knew how possessed people ought to behave, and it was this that allowed William Somers, Anne Gunter and many others to put on convincing displays of being afflicted by unclean spirits or by the machinations of witches. The second point is that the supposed victims of possession also fitted a widely recognized pattern. In theory, of course, anybody could be possessed by demons, and, in fact, a wide variety of people were thought to have been so afflicted. But what is striking in the English cases, as in the Salem outbreak or in the possessed nunnery at Loudun, was that it was overwhelmingly children or young people who suffered.

Reconstructing father–daughter relationships for this period is difficult. There was a body of normative literature published, but most of this was very conventional and stylised in its tone, and also surprisingly ungendered: the duties and responsibilities which parents and children owed each other were rarely discussed with reference to the specific problems facing fathers and mothers, and sons and daughters. There was, perhaps, a generalised feeling that mothers were more likely to be softer on children than fathers, and that it was advisable that the father's role should be more assertive as the child grew older. And, of course, children of either sex were meant to be obedient, dutiful, responsible and godly. The general assumptions about the female sex in this period may have meant that these qualities were more actively sought after and seen as more exclusively desirable in daughters than in sons, but the difference was one of degree. Perhaps one issue which was more acute was marriage, but even here the old image of gentry daughters being forced into dynasti-cally driven arranged marriages against their will is an overdrawn one, while the wives of sons, and especially of eldest sons who would inherit most of the family's property, was also of concern to parents. Relations between parents and children among the gentry, upper merchants and nobility were more formal than would currently be considered normal, while the religiosity of the time meant both that ideas about child rearing were couched in a distinctive rhetoric and that the objectives of bringing up chil-dren were closely connected to God's purposes. None of this implied that fathers were incapable of loving their daughters: when, to take one of many examples, the London craftsman Nehemiah Wallington lost a daughter during a plague epidemic in 1625, he was devastated. On Saturday night she had been well, and the last words her father heard her say, she 'then being merry', was 'father, I go abroad tomorrow and buy you a plum pie'. His 'sweet child' died at 4a.m. the following Tuesday, and Wallington, a Puritan, noted that 'the grief for this child was so great that I did offend God in it ... I was much distracted in my mind, and could not be comforted'.

The scattered evidence which we have suggests that, in the years around 1600 as at present, fathers' attitudes to their daughters could range from the doting to the abusive. Elizabeth Livingstone was a young gentlewoman who possessed both an extremely developed sense of godliness and a fairly disastrous father whose descent into a drunken and dissolute lifestyle appalled her. Yet she was troubled by what she interpreted as a lack of respect for him. 'I am commanded by God to honour my parents', she wrote in her journal in 1670, 'and yet without regard to this divine law ... I fail not with bitterness to censure my father for all his failings, and to discourse of them to many hear-ers, which now I am sensible is a very great wickedness in me'. Her feelings had probably been focused by her father's having arranged a marriage for her against her will, a marriage that took place later that year. Her father died a little later, and by Christmas Eve 1670 young Elizabeth was regretting her neglect of him, noting that 'even in his sickness, nay what is more upon his very deathbed, have I peevishly expressed my sense of his unkindness to me in things which I had reason to believe he bit-terly repented of'. Yet daughters could, if we may stay with this most serious of issues, resist parental pressure over marriage. Another man who probably made a difficult father was Sir John Oglander, a gentleman living on the Isle of Wight in whose diary grumpiness is raised to an art form. In October 1649 he was especially enraged when his daughter Bridget, against his will, married the son of Sir Robert Eyton. Bridget was lame and 'in years', as her father put it, and hence not the most marriageable of daughters, but Sir John was nevertheless hostile to her marriage to the son of Sir Robert, whom Oglander declared to be 'a swear-ing, profane man' that he had never liked. This match, wrote Sir John, 'was never with my approbation or good liking. It was her importunity that induced me to give way unto it, and she was resolved to have him whatsoever became of her, and gave me as much under her hand before marriage ... I beseech God to bless them and to make her happy, which I much doubt'. As this episode demonstrates there were limits to daughterly obedience, while it should also be noted that Oglander's spleen was mainly the product of an evident concern for his daughter's happiness, a reminder that even patriarchal fathers were not of necessity unloving .

In the modern societies that anthropologists study, possession by spirits characteristically afflicts the weak and disadvantaged: it gives the relatively powerless a temporary notoriety and moral leverage. This insight can be transposed back to the adolescent demoniac of early modern England. Child-rearing in Tudor and Stuart England can all too easily be caricatured as a round of unending physical and psychological brutality. Yet it remains true that, especially in gentry households, children and adolescents were expected to be seen and heard infrequently, and this expectation was probably stronger for daughters than for sons. Being demonically possessed turned the afflicted child or adolescent into the centre of attraction. Far from being subjected to the restraints of parental control and the discipline of the godly household, the young demoniac, convulsing, contorting, screaming and blaspheming, could completely defy the bounds of normally accepted behaviour, and yet be the recipient of sympathy, even approbation, rather than censure. Most episodes of possession, like Anne Gunter's, took place before a large and constantly changing body of spectators, with the possessed as the centre of attention. They were essentially theatrical performances, founded upon a script that all the participants unconsciously followed to a greater or lesser degree.

Moreover, the possessed child or adolescent had access to what might be described as licensed misbehaviour. To contemporaries the body of the suffering demoniac was envisaged essentially as a battleground between good and evil, a site of conflict where both physical and spiritual afflictions were being heaped upon one of God's creatures. The possessed, like those in the throes of religious ecstasy, were expected to decry the sinfulness and vanity of the age, an expectation that gave the young demoniac limitless opportunities to comment adversely upon the mores of the adult world. Individual adults, especially the doctors and clerics gathered around the sufferer's bed, could be mocked. Sexual misbehaviour, such a feature of the fits of the possessed nuns (many of them teenagers) at Loudun, was largely absent from English cases, although odd references to lewdness or indecency on the part of the possessed makes us wonder what was omitted from the accounts that have come down to us. What is obvious in the English narratives is that the behavioural script the possessed followed had them blaspheming and manifesting disrespect for God's word and for those who brought that word to them: as they were under the control of demons, little else could be expected. The beginning of a prayer or of a reading from scripture, the very sight of a Bible or a clergyman, could send demoniacs into ever more terrifying convulsions, in the course of which they would blaspheme ever more determinedly.

Possessed young people like Anne Gunter were, therefore, with whatever degree of consciousness, rebelling or seeking attention by inverting not only the disciplines of the household but also the disciplines of godliness. It is no surprise to find instances of group possession among the young nuns at Loudun, or the young girls, one of them a minister's daughter, at Salem: the repressive nature of the convent's Catholicism or of New England's Puritanism provided a cultural context.

Anne in her role as demoniac was in many ways an excellent example of this. Her conduct fitted the accepted and known behavioural template. She came, as did so many of those whose sufferings attracted public attention, from a good family and a reasonably high social background. And she was the right sort of age, a little older than Thomas Darling or Mary Glover, but

roughly as old as William Somers and some of the others Darrell
had helped. The numerous descriptions we have of her sufferings
in the Star Chamber dossier contain much that is familiar: the
fits, lasting one, two or even three hours, with their contortions
and trances; the presence in the sufferer of foreign bodies,
particularly those pins that witness after witness described Anne
as vomiting, or passing with her urine, or emerging from her
breasts and fingers; the way in which her sufferings intensified
when one of her supposed tormentors came to the Gunter house,
either coincidentally or as part of a staged confrontation. And, of
course, there is the very public, at times theatrical, nature of
her plight.

   Obviously, these descriptions of her sufferings raise all sorts
of questions. Anne, like the rest of the demonically possessed of
the period, was literally a 'body of evidence', something upon
which contemporaries could draw for proof of the ceaseless war
between good and evil. But for us, as for some of Anne's more
sceptical contemporaries, one of the biggest issues is the feasibility
of the physical contortions she demonstrated. (Some of the
descriptions of her symptoms have already been cited, but they
are worth repeating.) At one point, in the course of an especially
severe fit at her brother Harvey's house, a witness stated that her
torments were 'so great as they thought her bones would have
been disjointed'. Mary Thornebury of North Moreton, aged
about nineteen herself when she saw Anne in her fits, described
'the turning of her hands back, strange juggling & turning of her
eyes, going upon her ankles in a very strange and stiff manner'.
Gifford Longe, a Bedfordshire gentleman, told how he saw
Anne in 'a very strange agony of quivering & shaking', with
'a foaming of the mouth' and other 'fearful ... passions and
extremities'. Many of these accounts leave us with a sense of the
sheer violence of Anne's movements. Elizabeth Baker, aged

about fourteen when she attended Anne, told how the demoniac made the bed shake under her as she contorted. Thomas Bird, the minister from the nearby parish of Brightwell, saw Anne turn over two or three hundred times in one of her fits.

One of the themes that possession narratives help to open up is the history of the body. In Anne's case it was, of course, the female body, regarded by the male-dominated medical opinion of the period as irregular and unstable. A number of witnesses described Anne's body undergoing peculiar transmutations. The Oxford don John Prideaux recounted how at one point Anne suffered from 'a strange kind of swelling in her body', which grew to be as big as a man's head. Her body also became heavier, with that other Oxford don, Thomas Winniffe, commenting that she grew unnaturally heavy in her fits, and her neighbour the North Moreton yeoman William Sawyer confirming that she 'was much weightier in her fits, than she was out of them'. There were also the sympathetic symptoms when Elizabeth Gregory gave birth. There is that statement from Anne's mother that 'at the time when the said Elizabeth Gregory was in labour & travail of childbirth' Anne 'had a swelling in her belly as big as a great household loaf & cried out exceedingly with the extremity of the pain of that swelling'. Also, according to her mother, when Gregory was sick 'the said Anne should also be sick, & sick after the same manner as the said Elizabeth was'. And the modern observer trying to rationalize Anne's symptoms could add eating disorders to the growing list. She went for long periods without food, explaining to John Prideaux, for example, that 'the witches would not suffer her to receive or eat any meats'.

Her behaviour was not as unruly or subversive of the adult world as that displayed by some other demoniacs, perhaps because her sufferings were simulations under her father's direction. One or two witnesses record her striking out at those

around her, and William Field, a neighbour asked by Brian
Gunter to carry her home on one occasion, remembered how she
struck him several times and pulled violently at the hair on his
head. At another point she knocked a candle out of the hand of a
young Oxford don who was saying prayers by her bed. As
further evidence of disordered behaviour, Humphrey Tailor, a
gentleman from Newbury, recounted one incident when Anne
seemed to be attempting self-mutilation or suicide. He saw her
'take a knife in her hand & thrust the same into her mouth as
though she would have spoiled herself'. He took the knife from
her, and on future occasions she was not given a knife when she
ate at table.

Like other English possession narratives, there was little of
an overtly sexual nature in the descriptions of Anne's fits. Yet
there was something intrinsically sexual in the spectacle of a
twenty-year-old woman contorting and screaming on her bed,
usually with men present and taking an avid interest in her
movements. There were also considerable sexual overtones in the
descriptions of Anne's stockings and garters unravelling themselves and taking off of their own volition to leave her legs bare,
and of the bodice of her petticoat unlacing itself. There is the
evidence of Robert Vilvaine, who put his hand to Anne's breast
as her bodice unlaced itself, and there is William Harvey, a BA of
Exeter College, Oxford, and about a year older than Anne,
describing how in one of her fits her stockings and garters
removed themselves from her legs. She was at that point 'holden
in this deponent his lap', and one can only guess at the range of
reactions this may have provoked in the young scholar.

Something more of an overtly sexual nature is to be found in
the evidence of Francis Stewart, the young Scottish aristocrat
who seemed to have taken a fancy to Anne. He remembered one
occasion when he was holding Anne around the middle while

she was badly afflicted, and said that it was usual for one of those present (this was during Anne's stay at Thomas Holland's lodgings in Oxford) to hold her while she contorted in her fits. But Francis Stewart also told the Star Chamber of his first meeting with Anne. He saw her in Exeter College, striking and beating those around her as she had a fit, and expressed to Brian Gunter his worry that she would treat him in the same fashion. Gunter assured him that she would not. In fact, so Francis Stewart testified, Anne 'came unto this examinant, and put her head into his neck, and used him very gently'. Even when possessed Anne had enough sense to reserve special treatment for personable young noblemen with royal blood in their veins.

The broader theme of physicality appears in the accounts of the numerous occasions when, in hopes of proving or disproving the authenticity of her sufferings, Anne was subjected in her trances to various trials of her insensitivity to pain. A typical illustration of this is the evidence of Gifford Longe of Bedfordshire, one of the gentlemen who visited the Gunter household to observe Anne's sufferings. Longe said that Brian Gunter 'was desirous that this deponent should make what trial he would upon his said daughter' in hopes of demonstrating her insensitivity. The gentleman accordingly began by 'violently wringing of her little finger', and then progressed to 'violently pulling of the hairs of the temples of her head and moving and waving of other parts of her body'. Anne, possibly anaesthetized by a dose of sack and sallet oil, or the green mixture, showed no response, leaving Longe convinced that she was genuinely insensitive to pain and other stimuli while in her trances.

When the demoniac was conscious, compliance was meant to be replaced by demonically inspired defiance. One of those treated with insubordination by Anne was Thomas Bird, the minister of Brightwell, whom we have already encountered commenting on Anne's physical mobility in her fits. Bird, a man in his mid thirties who had known Anne and her father for about ten or twelve years when he gave evidence to the Star Chamber, told how, on one occasion, Anne in her fits tore hair from his beard. She threw it on the floor, but it had vanished moments later when he tried to pick it up. Anne told him that Elizabeth Gregory had taken the hairs to put them on the chin of her 'bun', or familiar spirit, and that it was 'a pretty sight'. The sceptical Wiltshire gentleman Thomas Hinton recalled another occasion when Anne, who 'seemed to be in great extremity ... fell into a bitter exclamation against Mr Bird, a minister', declaring that Elizabeth Gregory had told her that she would not recover from her fit 'unless that foul bird went out of the chamber, pointing at the foresaid Mr Bird the minister'. Neither the physical assault nor the play on his name dissuaded the clergyman from his belief that Anne's sufferings were genuine.

Hinton also gave telling details concerning the incident when Anne knocked a candle from the hands of a young college fellow who was trying to pray for her. As the young man began praying in 'a very decent manner', Anne, 'lifting up one of her legs in the bed', struck the candle into one of the young man's eyes, so that 'he was fain presently to deliver his prayer to a graver scholar'. Hinton told how 'he verily thinketh that at the instant of this accident he saw the said Anne Gunter give a sudden smile & turning her head aside, or rather as he remembreth putting her head under the clothes'. Anne was still capable of getting at least some fun from her situation.

In our attempts to understand what was happening to Anne, we have to accept the fact that, unlike Thomas Hinton, the majority of those giving evidence to the Star Chamber, certainly most of those who saw Anne suffering in North Moreton, and the group of Oxford dons that Brian Gunter rallied to his cause, seem to have had few doubts on the genuine and supernaturally directed nature of her sufferings.

But there is one important piece of evidence that bears out Anne's later contention that her father was behind her torments. When I first began to read the Star Chamber investigation of Anne's case, I was struck by the numerous descriptions of her father giving her that curious mixture of 'sack and sallet oil'. Where did the idea of using this mixture, for either making Anne better or rendering her unconscious, come from? The answer is from Samuel Harsnett. In his *Declaration of Egregious Popish Impostures* Harsnett describes one of the means by which Catholic exorcists made Friswood Williams, a girl aged sixteen, put on convincing displays of being possessed:

> Then they began to bind her with towels, whereat she was therewith cast into a great fear, and not knowing what they meant to do with her: being in this case, Mr Dibdale began to read in his Book of Exorcizing; and after a good while, seeing other alterations in her, that in the tokens of fear, which increased by reason of his words, and dealings, then they urged her to drink above a pint of sack, and sallet oil, being hallowed, and mingled with some kind of spices; when she took this drink, which they termed a holy potion, it did so much dislike her, that she could drink but a little of it at once, her stomach greatly loathing it, and then the priest said: all that comes from the devil, who hated nothing worse, than that holy drink: so as she was held, and by very force caused to drink it up at divers draughts. Hereupon she grew to be very sick, and giddy in her head, and began to fall into a cold sweat: verily then believing, that (as the priest said) it was a wicked spirit, that caused her to be in such case: whereas afterwards, when she better had considered of their dealing with her, she easily perceived, that the drink they gave her was such, as might have made a horse sick.

Harsnett also noted that doses of the sack and sallet oil were accompanied by burning brimstone and holding the sufferer's face over the fumes. All this, including the reference to the burning of brimstone, is very similar to Anne's account of the administering of sack and sallett oil to her, and it is certain that her father had access to knowledge of this technique. Gunter had a copy of the tract describing the Warboys case, and this was used to school Anne in simulating possession. He also had, he told the Star Chamber, a book written by John Darrell 'concerning some that were bewitched' and 'a book of certain persons said to be possessed with wicked spirits at Denham'. This must have been Harsnett's *Declaration of Egregious Popish Impostures*. Although Brian Gunter was to claim that he had not read this work until Anne was being held by the bishop of Salisbury, it seems obvious that he had in fact familiarized himself with it at an early stage in her sufferings and built on the use of sack and sallet oil that he had read about.

A case like Anne's invites analysis in terms of our current knowledge. The physical symptoms can be compared with those in modern cases of hysteria or related disorders, while the mental disorders can be explained in terms of modern psychoanalysis. But this could lead to the great danger that one encounters so often when modern knowledge is applied incautiously to early modern witchcraft narratives: a tendency not to explain phenomena but to explain them away. Trying to grasp the reality of Anne's experience is difficult: few sceptical observers at the time went into any detailed discussion of what the experience of simulation might have been like for the supposed demoniac.

One who did was Samuel Harsnett. In his *Fraudulent Practices of John Darrell*, Harsnett gives us his views on what the youthful demoniac was up to. Harsnett was a proponent of the view that many cases were pure simulation, the actions of boys who were unwilling to go to school or of girls who 'would be idle'. But he was also aware (and this logic would have become dominant even in many cases of simulation) of a rather more subtle set of factors that might be at play. He contended that the exorcist would frequently find young persons who were, in fact, suffering from a mild malady, would play upon their concerns over their sickness, and eventually come to convince them that their indispositions were of demonic origin, arguing that Satan was out to afflict the godly. They would also convince parents or masters, concerned about 'finding their children or servants somewhat drooping'. As Harsnett wrote, 'Now, there being no apparent cause of their dissembled sickness, they are driven to counterfeit, and to fall to those tricks, which they have heard of in others: wherein, if either their parents or masters begin to pity them, they run on in their knaveries above measure: but especially if they [i.e., those trying to aid them] begin to wonder at them, and to devise some remedies for them.' What might have begun as a minor prank, or a minor malady, once diagnosed as demonic possession, was likely to set in motion a sequence of events one possible outcome of which was an accusation of witchcraft against those thought to be causing the afflictions in question: for, as Harsnett commented with characteristic dryness, 'it seemeth a matter very pertinent to the dignity of the exorcist, that he be able to declare who sent the devil into his patient'.

It is worth remembering that Anne Gunter, her father and several others agreed that her afflictions began with what looked very like a natural illness. Anne, in her evidence to the Star Chamber, declared that her first sickness, in the summer of 1604, 'did hold her in such sort as it had been (as she thought it was) the disease called the mother', that is, hysteria, as a result of which she was 'much subject to swooning'. At this point, she was adamant, she did not 'believe or suspect that she was bewitched'. Her father testified that when she first fell sick it was 'as if she had the mother', although when she fell sick again in October 1604 the symptoms were 'more like the falling sickness', or epilepsy in modern terminology. Alice Kirfoote too was insistent that the initial symptoms suffered by Anne were 'swelling and swooning and so continued 4 or 5 days', adding that 'at that time there was neither speech nor suspicion of her being bewitched'. It would seem, therefore, that Anne was genuinely ill in the summer of 1604, and that her symptoms, like Mary Glover's, suggested that she was suffering from that typical female malaise of the age, hysteria.

After the onset of this 'natural' affliction, Anne found herself playing a role. As the next part of our story reveals, almost as soon as she was removed from parental control and was able to assess her situation undirected by her father, she confessed that she was pretending. For Anne it was parental pressure that was vital, as Darrell's influence had been for young William Somers. The clarity of the statement about her simulating possession, and her father's part in it, came when she gave evidence to the Star Chamber early in 1606. That was many months after she had escaped from Brian Gunter's control, after her situation had been given a distinctive spin, and clarified in a distinctive fashion, during lengthy discussions with Samuel Harsnett and others. What caused her to contort, scream, foam at the mouth, spit and sneeze pins and go into comas at North Moreton, at Stanton St John, at Oxford, or before the assize judges at Abingdon, initially may have been purely parental pressure, but one suspects that her motivation gradually developed into something more complex. Anne had been ill, and she and most others had diagnosed that illness, at least at first, as 'the mother', hysteria, a uterine condition peculiar to women, and to which unmarried women of Anne's age were thought to be especially at risk. But her father had cast her experience of illness into a new mould, and placed his daughter in a new role. This role, she rapidly discovered, was one that was both recognized and respected, by her neighbours, by her kinsfolk, by physicians, by clergymen, by the friends of her father, by Oxford dons, even by passing strangers who came to her father's house when they heard of her possession.

For the modern observer the first step towards understanding the experience of the sufferer in a case of demonic possession might be to seek an explanation based around two polar opposites: either simulation, or authenticity, in that some people did genuinely believe themselves to be possessed. One suspects, however, that in many cases matters were less absolute. The condition of many demoniacs lay, or perhaps more accurately oscillated, between these two extremes. An important initial step would be that youthful demoniacs, whether suffering from a natural ailment or simulating in the hope of getting attention, would be diagnosed by physicians and clergymen as suffering from a supernatural malady; they would then find themselves ensnared in a situation where they had no alternative but to act as though they *were* possessed. As this situation progressed, the sufferers (Harsnett's use of the word 'patient' is instructive here) would find themselves developing techniques for simulating their torments, displaying symptoms of increasing facility in order to meet the expectations of their audience. More physical factors would then come in. If, like Anne, the demoniac was not eating, food deprivation might alter perceptions and sensory states. This weakened condition would be aggravated by the physical and psychological stresses of simulating fits and trances, of keeping up a constant act. And, in Anne's case, a general disorientation would have been worsened by the effects of those doses of sack and sallet oil, and of the mysterious green potion that she was forced to drink. One suspects that, in her chamber in the North Moreton rectory, Anne's sense of what was happening to her as a result of outside forces, and what was being simulated, must have become very blurred.

But Anne's sufferings and accusations had not led to the conviction of her supposed tormentors, and after the Abingdon trial she continued to suffer her fits and trances, to spit pins and to call out against Elizabeth Gregory and the two Pepwell women. Within a few months her father was to make the disastrous miscalculation of bringing her afflictions to the attention of James I. And, as a consequence of this miscalculation, she was to encounter some men with very clear ideas about demonic possession.

chapter *eight*

ANNE MEETS *the* KING

WITH THE trial over, and the North Moreton women acquitted, the story of Anne Gunter's bewitchment should have ended. Animosities would have continued in the village (we can only imagine what it must have been like for an accused witch to go back to her community and attempt to reconstruct her life after such a trial), and Brian Gunter would doubtless have continued to feel aggrieved. But the tale of Anne's sufferings did not end with the trial, for both the symptoms of possession and her allegations against her tormentors persisted. A month or two after the trial officialdom acted. A number of those cases of possession and bewitchment that apparently flourished around 1600 were marked by the involvement of the local ecclesiastical authorities. As Anne continued to demonstrate her symptoms, the bishop of Salisbury, Henry Cotton, within whose diocese North Moreton lay, decided to intervene. Anne's sufferings, quite apart from causing a witch-trial, had attracted considerable local attention and involved a number of clergy both from the parishes around North Moreton and from Oxford. News of the case must have come to the bishop, and the failure of the trial at Abingdon to end matters must have led him to initiate his own investigations. Accordingly, around Whitsun 1605 Anne was taken from her parents and lodged in Cotton's residence at Salisbury.

Henry Cotton, bishop of Salisbury between 1598 and his death in 1615, was not a major figure among the Jacobean episcopate: indeed, his most memorable feat was the fathering of nineteen children, which may have placed restraints on the time and energy he had available for the pursuit of his career (his wife, appropriately, was named Patience). He was born in Hampshire, the son of Sir Richard Cotton, a privy councillor in Edward VI's reign; and the Lady Elizabeth, the future Elizabeth I, was his godmother, a sign of his family's acceptability in leading Protestant circles. He matriculated at Magdalen College, Oxford, in 1566, and then went on to take a series of degrees, culminating in his becoming a DD in 1599, when he was already bishop. By an interesting coincidence, when this last degree was conferred, the oration at the ceremony was given by Thomas Holland.

Cotton's clerical career had begun when he became vicar of Wanborough in Wiltshire, a parish, to note another coincidence, with which the Hinton family was connected, and he appears to have risen to episcopal rank in a fairly rapid, though by no means spectacular, fashion. He probably handled the Gunter case with considerable circumspection. The Wiltshire church courts were run efficiently while he was bishop, but accusations of sorcery or witchcraft were almost never heard before them, which suggests an entrenched indifference to such matters among the ecclesiastical leadership of the area. We have one very relevant comment from Anne herself. In describing how a trio of clergymen came to her in North Moreton, she said that although they offered her considerable assistance, they were not allowed to go through the formal process of fasting and prayer on her behalf, as the bishop of the diocese 'did not license or allow them so to do'.

Cotton himself did not testify to the Star Chamber, although evidence was taken from William Wilkinson, the bishop's chancellor, in effect his chief administrative agent, between 1591 and 1613. Wilkinson, a Doctor of Civil Law, was typical of the men in his position, with a good legal training and considerable administrative talents. These qualities were further displayed when he was chosen justice of the peace for Wiltshire between 1608 and 1613, which was probably the year of his death. Either he or the bishop called in assistance from local medical men. One of the women appointed to watch Anne while she was in the bishop's custody was servant to Richard Haydock, a physician who had just moved to Salisbury from Oxford. Another of those giving evidence was William Newcombe, an apothecary of Salisbury. He told how he visited Anne when, after a spell in the bishop's residence, she was moved to the house of Sir Giles Wroughton. Sir Giles was a member of one of the solid gentry families in Wiltshire, a justice of the peace and a colonel in the county militia, the sort of responsible person to whom a girl in Anne's circumstances could be entrusted. Newcombe visited Anne after she had been about ten days in the Wroughton household and witnessed one of her fits. This, he considered, 'was by her wholly counterfeited'. Anne's ability to convince was waning now that she was no longer on home ground. A number of those involved with the Salisbury phase of Anne's case also said how Bishop Cotton carried out experiments with pins that had been marked with a file. Anne's subsequent claims that she had vomited some of these helped confirm suspicions that she was simulating her bewitchment.

But Anne was not only failing to convince, she was also beginning to weary of the pretence. While at Cotton's house, she was looked after by two women: Joan Greene, a widow aged about fifty, was Richard Haydock's servant; Joan Spratt, aged twenty-eight, was the wife of a husbandman named John Spratt. Both women gave evidence of how Anne behaved in her fits and, like so many witnesses, were especially detailed in their accounts of Anne's doings with pins, including those that Henry Cotton had marked. On their account, Anne's deceptions with the pins, like the trickery with her hose and garters as described by Thomas Hinton and Francis Stewart, were very simple. She managed to convey them, presumably from hiding places in her clothing or bedding, into her mouth, and then, according to Greene, used 'some sleight or other with her finger to put them up higher into her nose or further into her mouth & then fell a sneezing & so void them out at her nose & mouth'. As she went through her fits she would also secrete pins in her cheeks, and sneeze or spit them out at appropriate moments. We can only conclude that, given Anne's ability to convince so many of those observing her that her problems with pins were of supernatural origin, many of those same observers who later gave evidence must have been very predisposed to believe in what they thought they were seeing.

The discovery of her sleight of hand with the pins helped convince both women that Anne's sufferings were simulated, or 'feigned', as they put it, and that she had previously secreted in her mouth or about her body the pins she sneezed and vomited. The women also noted how Anne seemed to go into her fits only when she thought that somebody was watching her. Greene and Spratt accordingly told Anne that they thought that she was simulating her symptoms, and that what she was doing in encouraging false accusations of witchcraft was dreadful. They suggested she confess everything to the bishop. Anne, willing to confide in these two women, who had perhaps shown her more sympathy and kindness than she had experienced for some time, cracked. She confessed to them that she was simulating, and was making accusations of witchcraft against Elizabeth Gregory at her father's instigation. She was very dejected at the situation in which she found herself, telling Joan Greene that she 'wished she had been buried when she was but twelve years old'. She went back to the origin of the problems, telling how 'variances & great troubles grew betwixt her father & some of the Gregorys' after a 'match at football', where fatal injuries had been inflicted on John and Richard Gregory. Greene urged her to admit every-thing to the bishop, who, she claimed, 'would quietly end all matters betwixt her father and the said women the supposed witches'. But Anne was aware of the possible consequences of this, having in all probability been warned of them before she left her father's house: if she confessed, she declared, she feared that 'her father should lose all his lands & so be undone'.

If the evidence of Greene and Spratt is to be trusted, Anne was now willing to confess that her sufferings were simulated, and that her father was behind the whole business. She had been counterfeiting possession for over half a year, and the experience was a wearing one. Moreover, she was now away from her father's control: Brian Gunter could neither instruct his daughter in what to do, nor stage-manage her alleged sufferings. In her new environment, despite the warnings she must have been given by her father, she felt that the pressure was easing. But she was not yet ready to tell her story to officialdom. Authority was male and, given her assumption that her father would be ruined if she told the truth, dangerous. Yet it is obvious that trust had grown between Anne and the two women attending her. They were of a lower social class than she, but both were older than Anne, and in the elder of the two women, Joan Greene, Anne had found somebody she could open up to. The first steps that were to lead to her remarkable confession to the Star Chamber had been taken. For shortly, unbeknown to her at that point, Anne was to pass under the scrutiny not of a couple of sympathetic women but of the King of Great Britain himself, James VI and I.

But before we turn to King James, we must take a detour. One of the unexpected pleasures of reconstructing the history of the Anne Gunter case is the way in which the process brings us into contact with so many of the minor figures of the early Jacobean period. We have noted how Joan Greene, the servant of a physician called Richard Haydock, gave evidence, but it is slightly perplexing at first sight that Haydock himself, who had presumably examined Anne, was not called upon by the Star Chamber. The reason for this is that between Anne's stay at Salisbury and the taking of Star Chamber depositions in 1606 the physician himself had been the perpetrator of another remarkable fraud exploded by King James. Haydock was of obscure parentage, a Hampshire man by origin, who was educat﹣ed at New College, Oxford, taking his BA in 1592 (by which stage he was already a fellow of the college), this being followed by a couple of higher degrees. He travelled on the Continent, and then returned to Oxford to study medicine. He left Oxford in 1605 to go to Salisbury, and may only have been living there a few weeks when Anne came into the custody of Bishop Cotton. During 1605 Haydock enjoyed a brief moment of fame when he claimed to be able to preach in his sleep. In his slumbers he would see visions and then a biblical text, on which he would expound at length, despite the distraction of demonic pinchings, most of his comments being hostile to the Pope and critical of the govern﹣ment of the Church of England. Haydock was summoned to court to display his powers before the King, but admitted that he was an impostor. James was evidently very taken by all this and, after Haydock had made a public recantation, wanted to set him up with a career in the Church. The impostor, however, was unwilling to take holy orders and returned to Salisbury, where he enjoyed a successful career as a doctor up to his death, which occurred shortly before the Civil Wars broke out in 1642. It is significant that James was exposing this fraud at about the same time as Anne Gunter was coming to his attention, and it is a happy coincidence that Haydock and Anne had met, albeit in rather strange circumstances, before they made their respective appearances at court.

Few English monarchs have enjoyed such a bad press as James I, king of England from 1603 but by that date already an experienced king of Scotland. Generations have been given a portrait of him that is little more than a catalogue of negative character traits. James, coming into his new and more sophisticated kingdom, has been regarded as politically inept, while his attachment to notions of divine right monarchy has been derided by historians and teachers raised with the traditional view of English constitutional history. His interests in philosophical and theological matters have been written off as pedantry, usually with a repetition of that old saw about James being the wisest fool in Christendom. His physical peculiarities, the rolling eyes, the uncertain walk, the tendency to slobber when he drank, the timidity expressed in his fear of assassination, all of these have been made much of. And, although it remains uncertain whether he was actively homosexual, his taste for personable young men caused complications for the smooth running of the faction politics of the period.

Recent re-assessments of James and his reign are beginning to provide a more rounded, and fairer, impression. Against his alleged political ineptitude has been set his record as a very effective ruler in Scotland, and it is possible to argue that he did a reasonable job as king of England. His taste for divine right monarchy was, in fact, widely shared by his subjects, while James, despite some early frictions, soon learned how to negotiate both the complexities of English constitutional theory and the practicalities of English politics. His pedantry was simply a reflection of the intellectual style of the period rather than of any individual quirks, while it is obvious that James, perhaps unlike any other British monarch, was somebody with sustainable claims to being a serious intellectual. He may not have been the most administratively gifted of rulers, and he certainly made some errors of judgement in his choice of favourites, but he was far from the royal disaster of historical myth.

James's interest in witchcraft has featured both in earlier interpretations that emphasized his wrong-headedness and in the more recent reassessments. He had played a central role in the first major Scottish witch-hunt. This occurred in 1590–91, and resulted in the torture and trial of at least seventy, and possibly more than a hundred, witches, an uncertain but large number of whom were subsequently executed. The crucial point in this incident was that the witches were thought to be threatening the King and his wife, Anne of Denmark; the problem was treason by sorcery rather than straightforward malefic witchcraft, and one of James's more troublesome noble subjects, the earl of Bothwell, was heavily implicated. The witches were accused of raising storms while James and his queen were at sea, of using image-magic against the King by melting a wax effigy of him, and of trying to poison the royal bed linen. The trials also introduced for the first time the full-blown demonological theories of the satanic pact and the sabbat into Scottish witchcraft history. The witches were supposed to have assembled, to the number of

300, in the church at North Berwick, where they performed obscene rituals in the presence of their master, the devil. Witchcraft in Scotland, although made a crime by parliamentary Act in 1563, had not been much prosecuted early in James's reign. The North Berwick trials of 1590–91 altered that: Scotland was to experience trials and executions, many of them episodes in whole waves of persecution, well into the eighteenth century. Despite the suspicion that the Scottish kirk was already a major influence on witch-hunting, it is impossible to deny James's involvement in the early stages of this process, while many have commented on how his arrival in England was followed, within a year, by the stringent witchcraft statute of 1604.

James's reputation as an enemy of witchcraft does not rest merely on his involvement in the North Berwick trials and the 1604 English witchcraft statute. James, that learned theologian and respected political theorist, was also the author of a tract on witchcraft, the *Daemonologie*. First published in Edinburgh in 1597, it was a perfectly conventional work on demonology, shorter than most, said little that was new and, like so many books in this genre, was as concerned with elite magic as it was with peasant *maleficium*. James was, of course, a proponent and theoretician of divine right monarchy, and the North Berwick witches had attracted his attention especially because of the threat they had supposedly offered to the royal person. Accordingly, it has been plausibly argued that the *Daemonologie* might be best interpreted in the context of James's other writings on monarchy, rather than as a free-standing demonological text. Yet the *Daemonologie* was widely read, and the fact that it was frequently cited by later English demonological writers shows that they felt it important that they had the authority of a royal demonologist on their side. Indeed, two English editions of the

book were published in 1603, the year in which James came to
the throne of England.

A closer examination of James's track-record in instances of
witchcraft while king of England, however, reveals that his attitudes were far removed from the propensity for rabid witch-hunting that has been attributed to him. The British Solomon, as
James fancied himself, was as likely to display his expertise in
matters of witchcraft by exposing fraudulent accusations as he
was by rooting out nests of malefic witches. Most of the relevant
cases came later in the reign, perhaps the most celebrated being at
Leicester in 1616, when James, travelling through the county,
saved five suspected witches after another nine had been
convicted on the evidence of a boy aged twelve or thirteen who
was displaying many of the same kind of symptoms as Anne
Gunter. Certainly, by the time of his death James's reputation
among his contemporaries as an exploder of false accusations of
witchcraft was equal to his reputation as a demonologist. James
seemed to make a distinction between sorcery aimed at himself or
the house of Stuart, which was likely to lead to the immediate
interrogation of suspects, and accusations between his subjects,
which were more likely to arouse royal scepticism. Unfortunately
for Brian Gunter, this was clear neither to him nor to anyone else
in the summer of 1605.

One of James's commitments during that summer was to
visit Oxford University, and on 27 August, after a leisurely
progress through the surrounding countryside, James, along with
Anne of Denmark and their son Henry, Prince of Wales,
entered the city, where they were to be entertained for three days.
The university went to considerable lengths to impress the new
monarch. More than two months before the visitation began, the
university authorities had sent out instructions to heads of colleges on how they and the members of their institutions were to

conduct themselves during the royal visit. Responsibilities for various aspects of the royal entourage's entertainment were allocated to different colleges, while all rails, posts, bars on windows, window casements and pumps were to be painted, all coats of arms were to be refurbished, and streets were to be swept clean. James was treated to scholarly disputations (in which he participated) in theology, medicine, civil law, moral philosophy and natural philosophy, heard numerous orations and verses in his honour, attended various plays and comedies, and enjoyed heavy dinners at a number of colleges. Reading the accounts of this visit, it is difficult to see how exactly James could have found time to meet humbler subjects who sought the royal presence: but we know that on James's first day at Oxford that Berkshire gentleman with strong Oxford connections, Brian Gunter, took his bewitched daughter to meet the King.

His motives in so doing remain uncertain, although a number of witnesses were insistent that it was essentially Gunter's decision. It is possible that he wished to reopen the case against his daughter's alleged tormentors, or that he was seeking favour or largesse from the King, or that he was simply hoping for royal sympathy that would allow him to regain face in his social world, and not least in North Moreton, following the acquittal of Elizabeth Gregory and Mary Pepwell. In fact, Anne was to meet with the King on four occasions in the summer and autumn of 1605. The first was at Oxford on 27 August, the last two at Finchingbrooke, near Windsor, on 9 and 10 October. There is some doubt as to the date of the remaining meeting, which occurred at Whitehall, but it seems likely that it took place in late September. Fairly soon after her first meeting, Anne was put under the charge of Richard Bancroft, with his formidable repu⁄tation as a sceptic in cases like Anne's, who in turned passed her on to Samuel Harsnett.

James received reports about the process of investigating Anne's case. The result of these, and of his meetings with her, was that he became convinced she was simulating bewitchment. She eventually confessed as much to the monarch. On 10 October, after what was to be his final interview of Anne, James wrote to his chief minister, Robert Cecil, the earl of Salisbury:

> For your better satisfaction touching Anne Gunter we let you wit that whereas not long ago she was a creature in outward show most weak and impotent, yet she did yesterday in our view dance with that strength and comeliness and leap with such agility and dexterity of body that we, marvelling thereat to see the great change, spent some time this day in the examination of her concerning the same. And we find by her confession that she finds herself perfectly cured from her former weakness by a potion given to her by a physician, and a tablet hanged about her neck; that she was never possessed with any devil nor bewitched; that the practice of the pins grew at first from a pin that she put in her mouth, affirmed by her father to be cast therein by the devil, and afterwards that and some other such pin pranks which she used together with the swelling of her belly, occasioned by the disease called the mother, wherewith she was oftentimes vehemently afflicted, she did of long time daily use and practice make show to be matters of truth to the beholders thereof; and lastly that she hath been very far in love with one Asheley, servant to the Lord of Canterbury, and is still, hath sought his love long most importunately and immodestly (in manner unfit to be written) and she doth now humbly and earnestly crave our furtherance that she may marry him; and this last is confessed also by himself. Whereof ye shall hear more by the next messenger; in the meantime we have sent you this letter enclosed for the better satisfaction of my Lord and yourself.

This letter would seem to mark a happy end to our story, with

Anne having confessed her deceptions, but having found love and marriage in the process.

Piecing together what happened after Anne first met the King in late August 1605 is an impossible task: there are too many gaps in the record. However, building on James's letter to Salisbury, it is possible to follow Anne's fortunes at least in outline. Her case was noted in a number of contemporary journals and chronicles. At the end of October 1605 Sir Roger Wilbraham, who combined his post as solicitor-general for Ireland with a number of other administrative responsibilities, noted in his journal that James 'by his own skill' had uncovered '2 notorious impostures'. The first of these was that of Richard Haydock, described in this source as 'a physician that made Latin & learned sermons in his sleep'. The other, almost certainly Anne, was described as 'a woman pretended to be bewitched, that cast up at her mouth pins, & pins were taken by divers in her fits out of her breast'. At about the same time Walter Yonge, Devon justice of the peace and MP for Honiton, wrote in his diary that 'there was a gentlewoman and near kinswoman to Dr Holland's wife, rector of Exon [Exeter] College in Oxford, strangely possessed and bewitched, so that in her fits she cast out of her nose and mouth pins in great abundance, and did divers other things very strange to be reported'. But by far the fullest account of James's meetings with Anne came in Robert Johnston's *Historia Rerum Britannicarum*, a Latin work published in Amsterdam in 1655. Johnston was a Scot, a burgess of Edinburgh, who was favoured by James and came south with him in 1603. His *Historia*, a chronicle of events in Britain between 1572 and 1628, contains a lengthy description of how James dealt with Anne:

At the time when the King was staying at Oxford a young girl of about eighteen years of age aroused the wonder of the people of Britain on account of her strange cleverness in deception, which imposed upon the astonished multitude. Whereupon James was seized with the wish to see someone so celebrated in popular report. Accordingly, she was at once brought to the King. To the great amazement of the bystanders she lacked all sense of pain when she was stuck with pins. The strangeness of this created great astonishment. Not only was this wonderful in the eyes of those who were present, but she also cast out of her mouth and throat needles and pins in an extraordinary fashion. The King, wondering where the numerous pins she vomited so suddenly came from, questioned her repeatedly, but she remained obdurate, claiming that this happened to her miraculously, and that the sense of feeling taken away from her for the time being would soon, by divine providence, return to her. The King being skilful in unravelling deceptions and considering the matter incredible, ordered physicians to determine whether this occurred by some natural cause or by human fraud. By recommendation of the theologians and the advice of the physicians, who differed widely concerning this novel and unusual affair, he committed the young girl and the investigation to the archbishop of Canterbury, in the hope of detecting the fraud. The archbishop, when he accomplished nothing by threats, warnings, and promises, called on the services of Samuel Harsnett, his chaplain, whom he honoured above others.

Johnston attributed to Harsnett the ploy of introducing Anne to a young man in the expectation that she would fall in love with him, and finished his account of the incident by declaring that 'in the end the credit for detecting the fraud was given to the King, and its perpetrators earned ridicule for their presumption'.

Two points come across very forcefully here. The first is that Anne's case was evidently the subject of considerable public interest. Like the Mary Glover affair three years previously, this was an incident of witchcraft that attracted widespread popular attention, and was also a source of controversy between learned divines and physicians. The second striking point is the way in which James handed over the case to Bancroft, who in turn entrusted it to Samuel Harsnett (it is interesting that in the opinion of our chronicler the archbishop honoured Harsnett 'above others'). Despite his reputation as a witch-hunter, James was perfectly happy to entrust the investigation of this puzzling case to an archbishop who was known to be sceptical in such matters.

Both James and Johnston mention the involvement of physicians in Anne's case, which leads us to another expert in matters of witchcraft and possession who helped investigate Anne in the autumn of 1605, Edward Jorden. Jorden was born in Kent in 1569, and went on to Cambridge, where he took his BA in 1583. He determined on a medical career and set off to study medicine at Padua, whose university housed the most advanced medical school of the period. Returning to England, Jorden rapidly became recognized as a doctor of considerable expertise, becoming a licentiate of the College of Physicians in 1595 and a fellow in 1597. After making an impact in the capital, he went to Bath and spent the rest of his lengthy career there, numbering Anne of Denmark as one of his patients during a visit the Queen made to that city. Although he is best known to historians of witchcraft for his tract on hysteria, published in 1603 in the wake of the Mary Glover affair, his fame among his contemporaries was founded on his *A Discourse of Natural Bathes and Mineral Waters*, a topic of obvious appeal to a doctor practis-ing in Bath. This work, first published in 1631, was regarded in the period as an important contribution to chemical studies, and was reprinted on four subsequent occasions. Its fourth edition, published in 1667, contains a short biography of Jorden written by another physician of some reputation in his day, Thomas Guidott. Guidott was full of praise for Jorden, whom he described as a doctor who 'had the applause of the learned, the respect of the rich, the prayers of the poor, and the love of all'.

In fact, the evidence that Jorden gave about Anne's afflictions to the Star Chamber was a little cautious, much of it reporting at second hand how she had fared while she was in the custody of Samuel Harsnett. He recorded how pins had been found in her stool while she had been in Harsnett's care, and also told how she behaved in her fits: she would 'cast & tumble about her arms, body and legs' and 'speak certain words', most commonly 'prayers for the release of her pains'. She called out against Elizabeth Gregory as the cause of her troubles. But he also noted, interestingly, that her last fit had occurred in mid September 1605, and that during her stay in Jorden's house she did not 'void any pins in her urine or otherwise nor swallow down any pin or pins or fall into any fit or fits, trance or trances that ever this deponent saw or heard of'. Jorden's wife Lucy also gave a short statement corroborating her husband's evidence.

A rather different account of Jorden's involvement was given by Thomas Guidott in his edition of *A Discourse of Natural Bathes and Mineral Waters*. When Jorden practised in London, wrote Guidott,

> there was one Anne Gunter troubled with such strange and unusual symptoms, that she was generally thought and reported by all that saw her to be bewitch'd. King James hearing of it, sent for her to London, and pretending great pity to her, told her, he would take care for her relief, in which thing he employed Dr Jorden, who, upon examination, reported to the King, that he thought it was a cheat; and tincturing all she took with harmless things, made her believe that she had taken physic, by the use of which, she said, she had found great benefit. The doctor acquainting his majesty that he had given

her nothing of a medicinal nature, but only what did appear to the maid, and also, that though when he repeated the Lord's Prayer, and the Creed in English, she was much out of order, yet at the rehearsal of the same in Latin she was not concern'd, the King was confirmed in what he had suspected before.

After hearing this account, the King reacted by 'dealing very plainly with her, and commanding her to discover the truth unto him', which Anne eventually did. She was at first unwilling, in Guidott's words, to 'disclose the juggle', but confessed all 'upon the King's importunity and promise to her of making up what damage should accrue from the discovery'. Anne told how, some time before, 'there happened a difference between a female neighbour of her father's and himself', and that 'having in his own apprehension no better way to be avenged of her than this, impiously caused his daughter, on the receiving of the sacrament, to engage to imitate one bewitched and ascribe it to that woman'. Anne, on her own account as reported by Guidott, complied, 'and acted this part in so exact and wonderful a manner, that she deceived all the country where she lived, who thought it to be a truth'. After her confession to the King, so Guidott tells us, 'she was very quiet, and the King giving her a portion, she was afterwards married, being, by this subtle artifice, perfectly cured of her mimical witchery'.

Guidott's comments make it clear that the main elements of the story of her sufferings that Anne was to give to the Star Chamber in February 1606 were already in place when she confessed all to the King in October 1605, and had obviously firmed up since her earlier confidences to Joan Greene and Joan Spratt at Salisbury a few months previously. It is also noteworthy, given her fear expressed at Salisbury that a confession would ruin her father, that James's promise of an indemnity, his 'promise to her of making up what damage should accrue from the discovery', seems to have been a major factor in her final decision to confess. Guidott's account also reintroduces the possibility that, if nothing else, Anne found love and possibly marriage in the course of her troubles.

Anne, indeed, made one intriguing reference to this last issue in her statement to the Star Chamber. When she was being taken into Harsnett's custody, she was told by her father 'to take heed she fell not into love or liking with any man while she was from him because that (as he said) might be a means to make her this deponent to disclose any secret though otherwise she had intended to have kept them never so close'. For the bulk of the population in Tudor and Stuart England, marriage occurred fairly late, normally after the bridegroom had entered a job or trade that would allow him to support a wife and family, and the bride, usually as a result of working as a servant in a farm or workshop, had also acquired a modest amount of money to put into setting up a household. As a general rule men were in their late twenties, and women a year or two younger, when they first married. But for the gentry, things were different. The economic constraints were not so marked, and their offspring tended to marry somewhat younger. Certainly Anne, aged twenty-one or so when she met the King, was at the age when a daughter of the gentry might expect to be married (her sister, Susan, was nineteen when she became Thomas Holland's wife). If we may trust the accounts of what happened to her in the autumn of 1605, we can safely infer that she herself had no doubts on this point.

James told how both Anne and Asheley, Bancroft's servant, had asked his permission to marry, and that Anne had sought the young man's love 'most importunately and immodestly (in manner unfit to be written)'. Robert Johnston, in his *Historia Rerum Britannicarum*, gives an account of the episode's background that does little for the credit of Anne's interrogators. Samuel Harsnett, he tells us, led by a hint from the archbishop ... induced a very proper youth to entice the girl into love, who discovering the secret and promising marriage easily procured her favour. Thereafter he gradually neglected her on the pretext of her magical vanities, and the infamy of witchcraft, widespread through all Britain. But she (as is the way with women) inclined to lust, revealed all her tricks, committing her reputation and safety to the care of the youth. Thus was fraud laid bare and detected by the lack of self-control in a woman.

The spectacle of the archbishop of Canterbury and his chaplain using a deceit of this kind is unpleasing, as is Johnston's attachment to the widespread view of his age, which portrayed women as morally, physically and intellectually inferior to men, and which saw lust as a female attribute. Yet if we pare away the misogyny, what can we make of this statement, of the King's reference to how Anne pursued the object of her affections 'most importunately and immodestly', and the worries expressed by her family, when she went into Harsnett's custody, that she might reveal all their secrets if she fell in love?

Anne was of an age when falling in love and marriage were felt to be appropriate for a young woman of her class. In an era that valued chastity, and especially virginity among unmarried women, sexual intercourse was definitely another matter. Anne, if we may trust the comments of James and Johnston, and the fears of her kinsfolk, was obviously thought by a number of those who knew her to be ready, both physically and psychologically, for amatory involvement and for the sexual relations that would, in the natural order of things, follow marriage. It may be appropriate when speculating on such matters to return to contemporary views on hysteria, 'the mother'. Anne herself in her evidence to the Star Chamber thought she had been suffering from 'the mother' when her afflictions began, and a number of the doctors examining her at that point at least investigated this possibility. In her last interview with James, Anne told the monarch of 'the swelling of her belly, occasioned by the disease called the mother, wherewith she was oftentimes vehemently afflicted'. And the uterine interpretation of hysteria that was standard in this period connected this 'disease called the mother' very directly to contemporary attitudes to the female body and female sexuality.

'The mother' was discussed at length in the main narrative of the Mary Glover case, written in 1602 by Stephen Bradwell. Bradwell was convinced that Mary Glover was bewitched, and he composed a lengthy manuscript account of her sufferings, to which was appended an even longer refutation of Edward Jorden's tract on hysteria. Bradwell was following the line, logical enough in contemporary interpretations of the malady, that hysteria was unlikely to affect Mary Glover, as she had yet to reach menarche (she experienced her first period while her sufferings were taking place, thus supporting Bradwell's assertion that the usual age for menarche in England was fourteen). He wrote that it was unusual for hysteria to afflict women before their eighteenth birthday (Anne Gunter was two or three years older than that), and quoted several authorities to the effect that hysteria was a disease of mature women caused by an excess of menstrual blood, by the need to conceive, or by the need for sexual activity. Given this third explanation, that Anne was suffering from 'the mother' allowed observers at court to dwell on her supposed immodesty and lustfulness: her hysteria could have been a sign that her womb needed unblocking through sexual intercourse. And for her part, it would seem that Anne experienced no problems in throwing off the restraints that had been placed on her in the Gunter household in North Moreton.

A further indication of this throwing off of restraints lay in the way Anne danced before the court with 'dexterity of body', in the King's phrase. Court culture was an ornate and splendid thing in the early modern period; historians of seventeenth-century England in particular have written about a marked divergence between a 'court' culture that stressed ostentation, fashion and magnificence, and a 'country' culture that stressed the more solid values of family, godliness and hard-headedness in business matters. Anne, arguably, had, unexpectedly and perhaps temporarily, crossed the boundary between country and court cultures. Raised in a small Berkshire village, subjected to the normal restraints imposed on the daughters of the country gentry and the abnormal pressures imposed on her by her father, Anne now found herself the centre of attraction in the strange and exotic world of the Jacobean court. The culture shock was a massive one, and doubtless there was much that scared her, not least being placed in the custody of Samuel Harsnett. But Anne had learned about falling in love, had confided in a king, and had danced before the court: one senses that in many respects her experiences in that autumn of 1605, in the course of her twenty-first year, were liberating ones.

Anne met the King for the last time on 10 October. James apparently planned another meeting, for 30 October, but it never took place. By that date Anne had been moved from Harsnett's custody to that of another clergyman whose career was on the up in the years around 1600, Richard Neile. Born in 1562, Neile had, when a boy, been fortunate enough to fall under the patron-age of William Cecil, Lord Burghley, and on the death of his patron had continued to be favoured by Burghley's son, Robert Cecil, later earl of Salisbury. Neile was to enjoy considerable professional success in the first half of the seventeenth century, a process that began when he became dean of Westminster early in November 1605. He was regarded by the upper reaches of the Church of England as completely trustworthy, and worked closely with Harsnett in the Anne Gunter business. His letter of 30 October, sent from his residence at Shenfield in Essex, told Salisbury that Anne was unable to meet the King at Ware in Hertfordshire as arranged. The letter from James setting up the meeting had arrived when he and Harsnett were busy, engaged in the process of examining Anne, while the two ecclesiastics 'had neither coach nor any other provision fit for her conveying thither'. Neile had therefore sent a servant to the King at Ware with letters asking that the meeting might be re-arranged for a later date at Whitehall or some other convenient place. He informed Salisbury that the investigations were proceeding well, in so far as 'whatsoever she has formerly confessed voluntarily, she has now confessed upon her oath'. Harsnett, he concluded his letter, 'commends himself very kindly to you'.

By the time Neile wrote, however, outside events had rather overtaken the Anne Gunter affair. Two or three days before Neile's letter of 30 October, the King and the higher levels of government had received their first warnings of the conspiracy that was to pass into history as the Gunpowder Plot, and the famous uncovering of that plot on 5 November 1605 meant that James had something rather more urgent than this fascinating witchcraft case to preoccupy him. Yet, as Guy Fawkes and the rest were racked and interrogated, somebody was orchestrating legal action against Anne Gunter and her father, with the result that proceedings against them were begun at the Star Chamber in February 1606. The proceedings, like most cases in which the Crown had an interest, were formally initiated by the King's attorney-general, at this point Sir Edward Coke. It is doubtful, however, if Coke had much of a direct interest in the case: although there is no unequivocal evidence, it seems safe to assume that the moving force behind the prosecution was that experienced exposer of fraud in matters of witchcraft, Richard Bancroft. As a privy councillor Bancroft would have been well placed to initiate such proceedings, while his influence in the affair is suggested by evidence that his chaplain, Harsnett, continued to play an active role in the case against the Gunters. Another letter from Richard Neile, endorsed '1606' but otherwise undated, shows how seriously Harsnett was taking the matter. Harsnett had been chosen vice-chancellor for Cambridge University, a prestigious honour and one not without its political overtones. Neile's letter told how Harsnett had decided to be admitted to his vice-chancellorship by proxy, as 'if he should now go down to Cambridge to be admitted he would greatly hinder the prosecuting of Anne Gunter's business', in which, wrote Neile, neither 'his majesty's learned counsel or any of the clerks of the Star Chamber' could do anything unless Harsnett or Neile himself were on hand. Some indication of broader governmental interest in the case, and the way in which that interest was being entrusted to Bancroft's associates, is provided by the £300 paid out by the Exchequer in March 1606 to Richard Neile, to be disbursed to help witnesses in the Gunter case with their expenses.

The Star Chamber has passed into historical myth as an unusually harsh tribunal, and it is true that its abolition by the Long Parliament in 1641 was occasioned by Charles I's use of it to chastise political opponents in the 1630s. The court was the Privy Council acting in a judicial capacity, and it features prominently in the traditional historiography of the Tudor period as the institution that Henry VII used to discipline recalcitrant noblemen in the aftermath of the Wars of the Roses. But in fact most of the court's business by 1600 or so consisted of suits between parties. It dealt with such matters as riot, riotous assault, assaults in general, defamation, perjury, fraud and libel, while it was also used to punish persons who were thought to have perverted the course of justice. Most of the plaintiffs using the Star Chamber were reasonably well positioned in the social hierarchy, and the ever expanding business of the court meant that, by the time of the Gunter affair, an institution that had initially been popular for the speed with which it dispensed justice was often taking several years to determine a case. The most severe punishment the Star Chamber could inflict was mutilation, usually by cutting off ears or slitting noses, but more commonly the court would imprison or impose fines.

As the Gunter affair demonstrated, the Star Chamber was routinely used to pursue offenders in whom the Crown was especially interested, and it was still, a century after the reign of Henry VII, well fitted for this role. It operated outside the common law, so there was no trial by jury: the privy councillors sitting in judgement made the decisions. Star Chamber proce‐ dures, however, depended on calling witnesses, and over sixty gave evidence in the Gunter case. The majority of them gave evidence on behalf of Brian Gunter, although many of the ques‐ tions in the interrogatories were designed to provide evidence for the prosecution. Surprisingly, among those giving evidence on Gunter's behalf were a number of men who had testified *against* him in those Star Chamber proceedings of 1601, which demon‐ strated the odium that he had attracted in North Moreton; while others, like the vicar Gilbert Bradshaw, had earlier been at odds with their contentious neighbour on other occasions. Elizabeth Gregory was evidently even more disliked in North Moreton than Brian Gunter. Maddeningly, we have no way of telling what decision the privy councillors sitting in judgement made on the allegations against Brian Gunter. Decrees of the court for the relevant years have long since been lost. It seems very unlikely, given Anne's full confession and the interest of Archbishop Bancroft, that Brian Gunter was found innocent.

Once the crisis of the Gunpowder Plot had passed, James continued to take an active interest in the case. Proceedings at the Star Chamber, as in other courts, could take a long time, and the suit against Anne and Brian Gunter helps demonstrate this point. On 20 February 1608 Sir Roger Wilbraham wrote to the earl of Salisbury, telling how

> this rainy day I moved his majesty upon the petition of Brian Gunter, to have his liberty upon surety [i.e., be released on bail] till the cause in Star Chamber be appointed and heard; the rather because all examinations are taken and the learned counsel have many great causes for him the next term, and this also a matter of great length. His majesty is very absolute to have it heard the next term, and when I told him the matter should be somewhat obscure, he said it was a plain cause by the daughter's confession after many examinations, etc.; and says the deferring thereof is only his dishonour and it shall be no longer deferred, and it was deferred the last term upon motion of the counsel to the end it might be heard this next term; and now he expects it to be heard, and the prisoner to remain as he does.

Much the same tone was set in a letter of 28 February 1608 sent to Salisbury by Sir Thomas Lake, one of the leading royal administrators of the period and a future secretary of state. In the margin of a letter about foreign affairs, Lake noted that, despite the importance of other legal matters, the King was anxious that the Gunter case should proceed the next law term, 'that this may have, if not a thorough proceeding, yet an entry upon the last Star Chamber day or some other day, and that no time be given to other men's causes before it'. Lake's comments reinforce the depth of James's interest in the Gunter case, which had been stressed by

Neile: 'he thinks his honour too far engaged in it to have it longer neglected'. James was obviously very keen to have the matter settled, and to have his interest in the Gunter affair vindicated.

Given this, it is a matter of great regret that decrees relating to the Star Chamber cases in this period have been lost. It may be significant that Wilbraham's letter mentions only Brian Gunter; his daughter had probably saved herself from punishment by confessing so fully, and by attributing her actions to pressure from her father. What happened to Gunter must remain a matter of speculation. He had, at the very least, experienced a lengthy spell in prison. Early in the Star Chamber proceedings he was held at Lambeth Palace, although it is uncertain whether he was still imprisoned there in early 1608, or whether he had been moved to one of the other London prisons. People imprisoned by the Star Chamber were often incarcerated in the Fleet Prison, whose walls abutted Farringdon Street. The Fleet was best known as a debtors' prison, and was thought of as a soft gaol by contemporary standards. Wherever he was, Gunter, as a gentleman of means, would have enjoyed a degree of comfort and special treatment. His experience of prison would not have been as unpleasant as that suffered by Elizabeth Gregory and Mary Pepwell as they awaited their trial in Reading Gaol a few years previously.

Even if judgement eventually went against him, it is very unlikely that the Star Chamber would have mutilated Brian Gunter for his offence. This punishment was largely reserved, as far as the gentry were concerned, for those found guilty of treason or sedition, and who were thus seen as more direct threats to the Stuart regime. Brian Gunter was able to return to North Moreton and continue the life of a gentleman; on the strength of the 1624 subsidy assessments, he remained the wealthiest man in the parish, suggesting that if he had been fined, it was not so

severely as to ruin him. Indeed, there is no mention of Brian
Gunter in the estreats of fines inflicted by the Star Chamber
noted in the Exchequer records, which means that any fine
imposed was never collected; while other sources that allow at
least a partial reconstruction of the outcome of the Star Chamber
cases in the relevant period make no mention of Brian Gunter.
The most likely outcome was that, on the strength of his
daughter's confession and pressure from the King, he was found
guilty, and sentenced to imprisonment and a heavy fine, the latter
being remitted if, as was so often the case, he made a full confession himself expressing his contrition and acknowledging the
error of his ways. It is also worth remembering that James had
offered Anne an indemnity if she confessed: perhaps he felt the
royal promise meant that Brian Gunter should escape severe
punishment after a suitable amount of grovelling on his part.

As for Anne, we can assume that the Star Chamber
investigations, however daunting they must have been on one
level, represented a release from her sufferings of the previous year
and a half, as well as, probably, a permanent escape from her
father's household. Her last fit, if we trust Edward Jorden, had
come in mid September 1605, and there was certainly no
suggestion from either the Star Chamber dossier or any of the
other documents of the period that they returned. Anne had
made her peculiar contribution to English witchcraft history. She
had been at the centre of a complex story that had begun in the
most familiar context for witchcraft-accusations, the push and
shove of disputes and personality clashes in the face-to-face
community of the early modern village, a story that had
concluded with her meeting King James, falling in love and
dancing before the court. This story had, en route, drawn in a
posse of Oxford dons, the judges and jurors who had been at
the trial in Abingdon, the bishop of Salisbury, such rising

ecclesiastics as Samuel Harsnett and Richard Neile, and that paragon of the physician's virtues, Edward Jorden, while Anne had also become, unwittingly, enmeshed in the high ecclesiastical politics of the day. For the daughter of a solid but hardly prominent gentry family, the experience must have been a remarkable one.

chapter *nine*

LOOSE ENDS, TIED
and UNTIED

W ITH THE conclusion of the Star Chamber proceed⁄
ings, Anne Gunter, having achieved rather more than
fifteen minutes of fame, passed out of the limelight, her story
buried in the Star Chamber archives, waiting for a historian to
find it and rconstruct as much of it as possible. But with the
story of Anne's bewitching at its end, we may now consider
the subsequent fortunes of those who were involved in her
sufferings.

It is, of course, easiest to trace the fate of the people whom
history has deemed important. James I, the most prominent
person to be involved in the Anne Gunter case, lived until 1625.
He was continually ill in his last years, suffering in particular
from arthritis. In the summer of 1624 the warm weather brought
him some relief, but with the onset of autumn arthritis returned,
his hands being so badly affected that he could not sign his name
on state documents. He spent Christmas at Whitehall, but was ill
and kept to his chamber. In March 1625, at Theobalds, the palace
built by Robert Cecil that James had obtained as a gift in 1607,
he suffered an attack of tertian ague, an acute fever that brought

on convulsions every two or three days. He suffered a serious
stroke as a result, and his last days were rendered miserable by
severe dysentery. His condition, despite the attentions of a
number of doctors, was terminal, and eventually, surrounded by
lords, servants, bishops and chaplains, he died on the morning
of Sunday, 27 March. His son, Charles I, followed him as king.

Of the senior ecclesiastics involved in the Gunter case,
Richard Bancroft was to die, after prolonged suffering from
gallstones, in November 1610. He was buried in Lambeth
Church, close to the archiepiscopal palace where Anne Gunter
and her father had been kept in custody early in 1606. Richard
Neile, the rising talent who had been involved with Samuel
Harsnett in investigating Anne and in orchestrating the Star
Chamber proceedings against her and her father, went from
success to success. In 1608 he became bishop of Rochester, and
subsequently went from bishopric to bishopric before being
elected archbishop of York in 1631. He was heavily involved in
royal service, regularly sitting, for example, to hear political cases
in the Star Chamber. He died in the cathedral close at York in
1640, and was buried in York Minster. His predecessor at York
was Samuel Harsnett, who had enjoyed a less rapid, if solid
enough, rise after his participation in the Gunter affair. He
became bishop of Norwich in 1619, an appointment that had
unfortunate consequences for East Anglia's Puritans, and was
elected archbishop of York in 1628, being sworn a privy
councillor the following year. An old man by that time, he began
to suffer severe ill health, and died in 1631. He was buried at
Chigwell in Essex, where he had held his first clerical living, his
resting place marked by a fine funeral brass. The two judges who
had tried Elizabeth Gregory and Mary Pepwell at Abingdon
died within a few months of each other. Sir Christopher
Yelverton passed away in October 1612, and was buried at

Easton Mauduit in Northamptonshire, where he had settled in the reign of Elizabeth I. His son, Henry, was to keep the Yelverton legal dynasty going by following his father's profession, although his fortunes were to suffer some downturns when he became enmeshed in the power politics of the Jacobean era. Sir David Williams died in January 1613 and was buried at Brecknock, although a portion of his remains, commemorated by a now long-lost monument, were interred in the parish church at Kingston Bagpuize. Alexander Chocke, the Berkshire JP who delivered such a full account of Elizabeth Gregory's trial at Abingdon, died in July 1607, less than a year after he gave his evidence to the Star Chamber. Thomas Hinton, the Wiltshire gentleman who turned the Abingdon trial in favour of the two accused witches, continued to live the life of a successful and locally important country squire, although he ran into severe difficulties when he was accused of fraud in 1616, and when he entered into litigation over debts owed to the deceased first husband of his second wife, Lady Mary Harvey. He died in 1635, leaving an extensive estate at Chilton Foliat in his native county. For reasons that remain unclear, four of his children developed ties with Virginia: two sons emigrated there, his daughter married Samuel Matthews, governor of the colony in the 1650s, and his eldest son, Anthony, was a merchant venturer in the Virginia Company. Another son, John, entered the medical profession and became physician to Charles I's queen, Henrietta Maria.

Sir Francis Stewart, the young Scottish aristocrat who was also sceptical about Anne's sufferings, and who was also apparently rather attracted to her, became thoroughly anglicized. His father had been killed in one of the classic incidents of Scottish noble feuding, but Francis was to become involved in London literary life, and may even have been associated with the famous circle of playwrights, poets, patrons and cognoscenti who came together at London's Mermaid tavern.

Sir Richard Lovelace, the justice of the peace who took the initial examinations of Elizabeth Gregory and her accusers, and who was also present at the Abingdon trial, did well in the following years, becoming Baron Lovelace of Hurley in 1627. His first marriage was to Catherine, the widow of William Hyde, and ended when she died in 1598. This marriage had brought Sir Richard important political connections, and his second marriage, to Margaret, daughter of Richard Dodsworth, a rich merchant tailor of London, resulted in Sir Richard fathering two sons and three daughters, and acquiring a massive fortune. It was said when he died in 1634 that he was worth £7,000 a year, and that his second marriage had brought him £50, 000. If it was Sir Richard Lovelace who made a fortune, it was that local notable whom Thomas Hinton had consulted before the Abingdon trial, Sir Francis Knollys, who was to score on longevity. He continued to involve himself in county matters in Berkshire and Oxfordshire, and then, in November 1640, was elected at the age of ninety to represent Reading in the Long Parliament. Described by a contemporary as 'the ancientest parliament man in England', Knollys, a Roundhead supporter, was to live to see his side's victory in the First Civil War, although his death in May 1648, two or three years before his hundredth birthday, saved him from having to experience renewed civil warfare, the execution of Charles I and the establishment of a republic.

Thomas Holland, Brian Gunter's son-in-law, died in March 1612 and was buried in St Mary the Virgin, the Oxford University church. In his will he left 20*s.* to the poor of his native Ludlow, and small amounts to various individuals. He made John Whetcombe, one of the clergyman who had given evidence in the Star Chamber proceedings, and who was now married to his daughter Anne, responsible for selling off some of his property and passing the proceeds on to his widow, Susan. This responsibility was to be shared by Holland's father-in-law, referred to respectfully as 'Mr Gunter'. The widow was made Holland's executrix. Apart from Anne's marriage, little is known of the fate of Thomas and Susan Holland's children, although their son William, who according to Gilbert Bradshaw had participated in a riotous assault on the vicar's wife in July 1620, became a captain in the service of Charles I. Susan herself survived her husband by a lengthy period, and was buried in the Church of St Peter the Bailey, on the western fringes of Oxford, on 4 March 1650.

The deaths of the villagers of North Moreton who knew Brian Gunter and his family, and whom we have encountered at so many points, are recorded in the village's parish register. Various Leavers, Fields and Maynes passed away, while the register also records the death of Alice Kirfoote in 1617, of Nicholas Kirfoote in 1625 and of Walter Gregory on 11 September 1629. It seems that both the Pepwell women returned to North Moreton and lived there until their deaths: a woman who was probably Agnes Pepwell (the name is given in a variant spelling) was buried in April 1612, and a Mary Pepwell was buried in December 1654. No mention is made of the death of Elizabeth Gregory, and one can only surmise that she died away from the parish. It is, however, noteworthy that the register records the burial of two other women described as wife of Walter Gregory: Mary, buried in 1617, and Margery, buried in April 1629. There may well have been more than one Walter Gregory in the parish, but it is safe to guess that at least one of these women was a second wife of the Walter Gregory who was Elizabeth's husband, further evidence that Elizabeth was dead. Edmund Dunch, lord of

North Moreton Manor when Anne Gunter had suffered her afflictions, died in 1623. We do not know when North Moreton's vicar Gilbert Bradshaw died, although it was probably shortly after he made his will in 1639. He had married a woman named Elizabeth Brasier about a year after his first wife died in the plague outbreak of 1603. Among the children she bore him was a son called Brian, possibly named in deference to the clergyman's difficult yet powerful neighbour.

Tracing the fate of Brian Gunter's two sons, Harvey and William, is impossible. Neither's death is noted in the North Moreton register, and searches of the standard reference works have provided no relevant information. Harvey, on the strength of his father's will, is known to have been alive in 1628, while the parish register for South Moreton notes the baptisms of two of his children in the 1610s, evidence that he was resident there at that time. Brian Gunter's wife Anne was buried on 27 April 1617 at North Moreton, being laid to rest, as was appropriate for the wife of the richest man in the village, in the chancel of All Saints' Church.

Brian Gunter returned to North Moreton after the Star Chamber proceedings of 1606–8 and resumed the life of a country gentleman, but there are strong indications that he did not grow old gracefully. In 1620 Gilbert Bradshaw initiated proceedings at the Star Chamber against Brian Gunter and others, Nicholas Kirfoote among them, asserting that Brian Gunter had been the ringleader in two riotous assaults on the clergyman and his family, disputes over tithe corn being the issue of contention. Bradshaw also asserted that Gunter had, over the previous fourteen years, threatened to force the clergyman out of North Moreton. He claimed that in the first riot, on 22 June 1620, Gunter had led a party that included his daughter Susan Holland and his grandchildren, William and Elizabeth Holland (the latter probably William's wife), as well as a cleric named Thomas Browne. The group had assaulted Bradshaw with 'pike staves, pitchforks, welsh hooks' and other weapons, and had taken away tithe corn. In another incident that occurred in the following month, Gunter led another small mob including, among others, Nicholas Kirfoote and four members of the Leaver family. This time 'cocks of tithe hay' were taken, and, according to Bradshaw, when his wife Elizabeth objected, 'the said riotous persons in scoffing and deriding manner uncivily turned her and tossed her over the cocks, and termed and called her Maid Marion'.

But death eventually came to Brian Gunter, and on 17 November 1628 he was buried in St Mary the Virgin in Oxford, described in the parish register as a *peregrinus*, or stranger. It is likely that he had fallen ill, and had gone to Oxford to stay with his daughter Susan Holland: it is perhaps fitting that he should be laid to rest near Thomas Holland, the son-in-law with whom he had apparently enjoyed good relations. He made his will shortly before he died. His son Harvey got his best suit of clothes and his 'sealing ring', and the will details bequests to several grandchildren, as well as to a number of others. Among these were the children of Thomas Browne, the clergyman who, according to Gilbert Bradshaw, had been involved in the second of the riotous assaults of 1620, and various members of the Fleets, a gentry family apparently related by marriage to the Gunters, to one of whom was bequeathed the Gunter family virginals. The associated probate records show that when Brian Gunter died he possessed £30 of clothes, £3 worth of books, a silver gilt dish valued at £5, 'a great seal ring and another gold ring' valued at £3, and a sword worth 10s. Gunter in his will made his daughter Susan his executrix: there was no unequivocal mention of his other daughter, Anne.

We come, indeed, to a complete impasse when attempting to reconstruct what happened to Anne Gunter. James I wrote in October 1605 that she had fallen in love with one Asheley, a servant of Archbishop Bancroft, that this love was reciprocated, and that the couple planned to marry with royal blessing and a dowry provided by the monarch. The tradition that she was married, with a portion from James, to a servant of the archbishop was current later in the century when Thomas Guidott published his edition of Edward Jorden's tract on mineral waters in 1667 (it should be noted that Guidott states that he never met Jorden, so the story cannot simply have been passed on at first hand). We have no real clue as to who Asheley was, not even a Christian name. An intelligent guess would be that he was a member of yet another gentry clan, the Ashley family, based in Dorset, which by the early seventeenth century had already produced a secretary of state and a serjeant-at-law, and from whose ranks was to be drawn one of the leading figures in Restoration politics, Sir Anthony Ashley-Cooper, earl of Shaftesbury. It has, however, proved impossible to find any trace of a marriage between Anne Gunter and anybody with the surname of Asheley or Ashley.

A possible alternative marriage partner for Anne is suggested by Brian Gunter's will. There may have been no explicit mention of a daughter named Anne, but Gunter did leave John Hartgill, Esquire, Anne his wife, and their three children 10s. apiece. It would be pleasing to think that this indicated that Anne had found a husband and a family life, but this conclusion is rendered suspect by a marriage licence allegation, dated 15 August 1621, held in the Guildhall Library in London, which relates to a marriage intended between Anne Gunter, aged nineteen, the daughter of Harvey Gunter, and John Hartgill of Kilmington in Somerset, gentleman, aged twenty-two. It would therefore seem that the Anne Hartgill mentioned in Brian Gunter's will was not his daughter Anne but rather her niece, the daughter of her elder brother Harvey. There are, in fact, scraps of evidence that suggest a number of connections between the Berkshire Gunters and the Somerset Hartgills. These were another locally important gentry family, who, like the Gunters, were involved in one episode that brought them a brief, if unwelcome, notoriety. Early in 1556 William Hartgill and his son John had been murdered at Kilmington by Charles, Lord Stourton, and four of his men, the climax of a vendetta that Stourton had conducted against the Hartgills after they had refused to help him force his widowed mother to agree not to remarry. Stourton was executed at Salisbury on 6 March 1556, and the servants who had aided him were executed at various locations in the area, their bodies subsequently hanged in chains.

There is a complication that prevents our simply concluding that the Anne Gunter who married into the Hartgills was not the one who has been at the centre of our story. The marriage licence allegation is struck through, evidence that it was not needed, and perhaps also evidence that the marriage did not take place. Genealogical sources for the Hartgills, dating from 1623, state that the young John Hartgill, his age given here as twenty-three, was married to the unnamed daughter of a Brian Gunter from Moreton in Berkshire. We are therefore left with a piece of contradictory evidence. It is inherently unlikely that it was Brian Gunter's daughter Anne that young John Hartgill married. She would have been at least sixteen years his senior, which would have made marriage unlikely in a time that thought rough parity in the ages of bride and bridegroom ideal, and that definitely felt that if one partner should be markedly older, it should be the groom. It is also unlikely, although by no means biologically impossible, that a woman married in her late thirties could have

given birth to three children, like the three young Hartgills men⁄
tioned in Brian Gunter's will of 1628. Yet the 1623 genealogy
was obviously drawn up by somebody with a good knowledge of
the Hartgills, and it was put together only a year or two after the
marriage in question had taken place.

There is another trace of a connection between the Hartgills
and North Moreton. In the only entry to mention the surname,
the parish register of South Moreton notes the birth of Mary
Hartgill, the daughter of John Hartgill (typically enough, the
mother is not mentioned), on 16 June 1622. This was just after
Brian Gunter had been the defendant in the Star Chamber suit
launched by North Moreton's vicar, and it is probable that
relations between him and Gilbert Bradshaw dictated that any
baptism of a grandchild should not take place in North
Moreton's church. Too much should not be made of this, but we
have seen how Anne's sister Susan had obviously chosen to have
her children baptized in her parents' parish church, perhaps
evidence that she had given birth in their home: possibly Anne
was the mother of this Mary Hartgill, and following a family
tradition. Despite the inherent implausibility created by the age
gap, it is just possible that this is evidence that Anne Gunter,
perhaps already a widow following a previous union, had made a
late marriage and produced a family at this time in her life.
Conversely, the parish register for South Moreton does note the
baptism of children of Harvey Gunter a little earlier than 1622,
suggesting he was resident there: it is therefore perhaps more likely
that it was Harvey's daughter who was the mother of the child
baptized at South Moreton, and also the Anne Hartgill
mentioned in Brian Gunter's will; she might have gone to South
Moreton to give birth near her parents.

Whatever course Anne Gunter's later life took, it is obvious
that her bewitching had strong resonances for her contemporaries.

A number of sources written at the time commented on her meetings with James, while, if Robert Johnston is to be believed, the affair attracted considerable public attention. There are some definite traces of an enduring knowledge of the case. The year 1606, which saw the instigation of the Star Chamber proceed/ ings against Anne, was also the year in which Shakespeare's *Macbeth* was first performed, and witchcraft and related matters were clearly of wider interest to the playwrights of the period. It has been suggested that a scene in Ben Jonson's *Volpone,* depict/ ing a fraudulent demoniac vomiting pins, was inserted as a refer/ ence to Anne Gunter's deceits. William Harvey, possibly the most distinguished English physician of his day, referred when discussing nervous systems in his lectures on anatomy some years later to 'Nan Gunter ... the mad woman with pins in her arms'. The case was also alluded to by the lawyer William Hudson in his tract on the Court of Star Chamber (it seems that the proceedings against Brian Gunter almost foundered on a legal technicality). Interestingly, however, Hudson, writing some two decades after the case was heard, remembered it as one 'where the King's attorney was plaintiff against Gunter for the impos/ ture of pulling pins out of the flesh of a young maid'. Thomas Fuller mentioned the incident, in the context of a more general discussion of fraudulent possession, in his important *Church History of Britain* (1655). 'Anne Gunter, a maid of Windsor,' he wrote, 'gave out that she was possessed of a devil, & was trans/ ported with strange extatical frenzies.' And, as we have seen, Anne's sufferings were mentioned by Robert Johnston in another work published in 1655, and by Thomas Guidott in yet another published in 1667.

What is the affair's broader significance? Surely as a witch/ craft case, the story of Anne Gunter has a number of unusual features. Most witchcraft cases, like this one, began with community disputes, but not many attracted the attention of learned men like the faction Brian Gunter tried to construct at Oxford, not many led to the bewitched party meeting the monarch, not many were the subject of full-scale investigations directed by central government. There are elements in the Anne Gunter affair that give it a wider importance in the history of witchcraft and, more particularly, offer a challenge to the notions about witch-persecution that are generally held today. The story of Anne Gunter shows us just how complex thinking about witchcraft was, how individuals like Thomas Hinton could reject the reality of witchcraft and possession, at least in specific instances, how judges could handle witchcraft cases with care, fairness and perhaps a touch of scepticism, and how a church establishment could be very sceptical about witchcraft, possession and related matters. Our views on witchcraft have been far too influenced by Arthur Miller's version of what happened at Salem.

Anne's case came at a significant juncture in the history of witch-persecution in England. Witch-trials were still to come, and in 1612 there was that famous local panic at Pendle in Lancashire, with ten executions, the worst English outbreak before the 1640s. But, generally, in the two decades that followed the Gunter case, witchcraft was an offence tried in the secular and ecclesiastical courts with increasing infrequency, was not given much attention by pamphlet writers and, after the publication of Richard Bernard's *A Guide to Grand Jury Men* in 1627, did not attract the talents of learned theologians. During the 1630s, on the strength of surviving documentation, the inhabitants of the five counties covered by the Home Circuit of the assizes brought only twenty or so accusations of witchcraft to court, none of which resulted in a conviction. Central government attitudes can be gauged by another incident originating in the Pendle region of

Lancashire, this time in 1633–4. Alarmed by what promised to be a massive outbreak of witch-hunting, the judge presiding over the initial trials contacted Westminster, and the boy whose accusations lay at the heart of the craze, his father and several of the suspected witches were hauled down to London, the witches being subjected to medical examinations by a team with William Harvey at its head. The case was exploded, and the boy confessed that he had made up a tale of being taken to a witches' sabbat because he was late getting the cattle home and was frightened of being chastised by his mother.

The slackening of interest in witchcraft, and in the prosecution of witches, which set in after the accession of Charles I in 1625 has never been fully explained. But one of the key elements in this process must surely have been a changing religious style among the upper reaches of the Church of England. The reign of Charles saw the gradual ascendancy of a theological tendency known as Arminianism. This was, in essence, a more relaxed form of Protestantism that downplayed the importance of predestination, a doctrine of central importance to Elizabethan and Jacobean Protestantism, and encouraged the decoration of churches and the elaboration of church ceremonial. Thomas Holland, while regius professor of theology at Oxford, tried to block Arminian teachings, as did John Prideaux after him, but a number of other figures in our story were associated with the spread of this new tendency. Samuel Harsnett was one of the few major Protestant figures to question predestination in Elizabeth's reign, and his election many years later to the archbishopric of York was to see presentments for witchcraft and sorcery in Yorkshire's church courts reduced to a trickle, a situation that continued when Richard Neile succeeded Harsnett as archbishop. Neile was a patron of that central personality in English Arminianism, William Laud, who became archbishop of Canterbury in 1633. When the political crisis that was to lead to the Civil Wars began, Laud was an obvious target for parliamentarian odium, and he was imprisoned in 1641; the dismantling of Charles I's ecclesiastical policy was symbolized by his execution in 1645. And it was in 1645 that there began the mass trials associated with Matthew Hopkins, in which over a hundred people were executed for witchcraft in England's eastern counties. The Civil Wars heightened religious ferment, unleashed an activist popular Puritanism, and diluted or destroyed those agencies of secular and ecclesiastical government that previously had been so crucial in dampening witchcraft accusations. The trials began again, as did the witchcraft pamphlets and the demonological tracts, while witchcraft's status as a serious matter of intellectual debate was re-established. Yet it seems very likely that if Charles had not committed that series of political miscalculations that led to the Civil Wars and all they entailed, witch-trials, as well as intellectual and theological interest in witchcraft, would have died out in England. As it was, the last-known execution in England for witchcraft came in 1685, the last conviction of a witch (the jury verdict was quashed by the judge) in 1712, the last major intellectual debate about witchcraft a few years later.

If we require an accessible and lasting reminder of Anne Gunter and her sufferings, we can go to the village where she lived. North Moreton is still there, set in a turning off the A4130 between Didcot and Wallingford. It continues to benefit from slight isolation, and it is an attractive place. There are a number of fine old houses around the middle of the village, although there is no way of establishing if any of these were inhabited by the villagers of four centuries ago. Stapleton's Chantry, the Gregory family's main holding, is identifiable, but there is some doubt over the fate of the rectory where Brian Gunter and his family lived. The relevant section of the *Victoria County History* for Berkshire claims it has long since been demolished, its site the location of the garden of a later vicarage, an imposing structure, now privately owned, with some sixteenth-century features. Local historians in North Moreton think that this residence, currently known as North Moreton House, was, in fact, the rectory once inhabited by the Gunters.

There are few amenities in the village, although there is a good and long-established pub, the Bear (another, the Queen Victoria, has recently closed), while the village has an active cricket team, founded by a paternalist vicar, Albert Barff, in 1858, and a Women's Institute, for both North and South Moreton, which has recently celebrated its seventieth anniversary. The population is around 275 adults and 60 children, probably a few more than in 1600 but less than in the late nineteenth century. There are still four working farms in North Moreton, although the bulk of the population, which includes many professionals, commute to towns in the area, or to London via Didcot, for their work.

All Saints' Church lies at the centre of the village, a strong and solid-looking building, strangely reminiscent of a crouching animal, its square, fifty-foot tower standing imposingly against the sky. The interior of the church is attractive but strangely austere, plain white walls virtually without decoration, although there is the splendid stained-glass. The church had, in fact, fallen into disrepair in the early nineteenth century, and any existing memorials or monuments were removed during the major rebuilding operations of 1855–8. The absence of a resident landlord family in the village means that there are none of those gentry monuments that are such a feature of England's parish churches. There are memorials to more recent losses, to the twentieth century's follies that claimed so many more human lives than did the witch-craze. Seven men from North Moreton died in the First World War; one of them, Herbert Butler, was twenty when he fell on the first day of the Somme offensive; another, Kenneth Bumpass, was just nineteen when he died while serving with the cavalry on the Italian front in 1918. The Second World War claimed two villagers, one serving with the Royal Air Force, one with the Royal Berkshire Regiment.

Yet there are two reminders of the passing of earlier inhabitants of the parish. Although memorials were removed in the 1850s refurbishment, some of the names that were on them were recorded on two small diamond-shaped plaques set in the floor of the church. These include some familiar surnames: a Mary Mayne, who was buried in 1776, a John Mayne, buried in 1810, a William Leaver, buried in 1742, and a John Leaver, buried in 1802. These plaques, together with documentation from the eighteenth century, demonstrate a final irony: long after their troublesome neighbour Brian Gunter had gone to his grave at Oxford, and long after his daughter Anne came to whatever end fate had decreed for her, the solid and well-established farming families, the Gregorys among them, maintained their hold on North Moreton.

NOTES *and* REFERENCES

ABBREVIATIONS

Berks. R.O.	Berkshire Record Office
D.N.B.	*Dictionary of National Biography*
Herts. R.O.	Hertfordshire Record Office
P.R.O.	Public Record Office
V.C.H.	*Victoria County History*

The Star Chamber proceedings initiated by the attorney-general against Brian and Anne Gunter in February 1606, P.R.O., STAC 8/4/10, are the main source for this book. The witnesses are listed alphabetically below, with the folio number within P.R.O., STAC 8/4/10, the date on which their evidence was taken, and details of whether they were giving evidence *ex parte* Brian Gunter (BG) or the attorney-general (AG). This should provide the interested reader the information required to trace the exact location of witnesses' statements referred to in the main text of this book.

list of witnesses

Benedict Allen, f. 46v, 21 April 1607, BG; Elizabeth Baker, f. 184, 9 May 1606, BG; Martha, wife of Richard Baker alias Tailor, f. 179, 9 May 1606, BG; Nicholas Baker, f. 169, 8 May 1606, BG; Richard Baker alias Tailor, f. 189, 9 May 1606, BG; William Barker, f. 212, 13 May 1606, BG; Margaret Bartholomew, f. 85, 26 July 1606, AG; Thomas Bird, f. 208, 10 May 1606,

BG; Roger Bracegirdle, f. 80, 5 May 1606, BG; Gilbert Bradshaw, f. 192, 10 May 1606, bG; Alice Buckeridge, f. 1v, 18 November 1606, AG; Alexander Chocke, f. 18, 30 November 1606, AG; Cuthbert Crooke, f. 3, 19 November 1606, AG; Richard Dakin, f. 206v, 10 May 1606, BG; Edmund Dunch, f. 5, 19 November 1606, AG; John Field, f. 178, 8 May 1606, BG; Mary Field, f. 1, 18 November 1606, AG; William Field, f. 190, 10 May 1606, BG; f. 89, 26 July 1606, AG; Thomas Fleet, f. 227v, 16 May 1606, BG; John Goodaye, f. 217v, 14 May 1606, BG; Joan Greene, f. 20, 4 December 1606, AG; Anne, wife of Brian Gunter, f. 201, 10 May 1606, BG; Anne, daughter of Brian Gunter, f. 121, 24 February 1606; Brian Gunter, f. 73, 30 January, also f. 95, 11 February 1606; Nicholas Gunter, f. 221v, 15 May 1606, BG; Anne, wife of William Gwillyam, f. 205, 10 May 1606, BG; William Gwillyam, f. 203,10 May 1606, BG; John Hall, f. 163, 6 May 1606, BG; John Harding, f. 6, 21 November 1606, AG; William Harvey, f. 153, 6 May 1606, BG; Richard Hawkins, f. 218, 14 May 1606, BG; William Helme, f. 148, 6 May 1606, BG; Thomas Hinton, f. 9, 24 November 1606, AG, also f. 57b, 21 April 1607, BG; John Hobgood, f. 51, 21 April 1607, BG; Susan, wife of Thomas Holland, f. 207, 10 May 1606, BG; Thomas James, f. 141, 6 May 1606, BG; Edward Jorden, f. 57, 21 April 1607, BG; Lucy, wife Edward Jorden, f. 60, 25 April 1607, BG; Thomas Kibblewhite, f. 47, 21 April 1607, BG; Alice Kirfoote, f. 87, 26 July 1606, AG; Nicholas Kirfoote, f. 90, 26 July 1606, AG; John Leaver, f. 226, 15 May 1606, BG; William Leaver, f. 156, 6 May 1606, BG; Gifford Longe, f. 202, 10 May 1606, BG; Richard Lovelace, f. 7, 22 November 1606, AG; Thomas Neighbour, f. 169v, 8 May 1606, BG; William Newcombe, f. 23v, 4 December 1606, AG; William Nicholas, f. 54, 21 April 1607, BG; Margaret, wife of William Orpewood, f. 52, 21 April 1607, BG; Thomas Palliser, f. 56, 21 April 1607, BG; John Pearse, f. 219, 14 May 1606, BG; John Prideaux, f. 143, May 1606, BG; Richard Pugh [Pewe], f. 217. 14 May 1606, BG; Margaret Rose, f. 223, 15 May 1606, BG; Anne, wife of Anthony Ruffin, 6 December 1606, AG; Edward Sampson, f. 46, 21 April 1607, BG; William Sawyer, f. 165, 8 May 1606, BG; Joan, wife of John Spratt, f. 19, 4 December 1606, AG; John Sudbury, f. 2, 18 November 1606, AG; Robert Tadmarten, f. 48, 21 April 1607, BG; Humphrey Tailor, f. 220, 15 May 1606, BG; Mary Thornebury, f. 182, 9 May 1606, BG; William Turner, f. 219, 14 May 1606, BG; Robert Vilvaine, f. 173, 8 May 1606, BG; Bartholomew Warner, f. 156, 6 May 1606, BG; Thomas Warwick, f. 59, 24 April 1607, BG; John Whetcombe, f. 55, 21 April 1607, BG; Robert Whisteler, f. 52v, 21 April 1607, BG; William Wilkinson, f. 23, 4 December 1606, AG; Thomas Winniffe, f. 171, 8 May 1606, BG.

PREFACE

The case of Anne Gunter has been familiar to historians of English witchcraft in a general way, but until now it has never formed the basis of a detailed
study. There is a brief account in Cecil L'Estrange Ewen, *Witchcraft in the
Star Chamber* (n.p., 1938), while a number of references to it are gathered in
Henry N. Paul, *The Royal Play of Macbeth: Why and When It was Written by
Shakespeare* (New York, 1971), pp. 118–27. The case's significance in legal
history is discussed in Brian P. Levack, 'Possession, Witchcraft, and the Law
in Jacobean England', *Washington and Lee Law Review*, 52 (1996), pp.
1613–40.

CHAPTER 1: ANNE'S STORY

For the physical setting of the Star Chamber, see J. A. Guy, *The Court of Star
Chamber and Its Records to the Reign of Elizabeth I* (London, 1985), pp. 1–2.
For other works relating to the Star Chamber, see notes to chapter 8. On
Lambeth Palace, see a A. C. Ducarel, *The History and Antiquities of the
Archiepiscopal Palace of Lambeth from Its Foundation to the Present Time* (London,
1785). Anne was probably held in one of the numerous chambers in the
palace, although Ducarel (p. 31) does mention a room off the porter's lodge
that was thought to have served as a prison at some point before the time
of writing.

CHAPTER 2: SOME UNEXPECTED CONSEQUENCES OF A
FOOTBALL MATCH

The Star Chamber proceedings giving descriptions of the 1598 football
match are P.R.O., STAC 5/L3/19, L31/124, L35/5. The parish register
entry is in Berks. R.O., MF 184 (microfilm of D/P86/1/1). The inquest on
Richard Gregory is P.R.O., KB9/698/387. The comments on football come
from an imposing compendium of early references to the game, Francis
Peabody Magoun, *History of Football from the Beginnings to 1871* (Stuttgart,
1938), pp. 21, 25, 33, 75, 92; the West Ham incident is recorded in the Home
Circuit Assize Indictments, P.R.O. ASSI 35/24/2/41. Phillip Stubbes's
comments on football come from his *The Anatomie of Abuses: Contayning a
Discoverie, or briefe Summarie of such notable Vices and Imperfections, as now raigne
in many Christian Countreyes of the Worlde: but (especiallie) in a verie famous
Ilande of Ailgna: together, with most fearfull Examples of Gods Iudgementes,
executed upon the Wicked for the same, aswell in Ailgna of late, as in other Places,
elsewhere* (London, 1583), sigs Pvi–Pvib.

For an introduction to North Moreton, see *V.C.H. Berks.*, vol. 3, pp. 492–8.

For Gilbert Bradshaw's will, Berks. R.O., D/A1/44/116a; Bradshaw's matriculation at Oxford is noted in Joseph Foster, *Alumni Oxoniensis : The Members of the University of Oxford 1500–1714* (8 vols., Oxford, 1891), vol. 1, p. 168. That the Gilbert Bradshaw matriculating at New College was the man of the same name who was vicar of North Moreton is strongly suggested by the following: Martin Colepepper, as archdeacon of Berkshire, was rector of North Moreton, and hence had the right to appoint its vicar; he was also warden of New College (Foster, *Alumni Oxoniensis*, vol. 1, p. 303). Information on North Moreton's church is provided by G. M. D. Howat, *All Saints' North Moreton* (Fyfield, Oxfordshire, 1997).

In reconstructing North Moreton, I have used: parliamentary subsidy rolls, P.R.O.: E179/74/231; E179/74/273; E179/74/283; E179/75/289; E179/75/329; E179/75/342; the parish register, MF 184 (microfilm of D/P86/1/1); the wills (all held at the Berks. R.O.) of Robert Adams, 1603; Margaret Bartholomew, 1631: Joan Field, alias Farman, 1590; Joan Field, 1647; John Field, 1620; Margaret Field, 1597; Robert Field, 1603; Thomas Gregory, 1574; Walter Gregory, 1629; William Gregory, 1555; William Gregory, 1634; Nicholas Kirfoote, 1625; Anne Leaver, 1593; George Leaver, 1587; John Leaver, 1627; Nicholas Leaver, 1616; Ralph Leaver, 1592; Thomas Leaver, 1595; William Leaver, 1607; John Tadmarden, 1591.

Manorial records consulted were the rolls for 1579–1621 (Herts. R.O., D/EAm/M42–61).

Churchwardens are noted in the visitation book, 1594–1596 (Berks. R.O., D/A2 e. 7). I have based my comments on church court cases on the Archdeaconry of Berkshire Act books for 1596–1608 (Berks. R.O., D/A2 c. 38–52), while I have also searched deposition books for 1590–94 and 1594–1600 (Berks. R.O., D/A2c. 154–5).

Basic details of the Dunch family's rise to local prominence are given in P. W. Hasler, *The House of Commons 1558–1603* (3 vols., London, 1981), vol. 2, p. 66. The continued importance of the Dunches in early seventeenth-century Berkshire is emphasized by Christopher G. Durston, 'Berkshire and Its County Gentry 1625–1649' (University of Reading Ph.D. thesis, 1977). I am grateful to Dr Durston for permission to refer to this thesis.

The standard work on the plague in this period is Paul Slack, *The Impact of Plague in Tudor and Stuart England* (London, 1985).

A basic genealogy of the Gunter family is provided by Elias Ashmole,

The Antiquities of Berkshire (3 vols., London, 1719), vol. 3, p. 215. A more detailed genealogy, although not very useful for our purposes, is held by the College of Arms, Bigland 19, f. 266. Other genealogies of the Gunter family from the relevant period, neither of them giving details of the branch in which we are interested, are held at the Bodleian Library, Oxford, MS Rawlinson, D 807, f. 58v, and D 865, f. 65v.

For Brian Gunter at Hungerford, Hungerford parish register (Berks. R.O., MF 134 1/1), and vestry minute book 1581–1623 (Berks. R.O., MF 136); and *V.C.H. Berks.*, vol. 4, pp. 184, 195.

Gunter's service as escheator is noted in A. Wood (ed.), *List of Escheators for England and Wales,* (List and Index Society, 72, 1971), p. 128.

The 1601 Star Chamber proceedings are P.R.O., STAC 5/L3/19, L31/124, L35/5. The dispute recorded in the manorial rolls over Gunter's entry into the rectory at North Moreton can be found in Herts. R.O., D/EAm/M50. For Dunch's Chancery suit against Brian Gunter, P.R.O., C2/237/17, and for Gilbert Bradshaw's Star Chamber suit against Brian Gunter and others, P.R.O., STAC 8/80/6. Tithe disputes involving Brian Gunter are noted in *The Thirty-eighth Report of the Deputy Keeper of the Public Records* (London, 1878), Appendix, 'Exchequer KR Depositions by Commission', pp. 211, 304, 508, which refers to P.R.O., E134/27ElizI/Nil8, E134/34ElizI/Hil26 and E134/5JamesI/Trin7. The last of these reveals that in 1607 William Gunter was tenant on land owned by his father in Shrivenham. Further evidence on the Gunter family's involvement in tithe collection is provided by a reference in a Signet Office docquet book to a lease of 1591 granted to Brian Gunter's wife, Anne, and to his sons Harvey and William, to the tithe lambs and wool in Shrivenham: P.R.O., SO2/1, December 1591. For the background to tithe disputes in Gunter's home area in this period, see D. J. M. Barker, 'Tithes in Elizabethan Berkshire 1558–1603' (University of Reading M.Phil. thesis, 1997). I am grateful to Mrs Barker for permission to refer to her thesis

Notes on Nicholas Kirfoote are held by the Berkshire Family History Society. The Kirfoote family's earlier involvement in the village is suggested by the presence of a Roger Kirfoote as vicar in the 1550s: Howat, *All Saints' North Moreton*, p. 3.

For the dispute between William and Richard Gregory, see 'Exchequer KR Depositions by Commission', p. 336. Depositions relating to William Gregory's tithe dispute with Thomas Heard appear in Archdeaconry of Berkshire deposition book, 1594–1600 (Berks. R.O., D/A2. c. 155), f. 46v. For Walter Gregory's breach of the peace, Herts. R.O., D/EAm/M55, and for his Chancery suit against William Dunch, P.R.O., C2/272/108. For the litigation between William Field and Robert Gregory at the Court of Requests, P.R.O., REQ2/39/85.

CHAPTER 3: MANY STRANGE TORTURES

This chapter is based entirely on witnesses' evidence from P.R.O., STAC 8/4/10.

One point that deserves further elaboration, however, is the location of Harvey Gunter's residence. This is usually referred to as 'Staunton' in Oxfordshire, in P.R.O., STAC 8/4/10. The two most likely locations are Stanton Harcourt and Stanton St John. These settlements are both about twenty miles from Oxford, Stanton Harcourt to the west, Stanton St John to the east. No manorial records survive for Stanton Harcourt, but a typescript copy of the village's very full parish registers held by Oxfordshire Archives reveals no references to Gunters. Stanton St John has no surviving registers for the relevant period, but detailed manorial records for the village survive in the Archives of New College, Oxford, which was the lord of the manor. Harvey Gunter, like his father at North Moreton, does not appear to have been a tenant of the manor, but the manorial rolls do record a Master Gunter being presented on 20 October 1607 for damaging the road in the manor by letting his sheep stray. Although not entirely conclusive, this does demon-strate that a man of gentry status named Gunter was farming at Stanton St John in the relevant period: New College, Oxford, Archives, MS 2601 (court roll of manor of Stanton St John). Martin Colepepper, who as archdeacon of Berkshire was rector of North Moreton, was also Warden of New College, and in this capacity was rector of Stanton St John, thus estab-lishing a possible line of connection between the son of the occupier of North Moreton rectory and the Oxfordshire parish: Foster, *Alumni Oxoniensis*, vol. 1, p. 303.

CHAPTER 4: WITCHCRAFT

There is a massive literature on the history of witchcraft. Perhaps the best general introduction is B. P. Levack, *The Witch-hunt in Early Modern Europe* (London and New York, 1987; 2nd edn, 1993). A shorter overview is pro-vided by Robin Briggs, '"Many Reasons Why": Witchcraft and the Problem of Multiple Explanation', in Jonathan Barry, Marianne Hester and Gareth Roberts (eds.), *Witchcraft in Early Modern Europe: Studies in Culture and Belief*

(Cambridge, 1996). Briggs's *Witches and Neighbours: The Social and Cultural Context of European Witchcraft* (London, 1996) is an excellent study of the social history of witchcraft in the early modern period, while perhaps the best study of how the interplay between popular and elite perceptions of witchcraft could work themselves out in one territory is Wolfgang Behringer, *Witchcraft Persecutions in Bavaria: Popular Magic, Religious Zealotry and Reason of State in Early Modern Europe* (Cambridge, 1997).

Modern thinking on witchcraft in early modern England was essentially established by Alan Macfarlane, *Witchcraft in Tudor and Stuart England: A Regional and Comparative Study* (London, 1970), which stressed the importance of interpersonal tensions in explaining English witchcraftaccusations, a theme that was reinforced by Keith Thomas, *Religion and the Decline of Magic: Studies in Popular Beliefs in Sixteenth and Seventeenthcentury England* (London, 1971). For a more recent overview, see James Sharpe, *Instruments of Darkness: Witchcraft in England 1550–1750* (London, 1996). The Warboys case is the subject of Anne Reiber de Windt, 'Witchcraft and Conflicting Visions of the Ideal Village Community', *Journal of British Studies*, 34 (1995), pp. 427–63.

Although some of their interpretations may now seem shaky, mention must be made of the works of three important pioneers in the history of English witchcraft: Wallace Notestein, *A History of Witchcraft in England from 1558 to 1718* (Washington, D.C., 1911); Cecil L'Estrange Ewen, *Witch Hunting and Witch Trials: The Indictments for Witchcraft from the Records of the 1373 Assizes Held for the Home Circuit A.D. 1559–1736* (London, 1929), as well as his *Witchcraft and Demonianism: A Concise Account Derived from Sworn Depositions and Confessions Obtained in the Courts of England and Wales* (London, 1933); and G. L. Kittredge, *Witchcraft in Old and New England* (Cambridge, Mass., 1929).

The involvement of women in witchcraft has attracted considerable attention resulting in a number of publications of varying quality. Three works that demonstrate something of the range of positions on the subject are: Marianne Hester, *Lewd Women and Wicked Witches: A Study of the Dynamics of Male Domination* (London and New York, 1992); Dianne Purkiss, *The Witch in History: Early Modern and Twentiethcentury Representation* (London and New York, 1996); and Lyndal Roper, *Oedipus and the Devil: Witchcraft, Sexuality and Religion in Early Modern Europe* (London and New York, 1994), especially chapter 9, 'Witchcraft and Fantasy in Early Modern Germany'. Two studies approaching the issue from English regional archives are J. A. Sharpe. 'Witchcraft and Women in Seventeenthcentury England: Some

Northern Evidence', *Continuity and Change*, 6 (1991), pp. 179–99; and Janet A. Thompson, *Wives, Widows, Witches and Bitches: Women in Seventeenth-century Devon* (American University Studies, 106, New York, 1993).

Full titles of the contemporary works on witchcraft referred to in the text are: Henry Holland, *A Treatise against Witchcraft: or, a Dialogue, wherein the greatest Doubts concerning that Sinne, are briefly answered* (Cambridge, 1590); William Perkins, *A discourse of the damned Art of Witchcraft. So farre forth as it is revealed in the Scriptures, and manifest by true Experience* (Cambridge, 1608); *A true and just Recorde, of the Information, Examination, and Confession of all the Witches taken at S. Oses in the Countie of Essex, whereof some were executed, and some entreated according to the Determination of the Lawe* (London, 1582); *The most strange and admirable Discoverie of the three Witches of Warboys arraigned, convicted and executed at the last Assizes in Huntingdon* (London, 1593): Reginald Scot, *The Discoverie of Witchcraft* (London, 1584); and George Gifford, *A Dialogue concerning Witches and Witchcraftes: in which is laide open how craftely the Divell deceiveth not onely the Witches but many other and so leadeth them awrie into many great Errours* (London, 1593), which was a more developed work than his *A Discourse of the subtill Practices of Devilles by Witches and Sorcerers* (London, 1587).

The Windsor witches of 1579 were commemorated in *A Rehearsall both straung and true, of hainous and horrible Actes committed by Elisabeth Stile, alias Rockingham, Mother Dutten, Mother Devell, Mother Margaret, fower notorious Witches, apprehended at Winsore in the Countie of Berks., and at Abington arraigned, condemned, and executed the 28 Day of Februarie Last 1579* (London, 1579). For a modernized version of the text of this pamphlet, see Barbara Rosen, *Witchcraft* (London, 1969), pp. 83–91. For a different perspective on the 1579 Windsor witches, see Richard Galis, *The Horrible Acts of Elizabeth Style* (London, 1579). I am grateful to Dr Marion Gibson for bringing this tract to my attention.

The letter containing the struck-out passage referring to Pepwell's confession is in the British Library, Additional MS 12497, ff. 197–8.

CHAPTER 5: THE OXFORD CONNECTION

My account of Oxford University in this period owes much to James McConica (ed.), *The Collegiate University* (vol. 3 of the History of the University of Oxford, Oxford, 1986), supplemented by Mark H. Curtis, *Oxford and Cambridge in Transition, 1558–1642: An Essay on Changing Relations between the English Universities and English Society* (Oxford, 1959) and Nicholas

Tyacke (ed.), *Seventeenth-century Oxford* (vol. 4 of the History of the University of Oxford, Oxford, 1997). Details on the number and composition of entrants to Oxford are given in Lawrence Stone, 'The Size and Composition of the Oxford Student Body 1580–1909', in Lawrence Stone (ed.), *The University in Society* (2 vols., Princeton, 1974), vol. 1, pp. 3–110. An excellent introduction to the city in the period in question is provided by the relevant sections of *V.C.H. Oxfordshire*, vol. 4, pp. 74–180.

Harvey Gunter's matriculation is noted in Foster, *Alumni Oxoniensis*, vol. 2, p. 620.

Basic details of Thomas Holland's life are given in *D.N.B.* For the funeral sermon, Richard Kilby [or Kilbie], *A Sermon preached in St Maries Church in Oxford, March 26, 1612, at the funerall of Thomas Holland, Doctor of the Chair of Divinitie, and Rector of Exeter College* (Oxford, 1613, which is supplemented by the comments of Thomas Fuller, *The History of the Worthies of England* (London, 1662), 'Shrop-shire', p. 9. For Holland's views on Elizabeth's Accession day, see Pamgctqiy *D. Elizabethae Reginae: A Sermon preached at Paul's in London the 17 of Nov Ann Dom 1599, the one and fortieth year of her Majesty's Reign. Whereunto is adioyned an apologeticall Discourse, whereby all such sclanderous Accusations are fully and faithfully confuted, wherewith the Honour of this Realme hath beene uncharitably traduced by some of our Adversaries in forraine Nations, and at home, for observing the 17 November yeerely in the forme of a Holy Day, and for the ioyfull Exercises, and Court Triumphes on that Day in the Honour of her Maiestie exhibited* (Oxford, 1601). I have given the full title to emphasize the piece's status as pro-Elizabethan propaganda. Holland's St Paul's Cross sermon of 1602 against exorcism is noted in R. P. Sorlien (ed.), *The Diary of John Manningham of the Middle Temple 1602–1603*, (Hanover, New Hampshire, 1976), p. 30.

For details of the Oxford personalities involved in the Gunter case, I have depended heavily on Foster, *Alumni Oxoniensis*; while further information on a number of figures is given in McConica (ed.), *The Collegiate University*. There are *D.N.B.* entries for John Hall, John Prideaux and Thomas Winniffe, as well as Thomas James, the Bodley's Librarian. Disparaging comments on Bartholomew Warner's abilities are made by Gillian Lewis, 'The Faculty of Medicine', in McConica (ed.), *The Collegiate University*, p. 237.

For Thomas Hinton's involvement as a militia officer and JP, see W. P. D. Murphy (ed.), *The Earl of Hertford's Lieutenancy Papers 1603–1612*, (Wiltshire Record Society, 23, 1969), pp. 122, 123, 173, 176, 177, 182. Giles Hinton's matriculation is noted in Foster, *Alumni Oxoniensis*, vol. 2, p. 718.

Biographical details of Sir Francis Knollys are given in Hasler, *The House of Commons 1558–1603*, vol. 2, pp. 408–9, and Mary Frear Keeler, *The Long Parliament 1640–1641: A Biographical Study of Its Members* (Philadelphia, 1954), pp. 243–4.

Francis Stewart's depositions are held at the Huntington Library, San Marino, California, Ellesmere Papers, MS EL 5955. This item is repro‑ duced by permission of the Huntington Library, San Marino, California. Some brief details about him are provided at the end of the *D.N.B.* entry on his father, James Stewart, second earl of Moray. This was the famous 'Bonny earl of Moray' whose death is commemorated and lamented in a border bal‑ lad, for the text of which see H. C. Sargent and G. L. Kittredge (eds.), *English and Scottish Popular Ballads*, (Cambridge, 1932), pp. 443–4. Anne's reactions to Francis Stewart suggest that he may have inherited some of the good looks and personal magnetism that popular tradition attributed to his father.

CHAPTER 6: THE WITCH‑TRIAL AT ABINGDON

The standard introduction to the assizes in this period remains J. S. Cockburn, *A History of English Assizes 1558–1714* (Cambridge, 1972). More detailed information, based on more recent research, is given by J. S. Cockburn, *A Calendar of Assize Records: Home Circuit Indictments Elizabeth I and James I: Introduction* (London, 1985). For the criminal justice system more generally, see J. A. Sharpe, *Crime in Early Modern England 1550–1750* (2nd edn, London, 1998).

Basic statistics for Home Circuit witchcraft prosecutions are provided by Ewen, *Witch Hunting and Witch Trials*, p. 99.

For Sir Thomas Smith's description of the criminal trial of the period, see his *De Republica Anglorum*, Mary Dewar (ed.) (Cambridge, 1982), p. 114.

The full text of the exchange between Edmund Anderson and Edward Jorden at the Mary Glover trial is given in Rosen, *Witchcraft*, pp. 314–15.

Biographical details of David Williams and Christopher Yelverton come from *D.N.B.*, supplemented by Cockburn, *History of Assizes*, pp. 142, 268–9, 293.

For details of Sir Richard Lovelace, see Hasler, *The House of Commons 1558–1603*, vol. 2, pp. 490–91, and *V.C.H. Berks.*, vol. 3, p. 155.

For the general references on county gaols in this period: Cockburn, *Calendar of Assize Records: Introduction*, Appendix 2, pp. 145–71; S. C. Ratcliffe and H. C. Johnson (eds.), *Quarter Sessions Order Book, Easter 1625 to*

Trinity 1637 (Warwick County Records, 1, 1935), p. 2; J. A. Sharpe, *Crime in Seventeenth-century England: A County Study* (Cambridge, 1983), p. 32. For the Berkshire county gaol, see the brief comments, which include references to the parish registers of St Mary the Virgin, Reading, in: Peter Southerton, *The Story of a Prison* (Reading, 1975), pp. 11–12. The references from Reading borough archives are given in *Diary of the Corporation of Reading* (5 vols., London, 1895–6), vol. 3, pp. 20, 260, vol. 4, p. 431. *V.C.H. Berks.,* vol. 3, p. 58, notes that the county gaol for Berkshire was moved from Windsor to Reading in the early fourteenth century.

The medical report on Anne is referred to in Sir George Clark, *A History of the Royal College of Physicians* (3 vols., Oxford, 1964–72), vol. 1, p. 198. For Vaughan's involvement with possession in Cheshire, see Kittredge, *Witchcraft in Old and New England*, p. 301. Bishop Aylmer's views on God's nationality are discussed in Patrick Collinson, *The Birthpangs of Protestant England: Religious and Cultural Change in the Sixteenth and Seventeenth Centuries* (London, 1988), pp. 4–5. Other information on Vaughan is drawn from *D.N.B.*

For details of Richard Fowler, see Cockburn, *History of Assizes*, pp. 316–17.

The trial of the Warboys witches is described in *The most strange and admirable Discoverie of the three Witches of Warboys*, sigs. O3v–P3.

The background to the 1604 witchcraft statute is in urgent need of reassessment: anybody setting out on this task will find a useful starting point in Kittredge, *Witchcraft in Old and New England*, pp. 307–13.

CHAPTER 7: DEMONIC POSSESSION AND THE POLITICS OF EXORCISM

The standard introduction to the theme of demonic possession in the early modern period remains D.P. Walker, *Unclean Spirits: Possession and Exorcism in France and England in the Late Sixteenth and Early Seventeenth Centuries* (London, 1981), although the interpretations offered there now look a little dated. For a short but more modern treatment, see Stuart Clark, *Thinking with Demons: The Idea of Witchcraft in Early Modern Europe* (Oxford, 1997), chapter 27, 'Possession, Exorcism and History'. Mention should also be made of Rebecca Louise Mullins, 'Children of Disobedience: Aspects of Possession in Early Modern England' (University of York MA thesis, 1997).

The significance of exorcism in the religious politics of Augsburg is emphasized in Lyndal Roper, *Oedipus and the Devil: Witchcraft, Sexuality and*

Religion in Early Modern Europe (London, 1994), chapter 8, 'Exorcism and the Theology of the Body'. A great deal has been written on the Salem trials, but there has been little that has concentrated on the sufferings of the supposedly afflicted girls at the centre of the witchcraft-accusations there. Although now very dated, Marion Starkey, *The Devil in Massachusetts* (New York, 1950), is still worth reading for its attempts to connect the girls' experience with Freudian psychology. John Demos, *Entertaining Satan: Witchcraft and the Culture of Early New England* (Oxford, 1982), examines New England witchcraft-accusations before the Salem outbreak, and is especially valuable for its detailed discussion of possession cases. Aldous Huxley, *The Devils of Loudun* (London, 1952), is a semi-fictionalized account of the possessions there.

Anybody wishing to understand possession in England in the years immediately before the Anne Gunter case should start with Michael Macdonald, *Witchcraft and Hysteria in Elizabethan London: Edward Jorden and the Mary Glover Case* (London, 1991). For the Catholic exorcisms of 1585–6, and for an appreciation of Harsnett, see F. W. Brownlow, *Shakespeare, Harsnett and the Devils of Denham* (Newark, Delaware, 1993). Contemporary publications on the Darrell affair are listed and discussed in Corinne Holt Rickert, *The Case of John Darrell: Minister and Exorcist* (University of Florida Monographs, Humanities, 9, Gainsville, Florida, Winter 1962).

Autobiographical details on Darrell, Bancroft and Harsnett are drawn from *D.N.B.*, augmented by the more recent works mentioned above. For a more general discussion of possession in early modern England, see Sharpe, *Instruments of Darkness*, chapter 8, 'Possession'.

The theatricality of possession cases in this period has been explored by Stephen Greenblatt, *Shakesperean Negotiations: The Circulation of Social Energy in Renaissance England* (Oxford, 1988), chapter 4, 'Shakespeare and the Exorcists', while the involvement of children and adolescents as victims of possession is discussed in J. A. Sharpe, 'Disruption in the Well-ordered Household: Age, Authority and Possessed Young People', in Paul Griffiths, Adam Fox and Steve Hindle (eds.), *The Experience of Authority in Early Modern England* (London, 1996). There is now a massive literature on the history of the family in the early modern period, as well as extensive source materials, both manuscript and printed, from which a history of father–daughter relations could be constructed. The examples cited are from a collection of extracts from diaries, Ralph Houlbrooke, *English Family Life 1576–1716*, pp. 18, 142, 209–10.

The quotation from Samuel Harsnett on the exorcists' use of sack and sallet oil comes from his *A Declaration of Egregious Popish Impostures, to with-draw the Hearts of her Majesties subjects from there Allegeance, and from the Truth of the Christian Religion professed in England, under the pretence of Casting out Devils* (London, 1603), pp. 38–40. See p. 171 of that work for the claim that the Denham exorcisms 'gained in a very short space, four or 5000 to be recon-ciled with the Pope'. The quotations from Harsnett on the behaviour of sup-posed demoniacs are drawn from his *A Discovery of the fraudulent Practices of John Darrell, Bachelor of Arts* (London, 1599), pp. 68–9, 36.

Thomas, *Religion and the Decline of Magic*, p. 489, notes the claims of the Jesuit Mission in England for the 1626 dispossessions.

For Francis Stewart's evidence, Huntington Library, MS EL 5955.

CHAPTER 8: ANNE MEETS THE KING

Details of Henry Cotton's life are given in Stephen Hyde Cassan, *The Lives and Memoirs of the Bishops of Sherborne and Salisbury, from the year 705 to 1824* (Salisbury, 1824), part 2, pp. 83–6. Thomas Holland's oration was pub-lished as *Oratio Sarisburiae Habita ... cum Reverendus in Christo Pater Henricus Episcopus. Sarisburiensis Gradum Doctoris in Theologia Susciperet, ex Decreta Convocationis Oxoniensis* (Oxford, 1599). For the possible connection between Thomas Hinton and Wanborough, *V.C.H. Wilts.*, vol. 9, p. 177.

Biographical details on William Wilkinson are given by Brian P. Levack, *The Civil Lawyers in England 1603–1641: A Political Study* (Oxford, 1973), p. 279. The running of the church courts in Wiltshire forms a major theme of Martin Ingram, *Church Courts, Sex and Marriage in England 1570–1640* (Cambridge, 1987). Ingram comments (pp. 96–7) on the paucity of accusa-tions of witchcraft before the Wiltshire church courts, especially by the early seventeenth century.

A number of contemporary sources refer to Richard Haydock: the basic information is gathered in *D.N.B.* Interestingly, it seems that Haydock took on William Wilkinson's residence at what is now 17 The Close in Salisbury after the latter's death: *Salisbury, The Houses of the Close* (Royal Commission on the Historical Monuments of England, London, 1983), p. 105.

For references to Sir Giles Wroughton's involvement in county adminis-tration, see Murphy (ed.), *The Earl of Hertford's Lieutenancy Papers*, pp. 47, 124, 125, 136, 159, 167, 168, 169, 172, 176.

For an important early statement of the revisionist view on James I, see Jenny Wormald, 'James VI and I: Two Kings or One?', *History*, 68 (1983), pp. 187–200, while a longer and more recent analysis of James's kingship is provided by Roger Lockyer, *James VI and I* (London and New York, 1998). Insights into revised thinking on James's involvement in witchcraft are provided by Christina Larner, 'James VI and I and Witchcraft', in Alan G. R. Smith (ed.), *The Reign of James VI and I* (London, 1973), and Stuart Clark, 'King James's *Daemonologie*: Witchcraft and Kingship', in Sydney Anglo (ed.), *The Damned Art: Essays in the Literature of Witchcraft* (London, 1977). His attitudes to witchcraft while king of England are summarized in Sharpe, *Instruments of Darkness*, pp. 47–50.

The stay of James, Queen Anne and Prince Henry at Oxford is described in detail in John Nichols, *The Progresses, Processions and Magnificent Festivities of King James the First, His Royal Consort, Family and Court* (4 vols., London, 1848: reprinted New York, 1973), vol. 1, pp. 529–61; pp. 508–10 provide a description of the Haydock affair, upon which I have drawn.

James I's letter to Salisbury of 10 October is preserved in British Library, Additional MS 12497, ff. 197–8; it is reproduced in M. S. Giuseppi (ed.), *Historical Manuscripts Commission: Calendar of the Manuscripts of the Most Honorable the Marquis of Salisbury, KG, KCVO, preserved at Hatfield House, Hertfordshire* [hereafter referred to as *H.M.C. Salisbury*], Part XVII, (London, 1938), pp. 450–51, where Bancroft's servant is named as Appleby, which would appear to be a mistranscription.

Other references cited are: Harold Spencer Scott (ed.), 'The Journal of Sir Roger Wilbraham, Solicitor-General in Ireland and Master of Requests, for the Years 1593–1616, together with Notes in another Hand, for the Years 1642–1649', in *The Camden Miscellany: Volume the Tenth* (Camden Society, third series, 4, 1902), pp. 69–70; George Roberts (ed.), *Diary of Walter Yonge, Esq., Justice of the Peace, and MP for Honiton, written at Colyton and Axminster, Co. Devon,* (Camden Society, 41, 1848), p. 12; Robert Johnston, *Historia Rerum Britannicarum ut et multarum Gallicarum, Belgicarum, & Germanicarum, tam Politicarum, quam Ecclesiasticarum, ab Anno 1572, ad Annum 1628* (Amsterdam, 1655), p. 401 (my translation); and Thomas Guidott's unpaginated 'A Preface to the Reader', in Edward Jorden, *A Discourse of Natural Bathes and Mineral Waters* (4th edn, London, 1667).

The full text of Bradwell's account of the sufferings of Mary Glover 'Mary Glover's Late Woeful Case, and her joyfull Deliverance', which includes his opinions on hysteria, is printed in Macdonald, *Witchcraft and Hysteria in Elizabethan London*, pp. 3–140. Ilza Veith, *Hysteria: The History of a Disease* (Chicago, 1965), is the standard introduction to hysteria as a historical phenomenon.

Biographical details of Richard Neile are taken from *D.N.B.* Neile's letter of 30 October is printed in *H.M.C. Salisbury, Part XVII*, p. 471. The disbursement of £300 to Neile is recorded in an Exchequer order book, P.R.O., E403/2725, f. 192v. An entry in the next volume in this series, E403/2726, f. 107v, suggests that this sum was paid in instalments of £100. Intriguingly, there is a reference dated 11 October 1605 to Brian Gunter being paid £25 'for charges by him disbursed to his Majesty's service being employed therein by his Highness's commandment': P.R.O., E403/2725, f. 114v.

For modern work on the Star Chamber, see: Guy, *The Court of Star Chamber*, which, despite its focus on the pre-1558 period, does contain numerous references to later practices; T. G. Barnes, 'Due Process and Slow Process in the Late-Elizabethan – Early Stuart Star Chamber', *American Journal of Legal History*, 6 (1962), pp. 221–49, 315–46; idem, 'The Archives and Archival Problems of the Elizabethan and Early Stuart Star Chamber', *Journal of the Society of Archivists*, 2 (1963), pp. 345–60. An important seventeenth-century guide to the court's workings is provided by William Hudson, 'A Treatise on the Court of Star Chamber', in F. Hargrave (ed.), *Collectanea Juridica* (2 vols., London, 1791–2), vol. 2, pp. 1–239, while insights into the business of the court in the period in which we are interested are provided by J. Hawarde, *Les Reportes del Cases in Camera Stellata 1593–1609*, W. P. Baildon (ed.) (London, 1894), which does not, unfortunately, mention Anne Gunter's case. The Privy Council registers for the relevant period, which might have contained references to the case, were destroyed by fire in January 1618: *Acts of the Privy Council of England, 1613–1614* (London, 1924), pp. v–vi. A vivid impression of life in the Fleet Prison early in the seventeenth century is provided by Augustus Jessopp (ed.), *The Oeconomy of the Fleete, or an Apologeticall Answeare of Alexander Harris (late Warden there) unto XIX Articles set forth against him by the Prisoners*, (Camden Society, new series, 25, 1879).

Details of estreated fines imposed at the Star Chamber are given in the typescript calendar 'Fines in the High Court of Star Chamber 1596–1641', T. G. Barnes (ed.) (American Bar Foundation, Illinois, 1971), held by the P.R.O. : as stated in the text, investigation of this source reveals no mention of Brian or Anne Gunter. Similarly, there is no mention of the Gunter case in the notes on Star Chamber proceedings over the relevant period contained in the archives of the Duke of Northumberland and calendared in the *Third Report of the Royal Commission on Historical Manuscripts* (London, 1872), Appendix, pp. 54–9. Consultation of a microfilm of the original documents confirms the impression created by this calendar: British Library, M.283.

Sir Roger Wilbraham's letter of 20 February 1608 is given in *H.M.C.*

Salisbury, Part XX, p. 76, and that of Sir Thomas Lake of 28 February 1608, ibid., pp. 87–8

CHAPTER 9: LOOSE ENDS, TIED AND UNTIED

I have taken the details of the final illness and death of James from an outdated but not yet superseded biography, D. Willson, *James VI and I* (London, 1956), pp. 445–7.

Details of the later careers of Richard Bancroft, Richard Neile, Samuel Harsnett, Christopher Yelverton and David Williams are taken from *D.N.B.*, augmented in Harsnett's case by Brownlow, *Shakespeare, Harsnett and the Devils of Denham*. Details on Alexander Chocke were kindly supplied by Henry Lancaster of the History of Parliament.

The account of Thomas Hinton's fortunes is based on S. Fry and E. A. Fry (eds.), *Abstracts of Wiltshire Inquisitions Post Mortem, returned to the Court of Chancery in the Reign of King Charles I,* (Index Library, 23, 1901), pp. 278–80, and information supplied by Henry Lancaster of the History of Parliament. Francis Stewart's taste in adult life for things literary is noted in the entry for his father, James Stewart, the second earl of Moray, in *D.N.B.*

Details of Sir Richard Lovelace's fortunes after 1605 are given in Hasler, *The House of Commons 1558–1603,* vol. 2, pp. 490–1.

The fullest description of Knollys's involvement in the Long Parliament is given in Keeler, *The Long Parliament,* p. 244. His support for the parliamentarian cause is noted in D. Brunton and D. H. Pennington, *Members of the Long Parliament* (London, 1954), p. 235.

Thomas Holland's burial is recorded in the typescript copy of the parish registers of St Mary the Virgin held by Oxfordshire Archives. His will survives in the Oxford University Archives, and is listed in John Griffiths (ed.), *An Index of the Wills Proved by the Court of the Chancellor of the University of Oxford,* (Oxford, 1862). Susan Holland's burial is noted in Andrew Clark (ed.), *'Survey of the Antiquities of the City of Oxford', composed in 1661–1662 by Anthony Wood. Vol. III: Addenda and Indexes* (Oxford Historical Society, 37, 1899), p. 264.

North Moreton parish register, Berks. R.O., MF 184 (microfilm of D/P86/1/1), for the deaths of local inhabitants and Gilbert Bradshaw's second marriage. Edmund Dunch's death is noted in the entry dealing with his grandson, also called Edmund Dunch and MP for Wallingford in 1640, in Keeler, *Long Parliament.*

For the Star Chamber proceedings between Gilbert Bradshaw and Brian

Gunter and his associates, P.R.O., STAC 8/80/6. Brian Gunter's burial is recorded in the typescript copy of the parish registers of St Mary the Virgin held by Oxfordshire Archives. For his will and probate inventory, Oxfordshire Archives, 25/5/36; b. 100, f. 7.

There are numerous references to Ashleys in the state papers and Privy Council documents in the years around 1600. A genealogy of the main branch of the family, leading to Sir Anthony Ashley-Cooper, is preserved in Bodleian Library, MS Dodsworth 71, f. 108. This contains no mention of Anne Gunter, nor does the more extensive genealogy of the Ashley-Cooper family given in John Hutchins, *The History and Antiquities of the County of Dorset* (4 vols., 3rd. edn, Westminster, 1861–70), vol. 3, pp. 594–5. One of the more frequently mentioned Ashleys, Sir Francis, an early seventeenth-century judge, had a wife named Anne, but his will makes it evident that her father was not Brian Gunter: Family Records Centre, London, microfilm PROB 11/171, quire 44.

For the marriage licence allegation between John Hartgill and Anne Gunter, see Guildhall Library, MS 10,091/8, 15 August 1621. For the genealogical details on the Hartgills, British Library MS Harleian 1141, f. 104, published in Frederic Thomas Colby (ed.), *The Visitation of the County of Somerset in the Year 1623* (Harleian Society, 2, 1876), p. 46. Details of the murder of William and John Hartgill are given in a number of sources: there is a brief account in J. L. Rayner and G. T. Crook (eds.), *The Complete Newgate Calendar*, (5 vols., 1926), vol. 1, pp. 24–9. South Moreton parish register, Berks. R.O., MF 184 (microfilm of D/P 87/1/1).

British Library, MS Harleian 1141, f. 104 notes an earlier marriage between the Hartgills and the Berkshire Gunters, and it is possible that there was a broad set of connections between the two families and others involved in our story. Thus the will of Thomas Harvey, parson of Brockley in Somerset, proved in 1582, has Brian Gunter as one of the overseers, and left sums of 40s. apiece to the clergyman's nephews, John and George Hartgill. It is possible that a connection with this clergyman or his family helps account for the Christian name of Brian Gunter's elder son, as Harvey was not a common forename in this period: S. W. Rawlins and I. Fitzroy Jones (eds.), *Somerset Wills from Exeter* (Somerset Record Society, 62, 1947), p. 128.

The standard introduction to the emergence of Arminianism in England is Nicholas Tyacke, *Anti-Calvinists: The Rise of English Arminianism c. 1590–1640* (Oxford University Press, 1987). Ibid., p. 72, notes Thomas Holland's opposition to Arminian teachings, and that this position was continued by John Prideaux. Official attitudes to witchcraft and witch prosecutions in the period of Charles I's Personal Rule have not been fully investigated. R. Trevor Davies, *Four Centuries of Witch Beliefs: With Special Reference to the Great Rebellion* (London, 1947), would now be regarded as an outdated work that was in any case marginalized by the sociological approach to English witchcraft history established in the 1970s, yet it does suggest interesting connections between witchcraft and the politics of the pre-Civil War period. For presentments at the Yorkshire church courts, see P. Tyler, 'The Church Courts at York and Witchcraft Prosecutions 1567–1640', *Northern History*, 4 (1969), pp. 84–110.

For the suggested association between Anne Gunter and Jonson's *Volpone*, see Paul, *The Royal Play of Macbeth*, p. 127. For the other seventeenth-century references: William Harvey, *Lectures on the Whole of Anatomy: An Annotated Translation of Prelectiones Anatomine Universalis*, C. D. O'Malley, F. N. L. Poynter and K. F. Russell (eds.) (Berkeley and Los Angeles, 1961), pp. 42–3; Hudson, 'A Treatise on the Court of Star Chamber', p. 212; Thomas Fuller, *The Church History of Britain from the Birth of Jesus Christ untill the Year MDCXLVIII* (London, 1655), book 10, p. 73. Harvey's reference to the Gunter case is discussed in Richard Hunter and Ida Macalpine, 'A Note on William Harvey's "Nan Gunter"', *The Journal of Medical History*, 12 (1957), pp. 512–5.

For the history of North Moreton, see *V.C.H. Berks.,* vol. 3, pp. 492–8. I am grateful to Professor G. M. D. Howat, who is preparing a parish history of North Moreton, for information about the modern North Moreton and for additional insights into its history. The Berkshire *Post Office Directory* for 1877 gives the population of North Moreton as 357 in 1871.

Additional information on All Saints' Church, supplementing Howat, *All Saints' North Moreton,* was kindly provided by Sabina Sutherland of the Berkshire Record Office. For a demonstration of the continued involvement of the old farming families in village affairs, see an agreement of 1719 concerning commons in the parish, Berks. R.O., D/EB/E3. The surname Gregory appears in the parish register throughout the eighteenth century: overall, the register contains over 300 references to persons named Gregory, making it the most frequently noted surname there.

INDEX

A

Abergavenny 32
Abingdon, Oxon xii, 19, 27, 80, 85, 102,
    111, 114, 125, 127, 130, 131, 166, 168,
    170, 195, 198, 199, 200
Adams, family 22, 31
Adams, Robert 14, 19, 22, 31, 38
Allen, Benedict 45
Anderson, Sir Edmund 122-3, 151
Anne of Denmark, Queen 176, 178, 183
Archpriest controversy 152
Argent, John 131
Armada, Spanish 50, 114
Arminianism 210
Ashampstead, Berks 58
Ashburnham family 27
Asheley, 180, 186, 204
Ashley, family 204
Ashmole, Elias 32
Assizes, courts of 19, 39, 67, 117–9
    criminal trials at 120–2
    at York, summer 1600 125
    Northern Circuit 124
    Oxford Circuit 117, 133
    South Eastern (Home) Circuit 118–9,
        122, 126, 208

Augsburg 143
Aylmer, John 131

B

Baker, Elizabeth 48, 50, 159
Baker, John 37
Baker, Martha 48
Baker, Richard 48
Bancroft, Richard xii, 3, 4, 144, 149–52,
    179, 180, 182, 183, 187, 191, 193, 198,
    204
Barff, Albert 211
Barker, Diana xiv
Bath 184
Bartholomew, Margaret 45, 59
Bernard, Richard 208
Bird, Thomas 109, 159, 161–2
Bishop, Goodwife 85
Bodin, Jean 74, 75
Bothwell, James Hepburn, earl of 176
Bracegirdle, Roger 7, 46, 58, 99
Bradshaw, Alice 31
Bradshaw, Amy 91
Bradshaw, Anne 31
Bradshaw, Brian 202
Bradshaw, Elizabeth (née Brasier) 202, 203

Bradshaw, Gilbert 21–2, 31, 35, 37, 44, 45,
        47–8, 49, 50, 51, 53–4, 58, 60, 63, 91,
        202–3, 206
Bradshaw, Henry 31
Bradshaw, Margaret 31
Bradshaw, Thomas 31
Bradwell, Stephen 189
Brecknock 123, 199
Bredon, Worcs. 101
Briggs, Agnes 146
Brightwell, Oxon. 109, 159, 162
Brossier, Marthe 144
Browen, Thomas 203
Buckeridge, Alice 12
Buckhurst, Thomas Sackville, Lord 97
Bumpass, Kenneth 212
Burghley, William Cecil, Lord 189
Burrington, Devon 102
Burton-on-Trent 148
Bury St Edmunds 149
Butler, Herbert 212

C

Calne, Wilts. 45
Calvin, John 75
Cambridge 16, 95, 107, 131, 183, 191
    Corpus Christi College 133
    Queen's College 148
Carter, William 62
Case, John 99
Chancery, court of 33, 39, 41
Charles I 101, 191, 198, 199, 201, 209, 210
Chelsea 112
Chetwyn, Mr 48
Cheyney, Dr 43
Chigwell, Essex 150, 198
Chilton Foliat, Wilts. 35, 199
Chilton Park, Wilts. 108
Chipping Norton, Oxon. 51
Chocke, Alexander 128, 129, 132–4, 199
Clarke, Edward 128, 129
Coke, Sir Edward 190–1
College of Physicians 130–1, 183
Cotton, Henry 4, 169–70, 171, 174, 195

Cotton, Sir Richard 170
Council of The North 124–5
counter-magic 60–1, 71–2, 76–7, 136
Cromwell, Oliver 16, 136
Cromwell, Lady Susan 136
cunning folk 4, 57–9, 72–3, 76–7, 84
Curwen, Hugh 149

D

Daneau, Lambert 74, 75
Darling, Thomas 148, 152, 158
Darrell, John 62, 148–9, 150, 152, 152–3,
        158, 166
Defoe, Daniel 30
Del Rio, Martin 74
demonic possession 7, 103–6, 131–2, 139–68
    passim
    in post Reformation England 145–9
    scriptural references to 140
    and young people 153, 156–7
Denham, Bucks 147, 164
Devell, Mother 81, 82
Dickinson, Roger xiv
Didcot, Oxon. 210, 211
Dodsworth, Margaret 200
Dodsworth, Richard 200
Dolman, Thomas 130
Donne, John 101
Downton, Wilts. 108
Dublin 125
Dunch, family 27, 39, 99
Dunch, Anne 46
Dunch, Edmund 39, 201–2
Dunch, Mary 39, 46
Dunch, William 34, 39, 41
Durston, Christopher xiv
Dutch Revolt 22, 92
Dutten, Mother 81, 82, 83

E

East Ham, Essex 16
Easton Maudit, Northants. 199
Edinburgh 178, 182
Edward VI 116, 170

Effingham, Charles Howard, Baron 125
Egypt 140
Elizabeth I 1, 2, 22, 74, 83–4, 92, 95, 97, 116,
    120, 145, 170
Elyot, Sir Thomas 16
epilepsy 43, 166
Essex, county gaol of at Colchester 126
    witch trials of 1566 in 77
    witch trials of 1582 in 78
Essex, Robert Devereux, earl of 97, 114,
    125, 150
Ewen, Cecil L'Estrange xiv, 118
Exeter cathedral 100
exorcism, contrasting Roman Catholic and
    Protestant opinions towards 142–3,
    146–7
Eyton, Sir Robert 155

F

familiars 47, 70–1, 85, 103, 162
Farnham Royal, Bucks. 82
Farnworth, Lancs. 149
Fawkes, Guy 191
Fenner, Edward 136–7
Field, John 14, 17
Field, Peter 29, 61
Field, Richard 25, 28 (senior and junior), 38
Field, William 25, 41, 48, 61, 160
Finchingbrooke, Berks. 179
Fleet, family 203
Fleet Prison 194
Flushing 114
football 14–7, 38, 51, 173
Fowler, Richard 133
Foxe, John 145
French, William 25
Fuller, Thomas 94, 207

G

Galis, Richard 81
gaols, conditions in 126, 194
Gaufridy, Louis 144
Gifford, George, 79–80
Glover, Mary 122, 123, 130, 131, 150–1, 153,

    158, 166, 182–3, 188
Gondomar, Sarmiento de Acuna count of,
    101
Gooderidge, Alice 148
Goring, Oxon. 127
Grandier, Urbain 144
Grays Inn 1, 2, 124
Greece 140
Greene, Joan 173–4, 186
Gregory, family 23, 40–1, 42, 51, 210, 212
Gregory, Elizabeth 8, 11, 17, 19, 27, 48, 50,
    51, 52, 53 – 4, 61, 68, 85, 86, 102, 103,
    107, 108, 113, 114, 126, 127, 137, 138,
    159, 162, 168, 173, 179, 194, 198, 199,
    200
    personality xii, 48–9
    suspected of witchcraft 6–7, 46–7, 54–5
    arrested, 55, 125–6
    tried for witchcraft at Abingdon 129–35
    no trace of details of death 202
Gregory, Goodwife 85
Gregory, John 14, 17–9, 34, 51, 173
Gregory, Margery 201
Gregory, Mary 201
Gregory, Richard 14, 17–9, 40–1, 51, 173
Gregory, Robert 14, 19, 23, 40, 41
Gregory, Thomas 40
Gregory, Walter xii, 42, 201
Gregory, William 14, 17, 23, 29, 40–1, 42,
    51
Guidott, Thomas 184–5, 186, 204, 208
Gunpowder Plot 190, 193
Gunter, family 32–3, 210–1
Gunter, Agnes (née Yate) 32
Gunter, Anne 1–13 *passim*, 43–8 *passim*,
    54–64, 66, 86–7, 99, 101, 102, 108–14
    passim, 115, 116, 118, 119, 139, 141,
    143, 156, 157, 168, 169, 174, 175, 178,
    183, 197, 212
    baptism 33
    appearance 4–5
    relations with father 11–2
    symptoms of bewitchment or possession
    43–8, 103–7, 109, 128–9, 132–5, 156,

158–9, 161, 165–6
contemplates suicide 12–3
simulates bewitchment or possession 3,
   7–10, 63, 110–3, 161–3, 166–7,
   167–8, 172–3
meetings with James VI and I 179–82,
   185–6, 189
in custody of Henry Cotton 4, 169, 171–4
in custody of Samuel Harsnett 4, 12,
   182–5, 189–90
at court 189–90
fate after Star Chamber proceedings
   204–6
significance of her case 208–9
Gunter, Anne senior xi, 29, 43, 47, 109, 202
Gunter, Brian xi–xiii, 14–9, 21, 25, 28–9,
   43, 45, 47, 50–1, 51, 52–3, 54, 56, 58,
   60, 62, 66, 72, 84, 91, 98, 99, 101, 102,
   106, 107, 108, 109, 111, 112, 114, 115,
   119, 125, 127, 128–31, 160, 161, 163,
   164, 166, 169, 173, 198, 200, 201, 204,
   205, 206, 207, 208, 212
personality 37–8, 38–9, 50–3, 202
economic activities 33–6
involvement in litigation 33, 34, 35–6,
   37–8, 39, 202–3
makes Anne simulate bewitchment or
   possession 6–12, 113–4
apparently affected by Anne's sufferings
   47–8, 106
builds party in Oxford to support witchcraft accusations 98, 102
conduct at Abingdon witch-trial 132–3,
   134, 135
motives in meeting James VI and I 180
trial by the Star Chamber 192–5
death 203
will 2034
Gunter, Edward 33, 34–5
Gunter, George 32
Gunter, Harvey 34, 37–8, 60–1, 91, 96, 102,
   104, 106, 158, 202, 203, 204, 205, 206
Gunter, John 33, 34, 36
Gunter, Nicholas 85, 87

Gunter, William 14, 19, 38, 202
Guy, John xiv
Gwillyam, William 84–5, 86

H
Hackney 147
Hall, John 100, 104
Hamden, George 113
Harding, John 101
Harrison, Thomas 132
Harsnett, Samuel xii, 12, 147, 149–53,
   163–4, 164–5, 167, 179, 182, 183, 184,
   186–7, 189–92, 196, 198, 209
Hartgill, family 205–6
Hartgill, Anne 204–6
Hartgill, John 204–6
Hartgill, Mary 206
Hartgill, William 206
Harvey, Lady Mary 209
Harvey, William, future clergyman 101–2,
   103–4, 105, 160
Harvey, William, physician 207, 209
Hatton, Sir Christopher 97
Hawkins, Richard 85
Haydock, Richard 171, 172, 174–5, 181
Headington, Oxon. 91
Heard, Thomas 21, 29, 34, 41
Helme, William 101, 103, 105, 111–2
Hemmingsen, Niels 75
Henri IV 144
Henrietta Maria, Queen 199
Henry VII 191, 192
Henry VIII 65, 97, 116
Henry, Prince of Wales 16, 101, 100, 178
Higgs, Goodwife 59, 60
Hinton, family 108, 171
Hinton, Anthony 199
Hinton, Giles 111
Hinton, John 199
Hinton, Thomas 45–6, 108–114, 127–8,
   135, 162, 199, 208
Holland, Anne 94, 201
Holland, Brian 94
Holland, Elizabeth 202–3

Holland, Henry 75
Holland, Susan (née Gunter) 46, 92, 93, 94,
    99, 103, 179, 186, 201, 202, 203
Holland, Thomas 92–4, 100, 111, 152, 161,
    170, 186, 200–1, 203, 209
Holland, William 35, 201, 292–3
Honiton, Devon 181
Hopgood, John 51, 53
Hopkins, Matthew 210
Horsley, Robert 28
Hoskyns, William 28
Houlbrooke, Ralph xiv
Houlbrooke, Margaret xiv
Hudson, William 207
Hungerford, Berks. 33, 36
Huntingdon 136
Huntly, George Gordon, earl of 113
Hurley, Berks 125
Hutton, Matthew 149
Huxley, Aldous 144
hysteria 6, 43, 112–3, 151, 165–6, 166, 187–8
Hyde, Catherine 200
Hyde, William 200

I

Isle of Wight 155

J

Jackson, Elizabeth 122, 123, 150–1
James VI and I xii, 4, 10, 16, 27, 88, 92–3,
    100, 101, 184–5, 186, 187, 188, 189,
    190, 193–4, 195, 204, 207
  reputation 175–6
  and witchcraft 75, 116, 176–9, 183
  death 197–8
James, Thomas 162
Jermin, Alexander 110
Jonson, Ben 207
Johnstone, Robert 181–2, 183, 186–7, 207
Jorden, Edward 122–3, 130–1, 151, 183–5,
    195, 196, 204
Jorden, Lucy 184

K

Kilby, Richard 93–4
Kilmington, Somerset 204
King's Bench, court of 18
Kingston near Lewes, Sussex 54
Kingston Bagpuize, Berks. 124, 199
Kintbury, Berks. 32, 36
Kirfoote, Alice 6, 8, 9, 10, 11, 12, 40, 51,
    53–4, 54–5, 58, 59, 119, 166, 201
Kirfoote, Nicholas 6, 10–1, 11–2, 25, 26, 35,
    40, 42, 45, 52, 23–4, 59, 61, 119, 201,
    203
Knollys, Sir Francis 114, 128, 200
Knowles, Nicholas 28

L

Lake, Sir Thomas 193
Lambeth church 198
Lambeth Palace 149, 194, 198
Lancaster, Henry xiv
Lancashire
  witch trials of 1612 in 208
  witch trials of 1633–4 in 209
Latton, Dorothy 124
Laud, William 209–10
Leaver family 23–4, 203
Leaver, Clement 23
Leaver, Denise 23
Leaver, Helen 23
Leaver, Isabel 23
Leaver, John 24, 25, 26, 49, 55–6, 125, 212
Leaver, Mary 23, 29
Leaver, Richard 28
Leaver, Raphe 24
Leaver, Thomas 23, 24, 26, 28
Leaver, William 23, 24, 25, 26, 28, 38, 41, 42,
    47, 48, 49, 54, 61, 212
Leicester 178
Leicester, Robert Dudley, earl of 92, 96–7,
    114
Leigh, Lancs 148
Levack, Brian xiv
Lincoln's Inn 133
Little Wittenham, Oxon. 21, 40

Livingstone, Elizabeth 154–5
London 20, 30–1, 84, 109, 130, 146, 151, 154, 199, 200, 209, 211
Longe, Gifford 45, 158, 161
Loudun 144, 153, 157
Lovelace Sir Richard, 55, 125, 128, 134, 200
Ludlow, Shropshire 92, 199

M

Maldon, Essex 79–80
Malleus Maleficarum 74
Manchester 15
Mansfield, Notts. 148
Margaret, Mother 81, 82
Marlborough, Wilts. 108
Marprelate controversy 149–50
Marseilles 144
Mather, Cotton 75
Matthews, Samuel 199
Mayne, family 22
Mayne, Francis 29
Mayne, John 23, 25, 28, 38, 50, 212
Mayne, Mary 212
melancholy 141
Middle Temple 123
Mill, William 2
Miller, Arthur 144, 208
Moray, John Stewart, earl of 113

N

Neile, Richard 189, 191, 196, 198, 209
Neville, Sir Henry 81
Newbury, Berks. 21, 57, 160
Newcombe, William 171
Nicholas, William 51, 53
North Berwick 177
North Moreton x, xv, 43–63 *passim*, 64, 66, 71, 72, 85, 90, 91, 94, 98, 102, 107, 108, 109, 111, 119, 125, 129, 138, 158, 162, 166, 169, 170, 179, 192, 194, 201–2, 202–3, 205, 206
   description, c. 1600 20–32
   descrption, c. 2000 210–2

Northwich, Cheshire 132
Nottingham 148–9
Nyndge, Alexander 146

O

Oglander, Bridget 155
Oglander, Sir John 155
Orpewood, Margaret 127
Oxford xi, xii, 5, 11, 43, 57, 63, 91–2, 95–7, 114, 115, 119, 163, 166, 167, 169, 171, 174, 178–9, 200, 201, 208, 209
   description of City c. 1600 90–1
   description of University c. 1600 94–7
   connections of North Moreton inhabitants with 20, 21, 91
   All Souls College xiv
   Balliol College, 92
   Brasenose College, 46, 91
   Christ Church College 113, 149
   Exeter College 3, 92, 97–8, 99, 100, 101, 110, 161, 181
   Magdalen College 101, 170
   New College 22, 174
   Queen's College 108, 111

P

Padua 184
parent-child relationships 153–6
Peckham, Sir George 147
Pepwell, Agnes xi–xii, 47, 55, 61, 68, 84–8, 102, 103
   character 26, 49–50
   reputation for witchcraft xi, 49–50, 127
   confesses to witchcraft 85–9
   death, 202
Pepwell, Mary xi–xii, 26, 27, 47, 49–50. 61, 102, 103, 104, 107, 108, 116, 119, 123, 126, 127, 137, 138, 179, 194, 198, 201
Pepys, Samuel 30
Perkins, William 75–7
Perry, William 147
Petre, Sir John 98
Petre, Sir William 97–8

plague, bubonic 30–1, 41, 54
poor law 69
psychiatry, and modern interpretations of
    witchcraft 65
psychoanalysis, and modern interpretations
    of demonic possession 164
Prideaux, John 100, 101, 103, 104, 106, 107,
    159, 209
Privy Council 83, 98, 152, 191

R
Reading 20, 21, 34, 81, 84, 85, 87, 114
    conditions in Berkshire county gaol at
    126–7, 194
Rome 140
Roper, Margaret 148
Rosimund, Father 82–3
Rougham, Norfolk 124
Rowe, Thomas 81
Ruffin, Anthony 11, 12. 56
Ruislip, Middlesex 15
Russell, Ken 144

S
Salem, Massachusetts, witch trials at 8, 75,
    143–4, 153, 157, 208
Salisbury 170, 171, 172, 174, 175, 185
Salisbury, Robert Cecil, earl of 88, 180, 181,
    189, 190, 193, 197
Sampson, Edward 54
Samuel, Agnes 137
Samuel, Joan 136
Samuel, John 136
Sawyer, William 44, 50, 52, 54, 57, 159
Schlutterbäurin, Anna 139
Scot, Reginald 78–9, 80, 88
Scott, David xiv
Seder, Mother 81
Shaftesbury, Anthony Ashley-Cooper, earl
    of 204
Shakespeare, William 100, 207
Sheils, Bill xiv
Shenfield, Essex 191
Shrivenham, Oxon. 36

Smith, Sir Thomas 120–1
Somers, Willaim 148–9, 158
South Moreton, Oxon. 49, 51, 55, 203, 206
Spinola, Ambrosio, marquis of los Balbases
    101
Spooner, Edward 23
Spooner, Richard 26, 55, 125
Spratt, Joan 173–4, 186
Spratt, John 173
Stampe, John 34
Stampe, Thomas 34
Stanton St John, Oxon. 60–1, 102, 104, 166
Star Chamber, court of xii, 17, 35, 37–8,
    125, 150, 191–5, 207
Stewart, Sir Francis 113, 160–1, 172,
    199–200
Stile, Elizabeth 80–1, 85
Stourton, Charles Lord 205
Stratford on Avon 100
Starkey, Nicholas 148
Stubbes, Philip 16–7
Sudbury, John 14, 19, 23, 29, 38, 41, 51
Sutherland, Sabina xiv

T
Tadmarten, Robert 9, 23, 28, 50, 51, 58–9,
    60
Tailor, Humphrey 160
Tailor, John 14, 38
Teversham, Cambs. 149
Theobalds 197
Thornebury, Mary 44, 158
Throckmorton, family 7, 62, 78, 107, 135–7
Throckmorton, Jane 136–7
Throckmorton, Joan 136, 137
Tilbury, Essex 50
tithes 29, 35–7, 39, 41
Townsend, Henry 35
Turnor, William 85

U
Uxbridge, Middlesex 15

V

Vaughan, Richard 130–1, 131–2
Vaux, William, Baron 147
Vilvaine, Robert 99, 103, 104, 105, 160
Virginia 199
Virginia Company 199

W

Wallingford, Oxon 43, 210
Wallington, Nehemiah 154
Wanborough, Wilts. 171
Warboys, Huntingdonshire
    witchcraft at 3, 62, 78, 107, 135–7, 146,
    164
Ware, Herts. 190
Warwickshire, county gaol of 126
Watts, Simon 14, 38
Wendore, John 57
West, Mr 48
West Ham, Essex 16
Westminster 1, 2, 13, 84, 117, 209
Weston, William 147, 152
Whetcombe, John 48, 102, 200–1
Whisteler, Robert 127
Whitehall 179, 197
Whitgift, John 149
Wilbraham, Sir Roger 181, 193, 194
Wilkinson, William 171
Williams, Sir David 123–4, 128, 129, 134,
    137, 199

Williams, Friswood 163
Windsor, Berks. 84, 85, 180, 207
    witchcraft case of 1579 at 80–4
Winniffe, Thomas 101, 103, 106, 159
Wiltshire, church courts in 170
Witchcraft 64–89 *passim*, 208–9
    English law and 115–6, 137
    trials for at south eastern assizes 118–9,
        208
    in Scotland 176–9
    'charity denied' model of 68–70
    and women 67–8, 72
    see also counter magic; cunning folk;
        familiars; witch's mark
witch's mark 71
Wormald, Jenny xiv
Wright, Katherine 148
Wroughton, Sir Giles 4, 171

Y

Yate, Agnes 32
Yate, Simon 32
Yelverton, Sir Christopher 124–5, 129, 137,
    198–9
Yelverton, Henry 199
Yelverton, William 124
Yonge, Walter 181
York 124, 125, 198